David Malouf

MANCHESTER
1824

Manchester University Press

CONTEMPORARY *W*ORLD *W*RITERS

SERIES EDITOR   JOHN THIEME

ALREADY PUBLISHED IN THE SERIES

Peter Carey   BRUCE WOODCOCK

Amitav Ghosh   ANSHUMAN MONDAL

Maxine Hong Kingston   HELENA GRICE

Kazuo Ishiguro   BARRY LEWIS

Hanif Kureishi   BART MOORE-GILBERT

Rohinton Mistry   PETER MOREY

Timothy Mo   ELAINE YEE LIN HO

Toni Morrison   JILL MATUS

Alice Munro   CORAL ANN HOWELLS

Les Murray   STEVEN MATTHEWS

Caryl Phillips   BÉNÉDICTE LEDENT

Amy Tan   BELLA ADAMS

Ngugi wa Thiong'o   PATRICK WILLIAMS

Derek Walcott   JOHN THIEME

David Malouf

DON RANDALL

Manchester University Press

Manchester and New York

distributed exclusively in the USA by Palgrave

Published by Manchester University Press
Oxford Road, Manchester M13 9NR, UK
and Room 400, 175 Fifth Avenue, New York, NY 10010, USA
www.manchesteruniversitypress.co.uk

Distributed exclusively in the USA by
Palgrave, 175 Fifth Avenue, New York, NY 10010, USA

Distributed exclusively in Canada by
ubc Press, University of British Columbia, 2029 West Mall,
Vancouver, bc, Canada v6t 1z2

British Library Cataloguing-in-Publication Data
A catalogue record for this book is available from the British Library

Library of Congress Cataloging-in-Publication Data applied for

ISBN 978 0 7190 6832 4 *hardback*
ISBN 978 0 7190 6833 1 *paperback*

First published 2007
16 15 14 13 12 11 10 09 08 07   10 9 8 7 6 5 4 3 2 1

Typeset in Aldus
by Koinonia, Manchester
Printed in Great Britain
by Bell & Bain Ltd, Glasgow

for Kim and Im

Contents

Acknowledgements

I have Bart Moore-Gilbert to thank - warmly - for putting me on to the idea of a Malouf monograph and facilitating my approach to the tirelessly helpful John Thieme, also to be thanked, and again warmly. Following the contracting of the book, Hamit Çalıskan, Assistant Chair of English at Bilkent, provided me the opportunity to create and teach a special upper-undergraduate elective in Australian literature. Subsequently, Carl Bridge invited me to undertake summer study at the Menzies Centre for Australian Studies, King's College, London. I thank Bilkent University for funding that research trip and various conference trips pertinent to my Malouf project.

In 2004, Bilkent University granted me a half-year sabbatical leave on the basis of an invitation to pursue my research and writing at the University of Western Australia. This particularly rewarding study leave was arranged – indeed, masterminded – by Kieran Dolin of UWA's Centre for Studies in Australian Literature. I thank him very heartily for all his work, and most particularly for the funding application he made to UWA's Distinguished Visitors Fund. I thank UWA for granting the requested funds. I also thank Van Ikin, generally for providing advice and orientation, and specifically for arranging an Honours seminar on Malouf for me to teach. I thank Brenda Walker for her heartening collegial reception and her interest in my study project, and Sue Lewis for so efficiently managing all practical matters. During my time at UWA, Delys Bird and Dennis Haskell took an interest in my work and encouraged me to submit a text to *Westerly*. Following peer review and a very helpful call for revisions, my article was accepted. I therefore thank the Westerly Centre at the University of Western Australia for permission to reprint material on *Remembering Babylon*, first published in *Westerly* 49 (2004). Subsequently, I successfully submitted an article on *An Imaginary Life*. Material from '"Some Further Being": Engaging with the Other in David Malouf's *An Imaginary Life*', *Journal of Commonwealth Literature* 41.1, is reprinted by permission of Sage Publications Ltd (©Sage Publications, 2006).

Finally, I would like to thank all those who have provided me the opportunity of talking through my work. At Bilkent, I thank the programme in Cultures, Civilisations, and Ideas, and particularly Trevor Hope, for inviting me to offer a conference paper and subsequently a colloquium talk. At UWA, the Discipline Group of English, Communication and Cultural Studies and the Institute of Advanced Studies generously offered me opportunities for public presentations. The Canadian Association for Commonwealth Literature and Language Studies (CACLALS) has twice accepted conference paper proposals on Malouf topics. My students, at Bilkent and at UWA, have done much to enrich my appreciation of Malouf. I particularly thank Yeşim Dikmen, Başak Ergüven, Gözde Köksal, Deniz Dönmez, Sedef Hasşerbetçi, Lucy Hopkins, David Leigh, John Stubley, and Victor Thomas.

Series editor's foreword

Contemporary World Writers is an innovative series of authoritative introductions to a range of culturally diverse contemporary writers from outside Britain and the United States or from 'minority' backgrounds within Britain or the United States. In addition to providing comprehensive general introductions, books in the series also argue stimulating original theses, often but not always related to contemporary debates in post-colonial studies.

The series locates individual writers within their specific cultural contexts, while recognising that such contexts are themselves invariably a complex mixture of hybridised influences. It aims to counter tendencies to appropriate the writers discussed into the canon of English or American literature or to regard them as 'other'.

Each volume includes a chronology of the writer's life, an introductory section on formative contexts and intertexts, discussion of all the writer's major works, a bibliography of primary and secondary works and an index. Issues of racial, national and cultural identity are explored, as are gender and sexuality. Books in the series also examine writers' use of genre, particularly ways in which Western genres are adapted or subverted and 'traditional' local forms are reworked in a contemporary context.

Contemporary World Writers aims to bring together the theoretical impulse which currently dominates post-colonial studies and closely argued readings of particular authors' works, and by so doing to avoid the danger of appropriating the specifics of particular texts into the hegemony of totalising theories.

List of abbreviations

Chronology

1934   David Malouf born on 20 March in Brisbane of Lebanese
            and English parents.

1947–50   Attended Brisbane Grammar School.

1951–54   Studied for honours degree in language and literature at
            University of Queensland.

1954   Graduated from University of Queensland.

1955   Junior Lecturer in English at University of Queensland.

1955–57   Taught in the Department of English at University of
            Queensland.

1958   Itinerant tutor for a Brisbane coaching academy.

1959   Left Brisbane for Europe and England.

1959–62   Lived in London and worked as a supply teacher, including
            one year teaching at Holland Park Comprehensive
            school.

1962   Published in *Four Poets*, along with Judith Green, Rodney
            Hall, and Don Maynard.

1963-68   English master at St Anselm's College, Birkenhead (UK).

1968   Returned to Australia.

1968-78   Senior Tutor, then Lecturer, in English Department at
            University of Sydney, New South Wales.

1970   Published first volume of poetry, *Bicycle and Other
            Poems*, in Australia (appeared as *The Year of the Foxes
            and Other Poems* in the U.S. in 1979).

1974   Published poetry collection *Neighbours in a Thicket*,

	which is awarded the Australian Literature Society's Gold Medal and the Grace Leven Prize for Poetry.
1975	Published first novel, *Johnno* (released in the U. S. in 1979)
1976	*Poems 1975–76* published.
1978	Second novel, *An Imaginary Life*, published in both the US (Brazilier) and the UK (Chatto & Windus). Became a full-time writer.
1979	*An Imaginary Life* chosen for the New South Wales Premiers's Prize.
1981	Published novella *Child's Play*. Poetry volumes *First Things Last* and *Selected Poems*.
1982	Published *Child's Play* in volume including the short stories 'Eustace' and 'The Prowler'. Published novella *Fly Away Peter* (issued in US as *The Bread of Time to Come*), which won the *Age* Book of the Year Award and, with *Child's Play*, the Australian Literature Society's Gold Medal.
1984	Published novel *Harland's Half Acre.*
1985	Short-story collection *Antipodes* received the Victoria Premier's Prize.
1986	Published *12 Edmondstone Street* and completed libretto for Richard Meale's opera *Voss*, based on the novel by Australian Nobel laureate Patrick White. *Voss* presented at the Australian Opera.
1987	Play *Blood Relations* first performed, and named winner of the New South Wales Premier's Prize.
1988	Awarded the Pascall Prize.
1990	Published novel *The Great World* (awarded the Commonwealth Writers' Prize, the Miles Franklin Award, and the Prix Femina Étranger) and wrote libretto for Meale's *Mer de Glace*, which premiered at the Australian Opera.
1992	*Poems 1959–89* published.
1993	Novel *Remembering Babylon*, named by *Time* as one of the best books of the year and shortlisted for the Booker Prize. Won the *Los Angeles Times* Prize for Fiction. Published opera libretto *Baa Baa Black Sheep*.

1994   Issued *Selected Poems, 1959–89*.

1995   Won France's Prix Baudelaire for *Remembering Babylon*.

1996   Published novel *The Conversations at Curlow Creek*. *Remembering Babylon* chosen as the first recipient of the Dublin IMPAC Literary Award.

1998   Delivered the annual Boyer radio lectures of the Australian Broadcasting Corporation: 'A Spirit of Play: The Making of Australian Consciousness', subsequently published as *A Spirit of Play*.

1999   Short-story collection *Untold Tales*.

2000   Published short-story collection *Dream Stuff*. Published opera libretto *Jane Eyre*. Selected, for career achievement, as sixteenth recipient of the University of Oklahoma's Neustadt International Prize for Literature. Autumn issue of *World Literature Today* (University of Oklahoma) dedicated to Malouf and his work. Won Lannan Literary Award for *Dream Stuff*.

2000, 2001   Special guest lecturer at the Brisbane Institute: 'The City as Artefact' and 'A Crisis for Poetry?'.

2003   Published the substantial essay 'Made in England: Australia's British Inheritance' in the twelfth issue of *Quarterly Essay*, subsequently shortlisted for the Alfred Deakin Prize. Awarded the Centenary of Federation Medal.

2004   Joint winner, for *Johnno*, of One Book One Brisbane award. Delivered Canada's annual Baldwin-LaFontaine lecture: 'Wisdom from a Tale of Two Nations'. The first non-Canadian ever chosen to give the lecture.

2005   Delivered the Australian Human Rights Centre's inaugural annual lecture.

2006   Plenary lecturer at University of Queensland's World Shakespeare Congress.

Contexts and intertexts

An examination of David Malouf's overall writing career reveals a remarkably continuous concern with encounters between self and other. What most distinguishes his work is its strong tendency to find in otherness (or alterity) the stimulus and orientation for a creative unsettling of identity. The other, in Malouf, does not typically enable a consolidation of selfhood, nor does it unproductively impede or confuse identity formation. Encounter with the other provokes creative self-transformation, a self-overcoming, a becoming other than oneself that responds to and moves toward the version of being the other manifests. For Malouf, the project of a human life should not be secure self-definition (though the author amply acknowledges the very human craving for such stability); a human life should remain on, or at least repeatedly return to, the path of becoming. Always, we should seek to become other than we have been, other than we are, and the other is the indispensable agent of our changes.

Malouf is both wilfully cosmopolitan and wilfully Australian, a writer of various worlds for whom Australian experience and identity represent an enduring but by no means exclusive concern. As his career progresses, Malouf shows an increasing interest in the cultural and racial otherness represented, for white Australians, by the Aborigine. He gives explicit argumentative expression to this philosophical and imaginative orientation, stating in his 1998 Boyer lectures, *A Spirit of Play*, that his work strives to integrate sympathetically and imaginatively with forms of Aboriginal culture and experience. However, the author never abandons his very broad sense of otherness as, most fundamentally, the not-I – all that stands beyond the tenuous and inescapably contingent border of the self. Even in his earliest work, Malouf often ascribes to landscape – particularly Australian landscape, and more particularly Queensland landscape – the self-unsettling power of otherness, and his value as a writer of place, of landscape, resides mainly in this. Social aspects of difference also assert their importance early on, and abidingly: in *Johnno*, the first novel, the title character's creatively challenging otherness for the narrator Dante has much to do with class difference; in the poetry and in the subsequent fictions, cultural differences – between Europeans and Australians, Americans and Australians, Asians and Australians – receive quite ample treatment. Masel speaks of Malouf's 'lack of anxiety' with respect to the assimilation and appropriation of otherness in all its manifestations, but this assessment is too absolute. Even in the relatively early *An Imaginary Life*, the focal character Ovid shows notable anxiety about the rightness of his assimilative, appropriative disposition with respect to the wild boy he encounters. Masel's accompanying idea that Malouf's sense of the self is 'essentially cumulative' is a more measured, more apt, assessment of his vision.[1]

In the first important critical monograph on Malouf, Neilsen characterises him as 'a post-Romantic writer',[2] thus aptly specifying the orientation of important aspects of the author's representation of subjectivity and landscape, his general sense of how human consciousness inhabits the world. Curiously, however, the major influence of Malouf's early career, the period of all his main poetic writing, is the modernist W. H. Auden. The influence is most pertinently stylistic, but Malouf's frequent adoption of Auden's characteristic tone, and thus, to a degree, his world-view, suggest this predecessor's more than merely technical importance. Auden is a key to understanding the *post*-Romantic thrust of Malouf's project, his will to update and rework Romantic thought and imagination in relation to the darkly shadowed experiential context of the late-modern epoch which Auden was among the first to document in poetic writing.[3]

Yet Malouf does not become un-Romantic in his quest to forge a post-Romantic writing. Already in the poetry of the 1960s and 1970s, and spectacularly in the 1978 novel *An Imaginary Life*, Malouf's work manifests its affiliation with Romanticism's legacy. The writing undertakes the detailed articulation of individual consciousness, portraying the 'I' self-consciously engaged in the processes of its becoming. This 'I', moreover, possesses a world-making power of imagination, and thus enables a creative conjunction between nature and consciousness. Malouf's portrayal of intense experiences of individual subjectivity and his affirmation of imagination's creative force recall Wordsworth, most particularly, among the Anglophone Romantics. But the Keatsian drive to push beyond the bounds of self, to imaginatively inhabit the other – the drive giving rise to the notion of 'negative capability' – is equally pertinent to the effective reading of Malouf, and especially of his imagined life of the poet Ovid.

Malouf also participates appreciably in the Romantic conception of the modern nation. His sense of the importance of language as a meeting-place for the negotiation of difference recalls Fichte's faith that the sharing of language founds all contemporary understanding within diversity and bears also the promise of ever improved, ever increasing understanding. In his sense of the individual and of the nation, Malouf is very much a writer of dawnings. Similarly Romantic in its provenence is his sense of the prevailing significance of the specificity of Australian landscape and of Australia's status as a continental island-nation, which recalls the Romantic affirmation of the nation-shaping role of geography most closely associated with J. G. von Herder. In *Fly Away Peter*, and still more clearly in *The Great World*, one can discern the influence of the Romantic conception of the need for nation-forging, nation-inaugurating epic. 'Most central to Malouf's work are the multivalent myths of Australian origins',[4] and as a maker of national myths, Malouf tacitly affirms the importance of a shared lore in the production of national consciousness – again a notion that is central to Romantic thought.

Neilsen, however, characterises Malouf as *post*-Romantic and not as a late-arriving Romantic. And he acknowledges that he is evaluating a writer who may be, in 1990, only in mid-career – a supposition that time has proved true. Only a few years later – but significantly after the appearance, in 1993, of *Remembering Babylon* – Nettelbeck usefully modifies Neilsen's assessment, affirming that Malouf combines 'Romantic idealism' with 'a post-colonial conception of language, world and subjectivity'.[5] She finds that Malouf coordinates with a particular transitional moment in Australia's cultural climate, when a 'tendency to look for national definition is ... being replaced by a more critical concern with the processes and effects of national myth-making' (i). He espouses the 'project of opening up the myths of our colonial past to reinterpretation'.[6]

The postcolonial frame of reference directs attention to a distinctly un-Romantic figure among Malouf's principal predecessors: Rudyard Kipling. As the writer who did most to establish English writing outside the British Isles and America – 'outside' both in relation to context and self-identification – Kipling merits a place in a good number of postcolonial lineages, but the link with Malouf is more than commonly close. The most immediately evident – and for some readers the most potentially problematic – similarity between the two writers is the preoccupation with masculine experience. A masculinist perspective typifies the male writers of empire, major and minor – not only Kipling, but also Conrad and Haggard, and Ballantyne, and Henty, and Wallace, and a long list of others now largely forgotten. It would be mistaken to say that Malouf shares with his imperial predecessors a sense that he inhabits a man's world, but male voices, male characters, and relationships between male characters, are unignorably prominent in his writing. Girls and women certainly are not such marginal presences as they tend to be in Kipling; in Malouf's prose fiction, female characters are numerous and often important, though never as important as the focal male characters. Detailed rendering of female perspectives only really begins with Imogen Harcourt, in *Fly Away Peter*, Malouf's third novel, but it is noteworthily present in all subsequent novel-length fictions. If women's perpective tends to reflect upon accompanying male characters, one should note that it often does so critically. The shortcomings of Lachlan, in *Remembering Babylon*, are never so clear as when seen through his cousin Janet's eyes; in *The Conversations at Curlow Creek*, Virgilia is both Adair's romanticised love-object and the most persistent and searching critic of his psychology and personality. Malouf, generally, is critical of the conventional codes of masculinity in ways that Kipling is not, although his exploration of masculinity is equally unrelenting. Indeed, Malouf's value as a contemporary writer resides in part in his critical re-evaluation of the codes of masculinity inherited from the imperial age.

Interestingly, a notable portion of Kipling's and Malouf's shared concerns serve to reveal what is arguably Romantic in the un-Romantic Kipling. Both writers make substantial use of the figure of the child. Malouf's most direct use of Kipling, in his libretto *Baa Baa Black Sheep*, admittedly makes the most use of Kipling's grim semi-autobiographical portrayal of a boyhood that is not at all in the Romantic vein. However, Kipling's Mowgli (who also finds his place in the libretto) and his Kim are significantly marked by Romantic conceptions of the child, and these boys find echoes in the wild boy of *An Imaginary Life* and in Gemmy of *Remembering Babylon*. For both writers (and for the Romantics) the child enjoys an intimate understanding of, a deep feeling for, the natural world. In such figures as Kipling's Kim and Malouf's Gemmy Fairley one also discerns the child's capacity to move back and forth across cultural borders and to grasp a variety of cultural idioms. The writers' use of the figure of the child reflects another, more broad-based shared orientation: responsiveness to the allure of the other. The child, particularly the wild child, does not yet have a fixed, socially assigned identity, and therefore represents otherness from the perspective of the fully socialised adult. Moreover, the child's own responsiveness and attraction to the other are assumed to be especially intense, multifaceted, and uninhibited.

For Kipling, however – and this is a principal source of dissatisfaction among his contemporary readers – the child's

access and mobility in relation to a diversity of cultural worlds
are recruited to the service of empire: Mowgli quickly becomes
first among brothers and ultimately achieves mastery of the
jungle, not simply inclusion; Kim's shape-shifting, his cultural
cross-dressing, is invariably an assertion of power, of power *over*
the other, and not the easy-going manifestation of democratic,
universal friendliness that it pretends to be. Kipling's imaginative engagement with otherness has always a certain stake in
domination; whereas Malouf's orientation is toward reconciliation, and this is increasingly the case as his career progresses.
Malouf nonetheless is keenly aware, as Kipling is, of power as
a key determinant of social relations. Will to power is part of
the composition of most of Malouf's more developed characters, even of the well-intentioned, generous-minded Frazer, in
Remembering Babylon, who takes it upon himself to account
for the black white man, Gemmy, and who feels slighted in
his authority when a decision about Gemmy is made without
consulting him. One may also note that violence, which associates closely with power struggles, is a quite prominent theme
in Malouf, albeit less so than in Kipling. Power in Kipling
inclines toward systematisation and control, and Kipling accepts,
as Malouf does not, the violence that favours the project of
power. Similarly, Kipling's mapping of diverse, concretely and
minutely detailed worlds, so characteristic of his texts, clearly
intends to enact the extension and consolidation of imperial
power. Malouf's mappings tend to be remappings, reconfigur-
ings of the world that acknowledge that the world can be – and
is – variously envisioned; Malouf's mappings counter rather
than confirm the perspective of power. Thus, Frazer's documentation of Queensland landscape sharply distinguishes itself from
Kim's investigation – one may say, his infiltration – of Indian
cultures. Kim is a bearer of the eye of empire; whereas Frazer's
vision challenges the pre-existing colonial understanding of the
land he studies. Malouf, however, does not oppose Kipling more
than he follows him. Kipling's ambivalence needs to be noted:
as his empire boys clearly demonstrate, Kipling's imagination
strains against established systems of imperial authority almost

as much as it favours them. Kim is never Colonel Creighton's minion, though he accepts the Colonel's offer of participation in the Great Game. Speaking of Kipling's relationship with empire and its ideals, Malouf writes, 'In the deepest part of himself, his imagination, he resisted' (*BBBS*, vi). One may say, then, that Malouf responds to Kipling by redirecting some of this predecessor's key initiatives, and also by attending to the resistance that shadows Kipling's portrayals of imperial power.

Comparison with Kipling brings Malouf into focus as a post-colonial writer, and so also – perhaps more – does comparison with Patrick White, the most compelling point of reference to be found among Australian writers, past and present. White precedes Malouf in his adoption of an international style and perspective, in his careful articulation of class and cultural difference, in his portrayal of the experience of exile, and in his recognition of the unsettling powers of Australia's natural landscapes. Indeed, much of Malouf's work undertakes to re-explore topics and concerns inaugurated by White. Certain of White's novels assert themselves as sources or templates for Malouf. Malouf's libretto for *Voss* derives directly from White's fiction, and frankly affirms its foundational importance. *Harland's Half Acre* (1984) can be read more effectively in the light of White's *The Vivisector* (1970). Malouf's painter is distinct from White's – certainly not a mere recapitulation – but some aspects of characterisation, notably the painter's obsessive commitment to his work, are shared, and for both painters the initiation to the life of art is an ordeal, and often harrowing. *Remembering Babylon* (1993) owes a portion at least of its achievement to the groundbreaking *A Fringe of Leaves* (1976). White, by his example, shows it is possible for a white writer to portray Aboriginal culture as more than simply 'primitive' and 'savage'. His novel also suggests that the white Australian's, or European's, experience of Aboriginal culture can be fortifying, self-regenerating, and not simply humiliating and traumatic (though it may be both of these as well).

A measured optimist, Malouf shows few or none of the corrosive and soul-pulverising aspects of White's vision, but he shares with his predecessor a multi-sited imagination and a perspective upon Australia that is not quite inside and not quite outside the place – intimately aware and yet detached. Certainly, Malouf's attempts, in *Harland's Half Acre* (1984) and *The Great World* (1990), to put forward an expansive but sharply, even in moments minutely, focused portrayal of Australian society must recall White's achievement in such works as *The Tree of Man* (1956) or *Riders in the Chariot* (1961). Malouf acknowledges White as an inspiring and yet somewhat daunting presence in Australian literary history: he opens new ground for fellow writers, but one must enter into a site of writing, Malouf concedes, 'always at the risk that he has been there before you'.[7] This somewhat ambivalent tribute may represent, however, a personal rather than a general response. Certainly, one does not discern in Peter Carey or Thomas Keneally the same felt need to grapple with White's legacy. Intense engagement with postcolonial questions is not continuous in Malouf's work, nor is it in White's, but both writers emerge within postcolonial experience and history, and White exemplifies an orientation of thought and imagination that Malouf takes up and pursues. A case for a postcolonial reading of *An Imaginary Life* needs to be made (and has been made), but one can scarcely begin to account for the whats and the wherefores of Malouf's accomplishment in *Remembering Babylon* and *The Conversations at Curlow Creek* without considering the postcolonial aspects of both works.

To further specify the postcolonial character of Malouf's writing, one can situate it within the body of writing originating in former settler colonies. Considered in this international frame, Malouf affiliates with Canada's Timothy Findley, whose novel *The Wars* (1977) bears immediate comparison with *Fly Away Peter* (1982), and to a lesser degree with Michael Ondaatje in such works as *In the Skin of the Lion* (1987) or *The English Patient* (1992). The most compelling point of comparison, however, is with South Africa's J. M. Coetzee, the 2003 Nobel laureate in literature and, coincidentally, a recent immigrant to Australia. Like Coetzee, Malouf manifests in his writing a deep-seated insecurity about belonging to one's place. What Bliss asserts about Malouf is equally – or more – true of Coetzee: both writers manifest the 'schizophrenia' of settler cultures, which arises from the settlers' being obliged to conceive of themselves both as 'colonial invaders' and as 'resistant imperial subjects'; both writers, and the characters they create, must wrestle, unceasingly, with 'the ambiguities of postcolonial status'.[8] In Coetzee's most representative and accomplished fictions – works such as *Waiting for the Barbarians* (1980), *Life and Times of Michael K* (1983), *Age of Iron* (1990), and *Disgrace* (1999) – characters are made to inhabit worlds that come to appear impossibly unjust. Malouf's vision is never so extreme, so exacerbated, but it shares with Coetzee's an intense and abiding concern with the marginalisation, disenfranchisement, and exclusion that are at work in the social order of the postcolony. His fiction, like Coetzee's, is significantly peopled with those who cannot discover a valid social belonging, either because they are directly submitted to alienating social forces or because they cannot accept their own possible belonging in the face of another's exclusion. Both writers are deeply ethical in outlook, perhaps ethical more than political; certainly, they both arrive at their political stances – against colonial or neocolonial social order, against racism – by following the paths of ethical analysis.

In comparison with Coetzee, however, as with White, Malouf is the more optimistic. Coetzee's protagonists typically fail in their quest to discover a workable resolution for the problems arising from difference – problems that are particularly pressing in the racially and ethnically mixed society of the postcolony. The Magistrate of *Waiting for the Barbarians* never arrives at a really clear understanding of his barbarian companion, nor of the nature of his feeling for her; in *Age of Iron*, Elizabeth Curren's quest to justify the politics of difference in the society of apartheid leads, with seeming inevitability, to self-immolation. Malouf's focal characters, however, quite dependably derive some benefit from the negotiation of difference: new clarity of understanding, more integrated vision, a new sense of self and of the world one inhabits. Like Coetzee, but again to a lesser degree, Malouf represents violence and violation in the social worlds he portrays, but his narratives retain, or at least return to, a measured hope for a better, more just, more fulfilling experience of self, of the world, of life – even of death. His capacity to maintain a utopian strain in his work most probably derives from his particular understanding of the core regime of the society of division, inequality, and injustice – what one may call, speaking in the broadest terms, the state of empire. Empire, for Malouf, establishes its reign over a world of essences; or, to speak with stricter accuracy, empire posits a world of essences over which it can establish and maintain its reign. In opposition to the rule of empire, Malouf fabricates a world in transformation, a world of transformations, which can never enduringly retain the structure of empire. Malouf's responsiveness to the allure of alterity, of difference, and to the personal and social transformations they can inspire, thus discovers its anti-imperial thrust.

The particular character of Malouf's writing and the assembly of its various literary influences and affiliations link with his biography in potentially elucidating ways. Born and bred in Brisbane, Malouf subsequently embarked on a period of international migration and eventually resettled in Australia (though not in Brisbane). This history of movement and self-transplanting, and especially the places it has included, has a palpable impact on his work. Malouf's early formation takes place in the social context of post-Second World War Australia. For him, as for others of his generation, this context contributes to a burgeoning new awareness of America and Asia, a new sense of Australia's place in a global assembly of nations and cultures. However, the Second World War experience in Australia has for Malouf a distinctly personal jagged edge (and his work, one may add, is full of edges): Malouf's Lebanese grandfather, his father's father from whom he inherits his surname, was temporarily submitted to arrest as a (potential) enemy alien, as the author himself records in the autobiographical essay 'The Kyogle Line'. This unpleasant incident recalls, and to a certain degree reinstates, an equally unpleasant history: Lebanese migrants had previously been 'grouped as undesirable Asians', an order that was not rescinded until 1926.[9] The war years, and those that followed, served to put Australia in closer contact with the world beyond its shores, but also awakened the history of Australia's problematically selective refusals of contact with the world.

Hodge and Mishra locate Malouf within the field of migrant writing, but as an example of 'reverse assimilationism', as an 'expatriate son of an assimilated migrant'. Australia, for Malouf, is a place of exile from which one 'exiles oneself'; indeed, it is not so much 'the place of exile' but more meaningfully 'the place of return'.[10] West pushes further with this thinking, declaring that a self-originating exile is 'the very ground of linguistic innovation and artistic redemption'.[11] And indeed, much of Malouf's writing seeks to find ways back into Australian culture and society, to envision Australia in ways that make it habitable, a place of meaningful, self-sustaining community. Malouf's belonging in Australia has been a matter of question, in the space of the author's own lifetime, and not only because he has resided in England and in Italy. He has been susceptible to construction as an other in the society of his birth. His attraction to otherness, and the high value he places on it, may well come out of his own historically ambiguous relationship with Australian identity. This same historically ambiguous relationship may shed light on other key features critics have discerned in Malouf: Neilsen sees that, in Malouf's work, 'nationality' or 'Australian-ness' are prominent among the abiding 'preoccupations', but also that Australia, in Malouf's representation, is 'a place we are still in the process of constructing culturally';[12] Scheckter argues that Malouf's writing shows a consistent concern with 'the exploration of historical influences upon a present consciousness'.[13]

In his poetry and again in the later-arriving autobiography, 12 Edmondstone Street, Malouf explores in considerable detail issues of cross-cultural migrancy as these pertain to his family and himself. However, in his fictional works, the main bulk of his writing, his consideration of migrancy becomes very broad-based and far-reaching: Australia takes shape as a nation composed of migrants and definingly characterised by ongoing multidirectional migration. Indeed, the tendency not to stay in one place, to move about the world, to err, emerges as the principal shared characteristic of Malouf's main characters. In his fictions, Australians travel to Europe, and Europeans to Australia. Australian soldiers, sent to Europe for the First World War, are shipped to south-east Asia for the Second; in both cases, the more fortunate ones travel back again, bringing experience of the Great World with them. Even the Australian characters who never travel beyond the shores of their nation-continent are strongly associated with movement within it. Malouf's Australia is a nation on the move, created and then repeatedly transformed by migrations.

Malouf is a writer whose main project is to rediscover and remake himself and his world. Not surprisingly, his career in poetry aims at a complexly detailed elaboration of personal experience, of the self and of the places of the self; his career in fiction moves dense portrayals of singularity in the first-person voice to the representation of a multiplicity of perspectives. The valorisation of multiplicity, in fictional presentation and in the social world, emerges out of a preceding valorisation of otherness. Malouf does not seek, however, to resolve difference or assimilate otherness; his sense is always that difference and otherness should be recognised, acknowledged, and valued.

The poetry

Although Malouf's international reputation is very much founded on his achievements in fiction, he began as a poet and was nearly two decades into his career before publishing his first substantial fiction. In his Preface to *Johnno*, Malouf offers some brief analysis of the creative process, in some aspects very practical, that initiated and sustained his first novel's composition. Forging the crucial first sentence of what will become the first novel entailed 'falling back on the open, undefended tone of poems ... written a decade before'. Further specifying his case, Malouf goes on to state that the first novel's central, generative problem – also in very real terms its inspiration – the death in 1962 of Malouf's friend John Milliner – had already been treated in the poem 'The Judas Touch'. 'But poems', Malouf concludes, 'are glancing affairs and I wanted to commit myself now to the steady gaze' (*J*, viii), seeming thus almost to disparage the achievements of his early career.

Dated May 1997, the Preface is a late-arriving, retrospective document, which needs to be evaluated with some caution. More than anything, it tells how the well-established author of prose fictions chooses to situate his inaugural career as a poet. Yet one cannot ignore that Malouf clearly sees his poetry as looking forward to his later-arriving prose fictions, and that he claims, moreover, to be putting aspects of real, remembered, writerly experience on record. Viewed in this light, his statements offer some justification for considering the poetic production, in relation to the overall career, as an apprenticeship, a forging of style and a preliminary mapping of topics and concerns. Some critics, one should note, have gone on record in favour of the prose fictions. Philip Neilsen, though at his time of writing the fictional career had not proceeded past *The Great World*, already opines that Malouf's 'reputation ... will ultimately be based on his fiction'.[1] Malouf himself has authorised the idea that literary 'excitement' in Australia shifts from poetry to fiction by the early 1980s.[2] Yet Ivor Indyk, publishing in 2001, affirms that the poetic career had a defining, and not merely initiatory, importance; that the internationally acclaimed writer of prose fictions has remained, essentially, a poet.[3]

Certainly, one cannot acquire a reading knowledge of the poetry and the prose fictions without recognising that they are of a piece, differently distributed in time but the products of the same hand. The correspondences between the two bodies of work are numerous and in some cases (as will be shown) quite exact. A good number of Malouf's favoured images and figures establish themselves first in the poems before impressing themselves upon the prose works; indeed, Malouf's personal image-repertoire shows itself fully furnished, or nearly so. Angels, which appear quite frequently in the prose works, are already present in the poetry, though appearing more frequently from the mid-1970s forward. Schoolchildren at play are 'like angels' who 'plunge into the sun' (*P*, 112); 'Angels' inscribe themselves on 'a blank page' (*P*, 131); 'dirigibles' are 'fat angels' (*P*, 147); caretakers are 'angels in rubber/ boots' (*P*, 214); 'a sullen angel' struggles against the world-as-it-is (*P*, 223). Malouf's angel is most fundamentally the attractive form of the stranger; however, the figure's repeated use works to produce the stranger as attractive, alluring, rather than fearful – an extraordinary being but not unrecognisable. The poetry celebrates 'the angel/ who comes to us in so many forms' (*P*, 231), but this preferred figure, the angel, is still a work-in-progress during the poetic career. Malouf does not yet seem entirely clear on the use he has for it. In later fictions, such as 1993's *Remembering Babylon*, angels have clearly emerged as beings that come from outside the usual frame of human lives and thus bear a challenge or message to these lives. Malouf's preferred angel, in other words, is ultimately an angel of annunciation, as is already suggested when he surmises that the crab-strangers of 'The Crab Feast', 'may be angels/ in the only condition/ our senses reach them in' (P, 184).

Malouf's abiding sense of an enlivening outside of experience, with which we can and do establish connection, also works itself in relation to delineation of edges. The edge or margin emerges quite early in the poems as an orientating image-concept. The poems emphasise the notion that Australia, the island continent, is defined by real terrestrial outline or edge, as in the case of 'Sheer Edge', a notable poem from the earliest collection, which situates itself 'Here at the sheer edge/ of a continent' (P, 14). This orientation of Malouf's vision endures in the fictions, even playing a crucial role in 'Great Day', the final and most substantial story in the 2000 collection *Dream Stuff: Stories*. Continental consciousness, very important in 'Great Day' and other short fictions, seems to emerge first in the poetry and out of edge-orientated thinking. Edge is 'at the centre' of Malouf's concerns; it is 'where things happen', the site of 'discoveries', 'metamorphoses', and 'revelations'. Edge is 'where inside and outside meet and sometimes interpenetrate'.[4] The edge may outline a place of darkness and danger – the not-yet-known and unforeseeable; 'In the Sea's Giving' considers, with a definite tincture of uneasiness, that the ocean beyond the inhabited edge of the continent imposes itself as 'A world so close that was not/ ours' (P, 148). Yet edge is also, Malouf elsewhere affirms, the place where 'may flower,/ precarious as weed/ or grey gull's nest, the moment/ of touching, the poem' (P, 14). The poetry, like the prose fiction, uses edge to set about 'proving there's another/ world to be grasped' (P, 136). Interestingly, the poem from which this last quotation is taken is titled 'A Critique of Pure Reason'.

Edge, of course, is space-defining, and its importance is part of Malouf's self-configuration as a writer of place. The will to discover and delineate the specific places in which experience unfolds shapes Malouf's writing career in all its facets and phases. Even memory, an equally durable aspect of Malouf's writerly orientation, tends strongly to be organised in relation to place: understanding remembered experience, and portraying it fully, entails rediscovering *where* one was. Barnard Turner affirms that 'the mind moving over a landscape' is the fundamental action of Malouf's poetic engagement with questions of identity, personal and national.[5] For Wallace-Crabbe, the poems 'celebrate the influence of benevolent places', revealing Malouf as a 'memorialist of mixed Arcadias', who 'reads landscape ... for signs of time regained'.[6] Even the very earliest published poems, such as 'At My Grandmother's', 'Childhood Illness', or 'Indoor Garden', confirm the pertinence of these observations. The close concern with the interrelations of place, memory, and sense of self may also be reflected by the poetry's frequent references to suburbs – which seldom appear as topics in the prose fictions. The poetry is, generally speaking, more personally orientated than the prose, and suburbs are – for Malouf as for so many other middle-class moderns, and especially in Australia – prominent in experience (if not always in esteem). Suburbs may also have attracted Malouf's early-career imagination because they are definitionally marginal spaces, but nonetheless may come to define centres as much as they are defined by them.

Turner finds the poetry notably regional in its attachment to South Queensland, and especially Brisbane, and somewhat regrets Malouf's wilful adoption of 'international style'.[7] However, Europe, in addition to providing measures of style, is an important sector in Malouf's assembly of significant places. The question, always, is the relationship of Europe and Australia, and more specifically, how much this place called 'Europe' is to be located inside or outside Australia. European spaces, especially those of Italy, but also of England and of other countries, are prominent in the early poetry collections and tend to receive a relatively independent consideration – they are among the places of the poet's larger world. However, a poem sited in Europe will often reflect upon Australia, as when 'Halfway Home' concludes, 'My blood beats south toward spring, another continent, the dawn' (*P*, 29). And travellers – these presumably are to be understood as Australian travellers – are noteworthily characterised as 'Double agents/ unfaithful to both worlds' (*P*, 93). Yet Europe observed by the alert writer-traveller can at times yield quite startling effects. Malouf's canny irony in 'At Ravenna' must seem slightly uncanny to the twenty-first-century reader. A composition of the early 1970s, the poem speaks of an encounter with 'one of the bright new Europeans', who voices 'a passionate conviction/ all Europe could be saved, one continent, one people undivided' (*P*, 109).

In the poetry and in the prose narratives, Malouf's principal place is the body. Dale and Gilbert find that 'metaphorisation of the body' orders much of the poetry and leads, by extension, to an 'erotics of place'.[8] Malouf's treatments of place frequently suggest the will to find or establish, in his words, 'some workshop where the world/ is one with our five senses' (*P*, 213). In many of the poems, and in much of the prose fiction that follows, Malouf strives, seemingly whenever possible, to encounter his world as a complete sensuous body, and not just as an eye or ear. The senses that actually contact and interact with the substances of the world are brought into play; things touched, tasted, or smelled often contribute indissociably to the composition of place. Thus, the first fact of a remembered childhood illness is 'His fingers quailed and lost their grip', and in a significant subsequent metaphor 'light turned sour upon his lids' (*P*, 5), as though the eye itself can be experienced as a tasting organ. The imagined plague-stricken city of 'From a Plague Year', although its representation puts forward political reflections, does not dwell in arid abstraction: plague asserts itself when 'pale flesh bruises/ black, then stinks and softens', and with plague's irresistible advance, the speaker concludes, 'It is death/ we suck on now' (*P*, 24).

Malouf imagines in terms of embodied consciousness, which is probably the main reason that his poems insistently represent the skull as the location of mental experience – rarely the head, and only very exceptionally the mind. In 'Air Rifle', 'new horizons/ open in a skull' (*P*, 48). Even those too-often-sentimentalised human figures, schoolchildren, find that new snow invades 'the spaces of their skull' (*P*, 49). Malouf chooses the uncompromisingly concrete skeletal structure, the hard casing the body provides for the mind. The skull is the camera obscura of which experience makes a camera lucida; it is also the bodily structure that best mimics the orb of the world. The prose poem 'A Poor Man's Guide to Southern Tuscany' situates experience within 'the horizon of the viewer's skull' (P, 192), almost as if the skull represented the hard outline of the globe, the three-dimensional map of the world.

Considered generally, the poems show numerous distinct merits as poetry – as writing within poetic forms and traditions. Numerous fresh and startling images take shape. A bicycle makes its appearance as 'this tall metallic insect,/ this angel of two geometries/ and speed' (P, 59). The early love lyric 'Poem' celebrates 'our pear-tree/ brimming with wasps' (P, 38). The tree as a figure of abiding and abounding life is still better realised in 'Evergreen', which portrays 'a bunya-pine, its roots/ deep in the 1880's, bubbling with doves' (P, 73). In both of these tree evocations, a shrewdly chosen action word – 'brimming', 'bubbling' – is the key to the writing's success. Very often Malouf's better effects emerge out of verb choices, as in the finely phrased affirmation 'It is ourselves/ we hoard' (P, 46), or in the palpable descriptive clause, 'children writhe out of our grip' (P, 51). The verb choices impress by their aptness, though frequently they are far from sweet, as in the following delineation of the brutal finality of a relationship's end: 'my father's tough heart slammed/ and shut her out' (P, 68).

The poetry, then, has specificity and integrity of its own, but does unmistakably look forward to the later prose works, with which it maintains a continuity of contents and concerns. Clear recognisable traces of key moments in the fictional works reveal themselves with dependable regularity in the poetic works. In the relatively early 'Glasshouse Mountains', 'sea lice,/ keen flakes of moonlight scatter/ and burn' (P, 34), looking forward to the tiny, teeming, luminescent sea creatures that cover the newly beached body of the child Gemmy in *Remembering Babylon* – which was published twenty-three years later. Another important image from the 1993 novel, the new-awakened, rearing snake that figures the rousing of Gemmy's dark and menacing memories, is suggested in the 1970 poem 'At Kew Gardens': 'At Kew, full circle/ season and century. The green vine rears/ like a serpent. Hear it softly coil and hiss' (*P*, 44). 'The City of God', another 1970s work, importantly manifests Malouf's interest in the Augustinian idea that will organise Janet McIvor's – or rather Sister Monica's – mature sense of the community of bees.

The powerful evocation of transformation, so crucial to the fullest achievement of *An Imaginary Life*, also finds itself anticipated in the poetry. In 'Asphodel', the nearly drowned child's return to life is mutation as much as restoration:

> Face down in the blady grass and pummeled alive again
>   I gagged
> on unfamiliar breath; my belly's
> mud gave up its frogspawn; waterspouts and cataclysms
> broke from my lungs. Filled
> a moment with its strangeness I discovered
> a lifelong taste for earth: gills flared
> at my throat, plant fossils sprouted in my thumbs. (*P*, 63)

'The Fables' similarly affirms that to properly understand a wood, you must 'rub fur/ in your groin and sense the hardening/ of fingernails, of toenails/ to horn' (*P*, 134). 'Stooping to Drink', from the award-winning 1975 collection *Neighbours in a Thicket*, must associate, in the mind of a reader of *An Imaginary Life*, with the splendid moment when Ovid dreams himself as a pool of water. As in the novel's passage, the poem emphasises water's reflectiveness and also its liquid receptivity to touch, to contact. The poet drinker collects together his experience fluidly:

> Taking all this in
> as the water takes it: sky
> sunlight, sweet grass-flavours
> and the long-held breath
> of children – a landscape
> mirrored, held a moment,
> and let go again (*P*, 112–3)

Here, as in the novel that will follow a few years later, Malouf articulates his sense of water's specific place in human experience and imagination: contact with water always breaks through surface; it reflects, and thus figures other bodies on its surface, but it also receives them, takes them in and holds them within its own body.

'An Ordinary Evening at Hamilton', another notable poem from the *Neighbours in a Thicket* collection, looks forward to the handling of domestic space one finds in the prose autobiography '12 Edmondstone Street' (from 1985's *12 Edmondstone Street*). Again, the concept of edge is saliently important, though its service as border or barrier is becoming decidedly uncertain, as in the autobiography. The poem presents the ostensibly enclosed house as marvellously, and alarmingly, open to the world beyond its bounds: 'The Pacific/ breaks at our table'. The choice of verb here introduces a genial ambiguity: are the ocean's breaking waves instances of housebreaking, or the easy, communal breakings of bread? 'Familiar rooms', the poem goes on to state, become 'exotic islands', and the house as a whole 'a strange anatomy of parts, so many neighbours in a thicket: hair, eyetooth, thumb' (*P*, 76). Here, as in '12 Edmondstone Street', domestic space manifests its exotic, uncanny aspects, also its heterogeneous multiplicity. The final mapping of inhabited space is in relation to the body, as is again the case in the autobiographical writing. In Malouf's own words, 'poetry begins/ as the body makes it' (*P*, 131). This anchoring sense of the body's insistent, even obstreperous, presence continues throughout the prose-writing career, but is perhaps most evident in the most recent full-length novel, *The Conversations at Curlow Creek*.

Malouf first articulates his rather fraught relationship with questions of genealogy in his poetry, though genealogical concerns contribute much to his autobiography, and to fictional works such as *Harland's Half Acre* and *The Great World*. 'Confessions of an Only Child' seems the first work to assert that genealogy is a path by which strangers enter our lives: one's nose may well be 'grandfather's', upon consideration; one may also note that 'the high cheekbones/ of parents and other strangers/ rise under the skin' (*P*, 65–6). Malouf's Lebanese grandfather is also remembered in 'Early Discoveries', where he is one set apart by having 'come too far from his century', by a 'foreign' odour, which may be 'garlic or old age', and by his life-sustaining collection of 'odd rites' (*P*, 69). The grandfather appears again, in the later poetry, as a kind of curiously proximate stranger, which is very much his role in '12 Edmondstone Street'. In 'To Be Written in Another Tongue', the tongue of the title is 'the language in which my grandfather/ dreams now he is dead'. The poem resolves its reflections upon the 'yearning/ of grandsons for a language/ the dead still speak'. This curiously pre-modern and non-Western notion of enduring ancestral presence, of the dead who still dream and speak, puts one in mind of the Aboriginal dreamtime. For the speaker, the language that makes the dead-and-gone present is a language of 'common objects' and yet, finally, 'strange upon the tongue' (*P*, 145). In this way, the tongue that is a language at the outset becomes at the resolution a bodily organ, or returns, one may say, to that originary status. The poetry that begins with the body also, it seems, seeks its way back to the body.

The poems evoke the native Australian notion of the dreamtime, which plays a particularly important role in the 1996 novel *The Conversations at Curlow Creek*, in several instances. 'Beside the Sea' presents time's interpenetrating moments 'slipping through/ from the now that is to the now that was or would be' (*P*, 228). In 'The Gift, Another Life', past, present, and future shiftingly cohabit, mingle and meld:

> We share
> our lives with ghosts, the future strikes
> clear through us, we are here
> and gone where crumbling paddocks dream
> their first green world ploughed under (*P*, 123)

Interestingly, it is in a paddock that Garrety of *Conversations* will have his most important, and most harrowing, dreamtime experience. But indeed, the correspondences between Malouf's imaginative productions are quite often surprisingly precise. The crucial final image of 1990's *The Great World* returns the reader to the child Vic striving to thread a needle. The same book explores, in the final passage and elsewhere, the notion of seeing the world through a needle's eye. In 'A Thousand and One Nights', one boy enters the 'life' of another 'through the eye/ of a tailor's needle' (*P*, 138); in 'The City of God' a host of nations is called upon to 'set off barefoot through the needle's eye' (*P*, 142); another 'needle's eye', another all-seeing point of passage, is hidden in the haystacks of 'Haystacks' (*P*, 216).

Concerning Malouf's place in the genealogies of poetic production, a few critics have agreed that W. H. Auden is the most notably influential of Malouf's poetic predecessors. Wallace-Crabbe finds Auden in Malouf, although he considers that Malouf is a 'poet of memory', and Auden very much not.[9] Sharrad also finds traits of Auden, and Malouf in interview has acknowledged Auden's influence.[10] Auden is evident in the often scrupulously dispassionate tone, and in the particular turning of certain images and phrases. So 'Health Farm', a short piece from Malouf's earliest independent collection, concludes, 'The lucky poor of course are always thin' (*P*, 32). The acerbic oxymoron 'lucky poor' already smacks something of Auden, but this foretaste comes through more clearly as the line goes on ironically to contrast the fatality of the poor person's leanness with the often fatuous aspiration to a trim, slender figure character-ising the Western middle and upper classes of the later twentieth century. One recalls Auden's writing of 'the poor' who are 'fairly accustomed' to their 'sufferings',[11] where irony quietly reminds us that the habit of poverty is neither fair-beautiful nor fair-just. The Auden tone and manner is again evident when Malouf, in 'Babysitting', represents Vietnam casualties as 'cold facts, the cold conditions of our time' (*P*, 45). As in Auden, one finds here a cool-headed coming to terms with the unacceptable, a sense that modern consciousness must maintain itself in contradic-tion with the heart's aspirations, with fully human sympathies. Thus, in 'Report from Champagne Country', a poem about war can become a 'Report' yet also find its source in the teasingly romantic 'Champagne Country'. And the shattering violence of war deaths can become 'shinbone, brain-pan, clavicle/ parting in a shambles' (*P*, 100). The human tragedy's absorption in the dull quotidian process of the world, such as one finds in Auden's 'Landscape with the Fall of Icarus', is noted also in Malouf, as when he ponders the ancient French battlefield:

> cattle stare into dead men's eyes, slow jaws mull over
> enigmas, energies at work down there, brutal illusions
>
> we are not done with yet, the good years go on happening.
> (P, 102)

The 'brutal illusions' are not yet clearly marked by Auden's impress, nor yet the dubious and deliberately facile mention of 'the good years', but the 'we' that conscripts us into a compromised group we would rather not be part of – that is unmistakably an Auden gesture. One recalls, for instance, 'the monstrous forms and lives/ With which we have nothing, we like to hope, in common' appearing in 'In Praise of Limestone'.[12] A similar 'we' appears in 'Natural History Museum':

> We are all exhibits here. In the greater dissolution
> that spreads beyond these walls, the wreaker's ball like a
>   pendulum
>
> swings through our days (P, 120)

Another such 'we' inscribes itself in 'News from the Dark Ages', where Malouf's speaker reflects, 'All/ that we do, all that we say/ betrays us', and then immediately urges, 'Forgive, since no man here is guiltless, the treason of clerks' (P, 106). Although this poem focuses upon Ezra Pound's Italian career, the notion of a modern universality of guilt is much more Auden than Pound (in any of his guises), and the combination of the highly emotive 'treason' with dull, everyday 'clerks' is entirely in tune with the Auden style.

   In both Auden and Malouf the dispassionate tone feels slightly feigned or forced. This is not necessarily a fault in either, as a feigned or forced dispassionateness may well be a pre-eminently modern disposition, the inescapably imperfect resolution of human sentience's strained relationship with the contradictions and dissymmetries of the modern experience. However, if poetic writing aims ultimately to produce a particular, new, and distinctive voice, then the voice of modern (feigned or forced) dispassionateness is Auden's more than it can ever be Malouf's. In this respect, Malouf may have taken too much from his distinguished forerunner, especially when one considers that Malouf's most modern reflections are typically in the manner of Auden. In 'A Poet among Others', one reads,

> And the state is everywhere. In a man's guts
> It aches, in the ear of corn it shouts its slogans, in a thick skull lodges
>
> its birdsongs like lead. (P, 107)

The diction – notably 'guts' and still more clearly 'slogans' – is distinctly Audenesque, as is the sense of the uneasy cohabitation of natural elements – 'the ear of corn', the 'birdsongs' – with the dominent, context-defining elements of human modernity. The subsequent sense of nature's abiding, curiously inviolate being – the grass that is 'innocent' and 'fortunate', and whose seed is 'unkillable' (P, 108) – also links with Auden's vision, as when, on the cold day of a poet's death, 'wolves ran on through the evergreen forests'.[13] However, the Auden intertext often appears more starkly, especially in the poetry of the early and middle period – that is, from the 1960s through to the mid-1970s – when Auden's influence is most insistently evident. So, in 'Elective Affinities', Malouf's 'all we doubted/ the instruments make plain' (P, 135) recalls Auden's 'what instruments we have agree' from 'In Memory of W. B. Yeats'.[14]

Even Malouf's rendering of erotic experience can show strong markings of the Auden manner, though Malouf's imagination is more autonomous, while remaining very modern, when in the realm of eros. Malouf's 'Escape from the City of Glass' speaks, in one of its moments, of

> lovers who sink down in a wood,
>
> dishevelled, lost, from the night's misunderstandings
> rise to find provisional happy endings
>
> in perfect rhymes and vows sworn fathoms deep,
> the promises imperfect lives must keep. (P, 147)

The contextualisation of tender, lyrical renderings with 'provisional' good fortunes and 'imperfect lives' recalls Auden in
works such as 'Lullaby', with its opening invitation, 'Lay your
sleeping head, my love,/ Human on my faithless arm', or again,
its characterisation of the beloved as 'Mortal, guilty, but to me/
The entirely beautiful'.[15]

The will to engage with and portray erotic experience,
however, is very specifically an aspect of Malouf's *poetic* writing
– Auden or no Auden; whereas, the details of sexual life very
rarely find their way into the fictions before the publication of
The Conversations at Curlow Creek. Love lyrics appear regularly
throughout the poetic publications, along with well-turned
momentary reflections upon the ways of eros in poems that
are not in the main about love. 'Easier', a particularly pleasing
love lyric, first offers a quietly humorous characterisation of
a relationship that has situated itself and achieved its proper
poise and balance: 'we make room/ for each other's oddities'.
But it moves surely toward the ordinary extraordinariness, the
moments of wonder, private yet shared, the 'night journeys hand
in hand/ across distances like Russia, touching/ down to find pale
sunstalks in our bed' (*P*, 47).

Of the erotic poems, 'The Crab Feast' is the richest. The last
and most accomplished of Malouf's longer poems, it is a sustained
yet pleasingly varied meditation affirming that discovery of the
other is the generative core of erotic experience. It also provides
the clearest demonstration that, in Malouf's vision, the object
of erotic feeling tends to be rather arbitrary, very commonly
chance-met rather than an effect of pre-established disposition.
In his 1993 monograph on Malouf, Indyk argues repeatedly for
Malouf's homosexual orientation. Indyk's main statement on
'The Crab Feast', however, is that it represents 'a philosophical
and visionary apprehension of the grounds of existence'.[16] This is
true enough, but fails to note that eros organises these 'grounds'
and does so rather whimsically, without clear reference to specifi-
able, socially-encoded sexual dispositions. The erotic object – and
this is not at all atypical in Malouf – takes shape in relation to

the cluster of affects it rouses in the lover who discovers therein his here-and-now version of the lover's role.

The crab is immediately established as an object of extreme delectation, a love object:

> There is no getting closer
> than this. My tongue slips into
> the furthest, sweetest corner
> of you. (*P*, 180)

The poem's third and fourth sentences then assert learning and discovery, intimate knowledge that melds the knower with the known:

> I know all
>
> now all your secrets.
> When the shell
> cracked there was nothing
> between us. (*P*, 180)

The poem's first movement (the first of ten) goes on to observe, 'knowing the ways/ we differ I'd come to think we must be one', lines which turn on the ambiguous use of 'must be': is the necessity, the 'must be', a matter of incontrovertible fact or intense desire; is one driven by the allure of difference to unite with the other, or is communion in a sense actualised when one recognises in the other a difference that can complete oneself? Certainly, the lover who consumes the other must also become for the other, for the beloved, a new site of being, must provide 'a new habitat under the coral/ reef of my ribs' (*P*, 180). Here, as elsewhere in the poetry (see also *P*, 82, 85, 87), the scene unfolds beneath moonlight; the moon, being the changeful star, oversees the processes of transformation. But the unfolding of this poem's narrative action occurs, more specifically, 'under the moon's/ ashes' (*P*, 180), at once evoking an impressive visual image – the scattered silver-grey light of moon on water – and suggesting, with the 'ashes' of the moon's reflected and reflective fire, that significant work of transformation has already taken place, preceding and enabling present experience.

In the poem's third movement the phrasing of 'the breaths/ we draw between cries' puts forward again a marvellously ambiguous image: these are the breaths between cries that mark the duration of a sexual encounter, but also the series of mortal breaths that measure our time between the birth cry and death's rough rattle. Love and life, then, share a structure; love, to put it another way, is principal among the life-drives. This generalised eroticisation of the mortal (and human) experience readily extends itself to elements of natural landscape: it is repeatedly applied to the crab quarry and also marks fireflies, those 'small hot love-crazed/ planets' (P, 182). The notion is classical: eros is not an exclusively human quantum; it is a multiform force within the world we inhabit, and one that links us to the world's other inhabitants.

In the fourth movement, the crab-hunter aims 'to learn/ how changeable we are'. His relation to the crab he hunts entails a wish 'to push on through' to new knowledge of life and death. Death confirms that change, radical change, is the mission of living being, the goal. But this sense of the need to change, to change in response to the other and toward the other, leads in the fourth movement to a troubled sense of isolation in difference: 'I watch and am shut out./ The terrible privacies!' (Malouf here allows himself an exclamation mark, which he very seldom does.) Though isolated from the natural other by 'pure humanity', the speaker claims, 'I look through into your life. Its mysteries disarm me' (P, 184). This hope that one can look into and apprehend the other's specificities, despite radical difference, develops further in the sixth movement – 'Drawn/ by unlikeness, I grew like you, or dreamed I did' (P, 184–5) – and in the seventh the other becomes the self's 'counterweight', although the two belong to 'different orders' of being (P, 185, 186).

Both self and other are 'beyond speech' (P, 188), yet the speaker/ crab hunter avows to his quarry, 'Our kinship is metaphorical' (P, 186), and finally asserts, 'words made you/ a fact in my head. You were myself in another species' (P, 188–9). The relation is created and sustained symbolically, in and by language, but it is, for all of that, a real transformation of the world's elements, a real creation and a *relational* creation, one that does not belong exclusively to either partner/participant: one that overcomes, moreover, their primary status as isolate beings, beyond speech. If the lover comes 'bearing a death' (*P*, 186), as he insists he does, it is both the Renaissance 'little death' that asserts life in the most energetic expending of it and also a dying into newness, into a different being newly formed and newly situated.

The poem ends with the assertion 'We are one at last', a communion achieved through 'a love feast' (*P*, 189) – the poem's last metaphor, though it is a metaphor the poem has worked to make ineluctable, literal. Where and how, this poem asks, do I begin and end, in relation to the other, to life, to the world? It concludes that I am, but not discretely; I situate myself in life and in the world, but I do so indiscriminately. The poem's final word, its last line and last sentence, is the command form 'Begin' followed by the full stop. (The much-evoked death clearly has no absolute finality; it is among the transformations.) In this final imperative is self-assertion but also the relinquishing of self; it is a command that makes self the object for the other to work upon. A poem, like other individual instances of creative, relational, erotic being, begins and ends in the same moment in the same place – or rather, begins and ends in any of its moments and any of its places.

The vision of 'The Crab Feast' does, then, examine the 'grounds of existence' (and finds them complexly erotic); it also, in the process, succeeds in outlining an ethics of subjectivity, portraying not simply how we experience our lives but how we *should* experience them. 'Magpie', listed among the 'New and Uncollected Poems' of *Poems 1959–89*, articulates key aspects of this ethics more programmatically, one may say. And given that this is not an erotic work, it carries the suggestion that eros itself emerges only in relation to still more fundamental drives that order the unfolding of consciousness. The magpie's specificity and value resides first and foremost in its being an agent of transformation: 'Magpie changes the subject, takes things out/ of themselves into second nature' (*P*, 217). This flighty being is a *bricoleur* of self-fashioning, avid for a diversity of elements, for all things in which difference dwells. It is specular speculative, a seeker of mirrors: '*I hoard them, I hang them/ in thickets where they double/ the sun*' (*P*, 218). The mirrors, significantly, are not for the reproduction of the self and its images, but for doubling and multiplying the elements in the world. The magpie of consciousness, through its reflections, makes the world's fullness all the more abounding. Crucially, 'magpie keeps/ touch with the ado/ he springs from' (*P*, 219). Here is no will to separateness, to detachment; this being made of the world's bustle and business wilfully remains there, in the thick (or, in the 'thicket', to use one of Malouf's favourite word-images). Entirely other-engaged rather than self-involved, the magpie does not even recognise its own egg – 'a stone with a pulse' – until it is hatched. Self-renewal, the production of self and the reproduction from self, comes only with the recognition of the broken stone's '*call-sign/ ugly-my-own creak creak*' (*P*, 220).

Malouf's poetic career can be envisioned as the initial forging of the ethics of subjectivity that is clearly and directly the organising topic of 'Magpie'. As in 'The Crab Feast' and in other poems, one discerns in 'Magpie' a strong commitment to experience that is creatively contingent, relational, and other-engaged.[17] Whether or not Malouf remains a poet in his prose-fiction career, it is clear that his intense concern with the mapping of subjectivity endures. The investigation of what the being is who says 'I', of how this being creates and sustains itself, is particularly apparent in the first prose works, which can be considered in part as exploratory experiments in the voicing of 'I'.

The narratiaves of 'I'

Johnno

The first three long prose fictions of Malouf's career, beginning with *Johnno*, are narrated in the first person. Only the first one, however, is strongly marked by Malouf's personal experience and history. Ovid, the first-person narrator of the second novel, is like Malouf a writer, and more particularly a poet; like Malouf and other Australians, Ovid undergoes a complex experience of exile. Yet Malouf's creation of Ovid nonetheless demonstrates impressive imaginative stretch, so distantly does the Roman poet's experience stand from that of the Australian author. Similarly, the narration of *Child's Play*, the third novel, is undoubtedly supported by Malouf's extensive experience of Italy, but the work's narrator, his intense interest in writing notwithstanding, is hardly legible as a Malouf persona. Even if the first-person presentation of *Johnno* arose as a more or less arbitrary response to the personal nature of the narrative material, Malouf clearly emerged from this writing with a desire to engage more fully with the potentialities, and limitations, of the perspective of singularity, of the individualised envisioning of self and world. The difference between *Johnno* and the frankly self-narrating *12 Edmondstone Street*, published four years after *Child's Play*, is in large part an outcome of Malouf's extensive experimentation with the first-person voice; the later text is so clearly preoccupied with founding (rather than merely assuming) the voice of individual selfhood, with finding the ontological and epistemological basis for the 'I' voice. Already apparent in *Johnno*, however, and in all the subsequent narratives of 'I', is the clear sense that, for Malouf, the 'I' confirms itself by writing itself into being; it is inseparable from acts of writing. In writing, the 'I' passes beyond its bounds and enters the world.

Reading the 'I' of *Johnno* as an initial instance of the self-forging autobiographical 'I' can scarcely be avoided. The autobiographical element is clearly suggested by Malouf's own commentary on the text, and particularly by his insistence on its being the seminal text in his initiation into the writer's life. It is a writing from life that confirms a life of writing. One finds, moreover, numerous fairly exact correspondences between the novel and the life: in the handling of the father's death, in the conversion of John Milliner to Johnno, and even in such tiny details as the dating – 1949 (the year Malouf turned thirteen) – of the grammar school magazine Dante finds among his schoolboy relics. Yet the novelistic aspect of the text, its status as fiction, is equally important. Malouf has placed *Johnno* in the world as a novel, and thus alerts his reader to his having taken liberties with his life's details. The novel is not his life, but a sense he has given it, a particular order he has made of it.

Weighing these two orientations, the autobiographical and the novelistic, one should expect *Johnno* to be more than usually marked by its author's personal investments. Certainly, Dante bears consideration as a kind of Malouf persona in ways that no other Malouf character does. He is a textual figure with the dual role of ordering a text and ordering a life. Dante's central presence strongly suggests that *Johnno* is a specific type of *Bildungsroman,* and not at all an uncommon type. Dante's life story recounts not simply the path from boyhood through youth to manhood, but – as in the case of Joyce's Stephen Dedalus or Proust's Marcel – the path, beset by challenges, impediments, setbacks, from boyhood through youth to artistry, or authorship. In the light of the clearly marked autobiographical aspect, one must consider Dante's journey as an allegorical version of Malouf's own. Although *Johnno* does not resolve itself upon Dante's arrival as an author-artist, the text is very much, in the autobiographical manner, a journey toward the signature, toward the right to sign oneself as an author – as 'David Malouf'. In his 1997 Preface to *Johnno*, Malouf clearly states the case: Dante must respond to Johnno's death by making a step 'in the direction of life', which is also, necessarily, a step 'in the direction of Literature' (*J*, xiii).[1]

To order one's reading of *Johnno* around a quest for authorship – and more precisely, for a valid postcolonial authorship – is to run counter to the prevailing view of criticism to date. Ivor Indyk sees the novel as being, not exclusively but substantially, a 'homosexual romance'; indeed, he affirms that 'the expression of homosexual love … elevates the novel to the realm of art'.[2] Thus, the novel's energising core is homosexual desire, ultimately unfulfilled – a view sustained by Kirby and, to a lesser degree, by Neilsen.[3] Taylor reaffirms the same basic line of argument, although, unlike his predecessors, he conceives of Johnno, not Dante, as the main subject of a desire that can never find adequate expression.[4]

Malouf's own objection to the understanding of *Johnno* as 'a gay novel in disguise' should be noted (*J*, x), but cannot of course be taken as definitive. Eve Kosofsky Sedgwick has deftly demonstrated that attentive readings can discover unavowed and unrecognised homosexual content in literary works.[5] The problem is that *Johnno* does not present itself very neatly for critical interpretation along Sedgwick's lines. To begin with, internal evidence shows that homosexual desire has an avowed place within the text. Dante speaks of being 'in love – once, not so briefly, with a boy from Sarina' (*J*, 109). A pair of 'queers' offer Johnno a trip to Hong Kong; he answers his friends' demand for details with 'one of his big, open grins' (*J*, 55). When Johnno later proposes to Dante a stint of tarting in Sweden, Dante's objection is clearly to tarting itself and not to tarting with male clients. And Johnno meets the counter-proposal – that he should be the 'male tart', but in Spain – simply by observing that the Spaniards lack money (*J*, 121). Most pertinently, however, one should note that the presentation of Johnno's one serious-seeming heterosexual romance, with Binkie, does not yield any of the intensified triangulated desire that Sedgwick's criticism delineates. Male rivalry does not take shape as the transfigured form of homosexual desire. Dante never shows any inclination to present himself as a rival for Binkie's love. He treats her, at times, as a new site of perspective upon Johnno, as a new source for knowledge of Johnno. She is legible as a site of emotionally charged negotiation between men, but she never appears as the substitute object of either man's desire for the other. While the objections here stated do not serve to dismiss the argument of the homosexual romance – and do not intend to dismiss it – they do provide an initial ground for proposing an alternative view of *Johnno*'s main quest, of its generative core. Johnno is certainly, for Dante, a path of homosexual love not taken, an alternative life unlived, as one sees most clearly when Dante recalls Johnno's confession that he sees Dante as an 'exotic' erotic object, a sort of 'foreign prince', and Dante avows, 'My mind had whirled, a whole past turning itself upside down, inside out, to reveal possibilities I could never myself have imagined' (*J*, 154). But this recognition of what Johnno has not been for Dante does not account, except partially and in negative terms, for the very real impact and importance of the experience he has had of Johnno. Johnno has not had the role of lover, so what then has been his role?

Right in the centre of the narrative, Malouf portrays an incident which, like the insistent return of the repressed, 'recurs'. This incident discovers more clearly than any other the key to Johnno's role in Dante's life and, one may surmise, to John Milliner's role in Malouf's. 'With a daring' frankly characterised as 'outrageous', Johnno 'would sweep through Barker's bookstore picking up books from left and right till the pile was so high under his chin that he could barely see. On past the cash desk, staggering slightly. Out into Edward Street. Where he would tumble the whole pile into a swing-top litter bin' (*J*, 87). Even the style of the passage sets Johnno in opposition to conventional cultural values. He picks up books from 'left and right' instead of the more usual right and left. The stack he assembles is represented as deliberately, ostentatiously excessive. He staggers, though only 'slightly,' at the very moment of passing the cash desk – as if to give authority a fair chance to catch him in the act. The description of his actions finally breaks, as it seems it must, into sentence fragments, as if such actions cannot be registered and contained within grammatical structures. As these stylistic perturbations register, the young man is attacking The Book or, perhaps more tellingly, the very understanding of texts as meaningful sites of social exchange.

The account of this recurring scene of theft and destruction is preceded, a few pages earlier, by Johnno's damning evaluation of Brisbane: 'Brisbane was nothing … A place where poetry could never occur' (J, 84). Pronouncements such as these also recur, in slightly altered versions, throughout the novel, and they are always delivered to Dante, the novel's Malouf-persona. Dante's brief but significant response, thought but unspoken, is 'Perhaps' (J, 84). Johnno succeeds in engendering doubts in the young would-be writer. Perhaps the project of writing the experience of Brisbane is impossible; perhaps, even if possible, it is pointless.

Johnno first enters *Johnno*, one should recall, as a perturbation of textual meanings and, most particularly, of the meaning of Dante's personal texts. As Dante sorts through the contents of his recently deceased father's house, through the contents of the last drawer of the last room, he finds himself amid the detritus of his own schooldays. Most notably, he finds texts: 'a sheaf (neatly folded) of "stories" [he] had punched out', and beneath this, 'the Brisbane Grammar School Magazine for 1949'. Flipping through the pages of the latter, he finds a photograph in which Johnno is a disruptive presence. He returns, or recurs, as the member of the 'Stillwater Lifesaving Team' who never was a member, as the interloper 'at the very edge of the picture', who is not 'staring out like the rest of us into some sort of rectilinear future', but 'staring diagonally out of the frame' (J, 10–11). And Johnno's grin is 'lopsided', his head 'oversized' and set off by the 'gold-rimmed glasses' that Johnno never wore. Everything about Johnno's presence in this picture – this photographic text – disrupts its aspirations to stable, convention-governed legibility. He destroys its archival value and more tellingly its thematic content – its affirmation of Youth, in a moment of confirmed achievement, gazing hopefully, confidently, and docilely – into a prospectively 'rectilinear future'. Johnno's disruption, however, appropriates the text in a very telling way, giving it a new, darkly ironic meaning he will later be called upon to consolidate. John Milliner, in 1962, drowns in the Condamine, in water too shallow to drown a man; his fictional counterpart, the false and falsifying member of the Stillwater Lifesaving Team, is destined also to drown in the Condamine, and his dead body is dragged out of the water by an erstwhile junior member of the Lifesaving Team.

The precise moment of the discovery is equally pertinent for the understanding of Johnno's perturbatory self-inscription in Dante's life – the life that has not yet been ordered as text. Dante rediscovers Johnno while sorting through – assembling, reading and interpreting – the traces of his dead father. This father, at once the source of the son's being and the ordering centre of his symbolic world, shares with Johnno, albeit less obstreperously, the tendency to place himself at odds with the world of texts. In this the two key figures align themselves, thus troubling Indyk's sense that the novel orders itself upon two principal and antithetical domains: 'the social world of the father and the world of homosexual romance'.[6] Johnno's main role in the novel may not be, then, that of the unavowed object of unfulfilled homosexual desire. He may serve, principally, as one of two key opponents in Dante's quest to affirm the value of texts and to find in texts a valid domain of masculine commitment and endeavour.

Even upon his death, the world of texts fails to lay claim to the recalcitrant father: 'on the morning of his funeral', a medical examination 'report' arrives and 'declare[s] him to be A1 in every respect' (J, 1). Like Johnno, Dante's father repeatedly refuses to acknowledge the value of texts and fails to establish any really workable relationship with them. Moreover, in the novel's early development, textual concerns are quite clearly coded in the feminine. Dante's mother is an avid archivist, a gatherer and producer of texts: 'Her dressing-table was the Library of Alexandria, a suburban V. and A.' (J, 6). His aunts, the 'father's sisters', take shape as text marshals, during their busy supervision of wartime mail (*J*, 29). But the father himself, Dante avows, 'had never, so far as I knew, read a book' (*J*, 5). Fatherly guidance includes the caution, 'You don't want to read *too* much', which the son interprets without hesitation or doubt: 'what he means is that books are useless ... and might even be a bit effeminate. He distrusts their influence on me' (*J*, 51). The father thus lends his authoritative voice to the placement of texts in a non-masculine, specifically feminine, social sphere.

Johnno's status for Dante, as a problem of Dante's personal history – and one that he feels he must resolve – arises most pressingly not perhaps in relation to his friend's defiant and corrosive negations but in the fact that Johnno strives at times, and invariably fails, to discover a productive relationship with texts. Certainly, Johnno consumes books, at times voraciously, but always in the manner of the addict rather than that of the impassioned lover. Particularly in the novel's later stages, he does not use books but uses them up. In Johnno's room in Greece, books once read find their way into 'a dusty pile in the corner, where silverfish nested – abandoned but not thrown away' (*J*, 133). This, however, needs to be understood as a shabby point of resolution at which Johnno's life with books sinuously arrives. The youth who steals and dumps Barker's books is still able to re-emerge some few years later as the impressively serious reader of the African period. In the Congo, Johnno, as always, considers books disposable, but the matter he reads then tosses is substantial: 'Schopenhauer, Berdiaev, Wittgenstein, Bonhöffer, Sartre – not to mention novelists old and new' (*J*, 107). The point is that such reading prepares for Europe, for life 'among civilized men' (*J*, 107). The reading aims to fill up the desperate emptiness of an Australian boyhood and youth; however, as one later learns, it fails to fulfil this aim. Johnno can only take his place in Europe as an Australian outsider, drifting unenlightened from Paris to Greece, from one empowered site of Culture to the next. Neither European books nor on-site European experience enables Johnno to transform himself.

Texts, for Johnno, come to represent a dependence he resents and resists, a craving he cannot master and from which he cannot free himself. Dante recalls, 'what Johnno called "life" … bore an uncanny resemblance, it seemed to me, to what the rest of us called "literature"' (J, 84). Yet Johnno's attempts to bring literature to life and to find a life in literature invariably take shape as curious mimetic stagings. His frenetic consumption of Dostoevsky yields drunken, semi-deliberate portrayals of 'Rogozin of *The Idiot*' (J, 84), and then, a little later, a truly embarrassing self-abasement 'before a holy man', in the manner of Dmitri Karamazov (J, 88). Johnno fails to make literature his own; he never attempts, so far as one can tell, to make a literature of his own. The project of self-fashioning in relation to cultural contexts takes its signal form, for Johnno, not as production but as evacuation; he resolves 'to shit this bitch of a country right out of my system', estimating, rather too optimistically, that the undertaking will require only seven years (J, 98).

The thesis Johnno's life comes to represent contains a two-fold impossibility: the impossibility of using European culture to remake and validate one's identity and the impossibility of authoring new texts – or at the very least a new 'life-text' – to sustain one's identity. Faced with these impossibilities, Dante must ask, is Johnno's case merely personal or is it his own as well? Or indeed, is this impossible case perhaps desperately and irremediably Australian?[7]

Dante, and by extension Malouf, must undertake a mastering of Johnno, which can have no other than a textual form. The would-be writer must become in fact a writer, an author, and he must write precisely those materials that Johnno, in word and deed, places outside the realm of text-making. He must write Brisbane, and thus affirm the city as a site of valid personal and social history. The documentation of Brisbane must therefore pass beyond what Indyk sees as the novel's deliberate use of 'inert detail' and its frequent 'denial of significance'.[8] The sheer force of accumulated detail combining with subtle heightenings of tone ultimately brings *Johnno* into accord with a fundamental conviction characterising Malouf's fiction: all worlds are full; no place is an empty place. Like Ovid's Tomis, like Reverend Frazer's northern Queensland, Dante's Brisbane comes to yield up its specific version of fullness and multiplicity, in dawn rambles through a city strangely refreshed, inchoate, or in the strange sights of a flood time, 'a month of wonders' (*J*, 100). Even the unpromising patio-bar of the Grand Central Hotel renders the 'flamboyant tarts' who contribute an abundance of precise and lustrous details to Dante's portrayal of his city's life (*J*, 70).

Of course, still more crucial than the writing of Brisbane is the writing of Johnno. He too, along with the world he both represents and denounces, must be submitted to the dominion of text. There is no other way to prove Johnno wrong, no other way for Dante to free himself from Johnno's daunting influence. From this perspective, Johnno's is an enabling death, one that looks forward, in a quite precisely parallel way, to the deaths of the gifted or favoured elder brothers in *An Imaginary Life* and *Child's Play*. Like Ovid and the author (of *Child's Play*), Dante is empowered by a brother's death, released into fuller life and enabled to take up the role of author. Johnno, once dead, can be written.

Establishing a textual mastery over Johnno is rather a tricky business requiring careful handling. First of all, one must not lose a sense that Johnno has a case, a valid one in some ways – or at least one that he shares in part with others. His attitudes, his argumentative positions (if one can call them that), are almost always extreme but not always eccentric. Dante shares, in various moments, his friend's dismissive view of Brisbane and Australia, and also his sense that grander, richer life-possibilities – such as those represented in literature – are only to be found elsewhere. Johnno, one must recognise, is representative as well as idiosyncratic. 'This business', Malouf affirms, 'of turning to literature as a guide to the passionate life and finding ordinary life, life at home, by comparison thin and inauthentic, was a very Australian pastime when I was growing up, and still is, perhaps' (*J*, xii).

And yet Johnno *is also* different, distinct, and most emphat-ically so in his relentless nay-saying, his refusal of conventional patterns for living. He says 'no' to many things to which one *should* say 'no', and Dante, among others, needs the challenge offered by Johnno's fractiousness. Dante must learn to question his commitment to 'rules and regulations', disciplined 'character-building' and 'moral backbone', his docile belief in 'the dogma that if what you *didn't* like doing was good for you what you *did* like doing was not' (*J*, 38). Johnno suggests to the young Dante 'a marvellously liberating alternative to [his] own wishy-washy and hypocritical niceness' (*J*, 48); Johnno's lesson *is* subversive[9] – and, one may add, needfully so. What Dante learns from Johnno is, and must be, a lesson for writing as well as for life: to write from the perspective of established convention is to be written in advance, pre-scribed; it is to produce a writing that accumulates but does not intervene. Accumulation without intervention typifies Dante's world. He finds it most notably in his parents' lives. And he finds it in a final and defining moment, in the funeral eulogy offered to Johnno – who, unfortunately, is no longer able to resist. Subsumed within the old rhetoric of Great-War deaths, Johnno takes shape as another 'golden youth cut off in the fullness of his promise' (*J*, 157); he becomes 'an insubstantial abstract of such empty recommendations as "devoted son", "loyal friend", "a splendid example to us all"' (*J*, 158). It is against this particular textualisation of Johnno that Dante must compose his own.

In many ways Malouf is a deeply affirmative literary voice; he finds much in life and in the world to which he wishes to pronounce a validating 'yes'. But one must recognise that the affirmations are selective, and that all of them are founded upon an initial, energising 'no'. In Malouf, there is a clear sense that writing, in so far as it intervenes, must say 'no' to the world-as-it-is before it can begin to say 'yes'. If one's world and one's place within it are perfectly fine just as one finds them – why write? Johnno first serves to pinpoint this brief but troubling question; he then develops as an embodiment of the 'no' that yields the 'yes'. For these reasons Johnno must be written into, rather than out of, Australia's story of itself. Yet text remains for Malouf an ambivalent site of investment: text emerges out of, and works within, the social world. The social world – to which one must at times say 'no' – inhabits texts too deeply, too thoroughly. In

Johnno, one can locate the first major inscription of a disposition – call it a deep distrust of the values of the collective – which will mark Malouf's writing throughout the development of his career. However, the equally characteristic urge to rework and transform the values of the collective is also present, as one can observe most notably in Dante's final return to the texts of the father.

Early in his novel, Malouf presents Dante's familial world, in part, as a cluster of counter-empires: the mother has her personal V. and A. collection of heirlooms and also her particular version of English manners, which she imposes on her household; the aunts' unyielding 'grip' upon the wartime mails wilfully counters the efforts of the hostile 'Japanese Empire' (*J,* 29). Most curious and compelling, however, is Dante's uneasy experience of his dead father's house as 'an abandoned empire' (*J,* 7). Although the father is 'comfortingly foreign' (*J,* 5), particularly in relation to the mother's scrupulously English, suburban-imperial style, he too gives shape to his own version of imperial culture, a version that consolidates itself – surprisingly, and yet unsurprisingly – in textual forms. The first of the father's books – there are two, in fact, that he not only 'consult[ed]' but 'owned' – is even *authored* by the father. It is a ledger containing one solitary text, which is at once a measurement of social developments and an *autobio-graph* (that is, a life's personally composed grapheme, its singular, integrated instance of writing). The father's graph presents nothing less than 'the record, crudely projected, of his life, and at the same time the map of an era' (*J,* 167). Malouf's prose, through a play on the word 'line', suddenly presents the taciturn, book-despising father as a poet of the graph: 'That line on the page was what he had tuned his soul to' (*J,* 167). The other volume, a popular biography of colonial entrepreneur James MacRobertson, Dante characterises as his father's fondly cherished 'success story' and as 'the palpable record of a great national mythology' (*J,* 168). It is another sketch of the father's inner life – personal, peculiar, and yet profoundly social. The father's textual proclivities thus outline, albeit imperfectly, a potentially postcolonial enactment of imperial culture, a somewhat crude model for Dante's own future in the realm of text. The father, like the mother and the aunts, reworks imperial culture through his particular ways of inhabiting it. In this, he is counter-imperial rather than anti-imperial; his action is modestly 'oppositional', in the sense this term has acquired from the work of Michel de Certeau.[10] The father inhabits a world structured by empire, but activates its elements and its spaces of culture in distinctly motivated and therefore potentially transformative ways. Here again, one may find that the father does not differ so very much from Johnno – and still less from Dante.

Johnno's validating return to the father, and to the father's personal scripts, may lend some nuance to the reading of the novel's final lines: 'Maybe, in the end, even the lies we tell define us. And better, some of them, than our most earnest attempts at the truth' (*J*, 170). One may feel inclined to find here the rather facile dodging of an overly autobiographical interpretation of the novel; autobiography gives precedence to fiction as the narrator admits that the book contains lies, fabrications. But considered in the light of de Certeau, one may interpret the final statements as the affirmation that a writer defines himself, and his intervention within the realm of writing, by the innovating twists he gives to the conventions of literary practice. The postcolonial writer, one should add, may make use of the imperial forms and contents of his world, but in making use he is obliged to transmute.

An Imaginary Life

An Imaginary Life is quite readily legible as an Australian writer's novel if one considers it in the light of its predecessor. Ovid's experience of Tomis recalls, by way of analogies, Johnno's or even Dante's sense of the Brisbane experience. Ovid understands his new location as the outermost margin of empire – what would be, in Johnno's idiom, 'the bloody arsehole of the universe' (*J*, 83). Ovid is acutely aware, moreover, that he is in exile from an empire that has the power to stifle voices representing orders of experience other than those it authorises – and this also continues from, and yet extends, the concerns of *Johnno*. What most links *An Imaginary Life* to *Johnno*, however, concerns Malouf's evolving vision more than discernible Australianness. In both novels a central character and first-person narrator confronts a second character whom he experiences, at once, as his antithesis and his double, as an insoluble puzzle and also as the key to an understanding of himself. Ovid's richly allegorical story pursues this close pairing of main characters – one of whom is the narrative 'I' – more intensely and complexly.

As David Malouf acknowledges, little is known of Ovid's life, and still less about his exile, which was decreed by Augustus for unrecorded reasons. Interestingly, Malouf has suggested that this dearth of facts was 'useful' for his writing of 'a fiction with its roots in possible event' (*IL*, 153). The decision to write an imaginary life for Ovid is based on a primary recognition that history is synecdochic, that our sense of the past is necessarily partial and gapped. More compelling, however, than this recognition – which is not extraordinary, after all – is the writer's response to it, his clear sense that the facts of history, whether meagre or plentiful, require a work of synthetic imagination.[11] To make history – to compose it, to write it – one must imagine it, bridge its gaps, remake as seemly wholes its fragments. This is not perhaps an understanding so much as it is a disposition with respect to history, but this disposition, in Malouf's case, is potentially enabling. It relieves the writer from the burden of a constituted past that leaves him belated, unaccounted for, unfounded. It conceives of history – too often appearing as the record of exclusions, limitations, and constraints – as an energising field of multiple possibilities. And in Malouf's specific case it allows for an inaugural act, for the bringing of newness into the world. Our only integrated history of Ovid's exile is Malouf's fictional one, even though it is other than history in both conception and execution, even though it is history slipping into story. History may be the initial instance of the otherness Malouf pursues, by various paths, throughout *An Imaginary Life*. In relation to our lived experience of time, history signals individual incompleteness, manifests the ever-more-than-I that cannot be mastered and assimilated, but also opens a field of discovery, of new and greater possibility.

Malouf elaborates a suggestively postimperial conception in writing out his other-history. He understands his writing as a subversion, as a writing that inscribes itself below established, authorised meanings, a writing that aims to unsettle – and even undermine and unfound – such meanings. The Ovid of Malouf's imagining deliberately subverts imperial structures of meaning. This poet self-consciously turns his verses against the authorised writing of the Augustan age, which he sees as 'solemn, orderly, monumental, dull' (*IL*, 26) – a writing of empire in its most stultifying form. But Ovid nonetheless makes use of the imperial monuments, turning them away from their intended purposes, striving to produce an other-than-imperial writing that others imperial writing. Quite early in the novel, Ovid metamorphoses the meaning of the monumental Portico of Marcellus: 'in the shadow of a portico dedicated by [Augustus's] sister to her faithful husband, someone tonight is being fucked; because in a poem once I made it happen, and made that particular act, in that particular place, a gesture of defiance' (*IL*, 27). This writing evidently is not only subversive but inaugural; it succeeds in remaking the world. Yet Malouf's Ovid does not simply oppose, or defy, imperial culture in a straightforward counter-discursive act. He reworks and supplements, thus transforming the meaning of the imperial given and creating the possibility of new and different life for his social world. Unsurprisingly, Ovid associates his writing's desired effects with sexual acts. In sexual acts one ventures and risks identity in encounter with an other, and finds oneself (hopefully) both energised and transformed.

The word 'desolateness', however, orders Ovid's earliest reflections upon his place of exile, recalling innumerable colonial renderings of Australia as the most extreme form of *terra nullius*, as a land intransigently strange, empty of and even hostile to productive human intentions. But more crucially, the cosmopolitan Roman poet feels he is in exile more from a culture than from a homeland. Ovid thus takes shape as a quite precise figuring of the settler-exile: although he opposes imperial forms of culture while inhabiting the empire's centre, he experiences himself in exile as a displaced piece of empire. He must half-discover and half-forge an other version of himself. And indeed, *An Imaginary Life*'s affiliation with postcolonial topics and concerns is most compellingly evident in its intensive meditation on questions of difference and alterity, which preoccupy the poet-exile, and in its eventual organisation of these questions in relation to situations of intersubjective encounter and exchange.

Criticism that seeks to specify the novel's postcolonial thrust has emphasised its preoccupations with language – with language as a topic of the fiction as well as its vehicle. (Language, as will become clear, is also a principal path for the pursuit of the other.) Patrick Buckridge argues that Malouf's originality, in *An Imaginary Life* and in subsequent fictions, resides mainly in his particular 'grammar': this grammar marks Malouf's writing as distinctly postcolonial; it is 'his own in a way that nothing else in his writing is, or can be'.[12] Suzie O'Brien finds that Malouf's imagining of Ovid's story rejects imperialist knowledge systems and contributes to the rich 'wilderness of dialogical possibilities', which, for O'Brien, is the space of postcolonial enunciation.[13] Gareth Griffiths follows a similar line, asserting that the novel's 'discursive features' – its concern with 'linguistic displacement', exile, and 'cross-culturality' – mark it as 'characteristically post-colonial'.[14]

By taking up Buckridge's grammatical orientation and refocusing it in relation to dialogue, displacement, and cross-culturality, one can discern in Malouf a closely ordered yet vigorous grammar that shapes his envisioning of the allure of otherness and of the role of otherness in creative self-fashioning. Particularly noteworthy are verb-phrases using such constructions as 'out into' or 'up out of'. 'Out into' suggests movement out of self, out of familiar space, and into newness, spaces of venture, experiences of otherness; 'up out of' lends to outward movement a sense of progress, development, 'heightened' experience. Thus, Ovid observes the wild boy, the Child, as he gains confidence in the strange new world of a human household: the boy begins 'to move out into the room'; Ovid also witnesses him 'reaching up out of himself' (*IL*, 79). Ovid imagines the Child's birth as a 'push out into the world' (*IL*, 89). He observes the Child looking out a window, and surmises that the boy must be 'dreaming himself out into the winter countryside' (*IL*, 114). Following the inspiration he takes from the Child, Ovid concludes that he must 'try to leap up out of [him]self' (*IL*, 97), ultimately arriving at an ethos recalling that of Tennyson's Ulysses: ageing men, and especially ageing poets, must 'push up off their deathbed and adventure out into the unknown'. Indeed, this 'pushing out', this traversing of conventionally presumed 'limits' emerges at last as the key to an understanding of the meaning and purpose of a human life (*IL*, 135).

A closely related grammatical pattern orders itself around innovative uses of 'forward', 'further', 'beyond', and related word-concepts. Ovid imagines his physical frame 'breaking forth' and 'bursting forth', seeking new forms for itself (*IL*, 148). The Child also ends the story 'already straining forward to whatever life it is that lies out there beyond our moment together' (*IL*, 149). Indeed, the thrust toward 'further being' effectively orders the novel's closing passages (*IL*, 150), which turn upon movements between 'here' and 'there'. As the work moves toward 'I am there', its peculiarly open closing statement, the energised oxymoron 'out here' occurs twice (*IL*, 148, 150). (I characterise 'out here' as oxymoronic, because 'out there' would be a more common-place construction: 'out' is usually situated 'there' at a certain distance from the locus of the speaker/observer.) Following the two instances of 'out here', one finds 'The Child is there' (*IL*, 151), occurring as a single-sentence paragraph that initiates the final passages. The Child is present, but apart from the observing self, distinct, there not here. This returns us to the narrative's opening enunciations, where one also reads '*The child is there*' (*IL*, 9). But in this first instance the perspective is that of a child – a child Ovid once was, a child whose sense of separate selfhood has not yet consolidated itself; whereas, the second instance enunciates the perspective of one who is near death and ready to release himself from the reign of separate selfhood. Therefore, the short sentence that quite famously closes the narrative – Ovid's final 'I am there' – needs to be read with the recognition that the location of the first person is almost invariably 'here'. In the conventional grammar of everyday speech, *I*, most typically, am *here*. Ovid, however, in making his passage toward death, becomes other than himself, discovers the site of the other, transports his consciousness (in its final moment) from the 'here' of self to the 'there' of the other.[15] The exiled cosmopolite becomes more meaningfully the poet of metamorphoses, of transformations – of transmutations, transfers, transits, translations – of all the 'trans' words that occur with notable frequency in Malouf's writing, the 'trans' words that delineate movements across, from here to there, from one location or state of being to another.

Malouf's grammar is evidently spatially orientated, locational. It situates and resituates. This grammar not only foregrounds the importance of language as a focus of concern, it shows that Malouf seeks a language of situation and transit, a language fundamentally preoccupied with place and with movements within and between places. On occasion, this preoccupation with the relation of language to place finds explicit expression, as when Ovid describes the landscape of his exile as 'a vast page whose tongue I am unable to decipher, whose message to me I am unable to interpret' (*IL*, 17). Faced with this initial illegibility of his new world, Ovid's project becomes that of discovering and learning an appropriate language of place. This project is not only grammatical; it is also very thoroughly and methodically configured. The figure, always a prominent element in Malouf's prose, is the use of language that spatialises, giving language a shape and location that is, as it were, right there before our eyes. In the figure, language takes place.

Responding critically to European folk-tale traditions, Malouf first uses the figure of the wolf to represent alterity as a locus of misrecognition, a manifestation of othering that deforms. The wolf is the othered other created by the social world, the other estranged and remade as a site of fear and disavowal. This psychosocial dynamic that creates the wolf as the wild, threatening other is clearly portrayed right at the start of the novel, in an alarmingly concrete imaging. As a child of perhaps five or six, Ovid confronts a wolf's head hacked off by hunters, a head 'with ropes of dark blood hanging from it' (*IL*, 10). This horrifying, and horrifyingly partial, presentation of the wolf emphasises not lupine violence but human violence motivated by fear and undesired recognition – human violence that is done to the wolf. Intuiting perhaps that the wolf's message of terror is in fact a human message, the child Ovid is moved to envision the wolf as 'kindly', as mysteriously yet deeply connected with humankind. This thinking leads, in short order, to a transformative rendering of the wolf figure; the wolf figure gives rise to wolf-men or lycanthropes:

> *They close their human mind like a fist and when they open it again it is a wolf's paw. The skull bulges, the jaw pushes out to become a snout. Hair prickles down their spine, grows rough on their belly. The body slouches and is on all fours. The voice thickens. It is the moon draws them on'* (*IL*, 10).

The passage is almost alarmingly concrete and physical. It emphatically stages transformation as a bodily event, insisting on the strain of transformative force against the resistance of pre-established form and structure. It is not easy for the human being to find the kindliness of the wolf, and yet this finding is clearly necessary, irresistible.

Even as lupine imagery moves toward hybrid or syncretic imagings, so do Malouf's other engagements with folkloric or mythic figures – most notably, with respect to his handling of horses and centaurs. However, the narrative is figuratively ordered at all levels, and Malouf also makes ample use of figures that have a more restricted rhetorical and symbolic register – such as the figure of the circle. Malouf is clearly aware of this figure's association with completeness, closure, symmetry, with that which eternally returns. But the textual will to circularity, so clearly inscribed through the reiteration of the novel's beginning in its moments of resolution, is also repeatedly challenged. Thus, even while working within the circle figure's more limited signifying range, Malouf still is able to multiply and transform the meanings of his figure.

In Malouf's view, the closed circles of selfhood and community must be broken, opened, and then creatively reconstituted.
The circle figure is introduced quite early: Ovid's magnificent
dream-centaurs, harbingers of greater, fuller life-in-transfor-
mation, are seen to 'wheel in great circles' around the dream-
persona (IL, 24). A little later in the text, Ovid's first hunting
mission is strongly marked by the circle figure. A ritual that
gathers the hunters in a circle marks their departure. The first
phase of the hunt orders itself upon a visit, on horseback, to 'a
huge natural circle' (IL, 43), the burial site of the horsemen-
hunters of the Getae people. Here, the hunters undertake new
ritual enactments involving circular movements on horseback,
and in this narrative sequence the purpose of the circle figure is
first clearly portrayed. The element of horsemanship is suggestive because Ovid, though he has never previously given any
importance to the fact, is by birth a member of Roman society's
equestrian order. The exploration of his own horsemanship, once
combined with the circle figure, leads Ovid back to his past; his
mind returns, comes around, comes full circle, to that beginning
point of his adult life which is marked by the death of his elder
brother and a consequent alienation from his father. Through
circular movement the mind renews experience, discovering
new meanings, new clarity of self-understanding. It is a rediscovery that frees Ovid from the burden of the past; he breaks, it
seems, the circle of time by first retracing it.

The circle figure, however, functions differently when the
narrative addresses the approach to the other rather than the
consolidation of selfhood. It is significant, in this respect, that
circular movements fail when these are first used to search for
the wild boy, the Child; the horsemen 'circle round the same few
hundred yards of forest as in a dream' (IL, 49) – indeed, as in
Ovid's dream of centaurs – but the Child, the organising centre,
proves to be elusive, unlocatable. This new sense of the circle
is clarified a little later in a deer-hunting episode. The village
shaman draws a magic circle to enable a psychic journey beyond
the bounds of self. By first configuring the sphere of the self, the
shaman can then pass outside it, into the immense and potentially

threatening realm of the not-I. The hunters witness this ritual while seated 'outside' the circle, 'in the growing dark' (*IL*, 51), thus emphasising that the self's others are to be situated, necessarily, outside the bounds of self, never within. Interestingly, the hunters are seated in a circle for the second sighting of the wild boy. The circle in this case is clearly a figure of community, which the approach of the outsider disrupts. Yet one should note that the men look at each other and at the wild child 'over the rim' of the drinking cups held up to their lips (*IL*, 59); they peer over the containing, circular rim of self – an imaging that again stresses the insularity of self, even of the self in community, and the intransigent exteriority of the other. Evidently, Ovid begins, at this point, to appreciate the meaning of the circle as boundary between self and other, between community and outsider: he subsequently places his Child-seeking lure, a bowl of gruel, 'just at the edge of the fire's circle, where the dark begins' (*IL*, 60). The sense is that one must pass beyond, break out of, the containing circle of selfhood to contact the other. Indeed, given that what is offered is a bowl, a hemispherical vessel, a figure of contained selfhood, it seems that one must effectively exteriorise the self, risk the self beyond the border of its security. These meanings are still clearer when Ovid dreams himself as a pool of rainwater that 'break[s] in circles' upon the contact of a deer who drinks from him. The circles of self are broken, the self breaks in circles, upon contact with the other. This evocatively erotic experience is exhilarating but also 'fearful' (*IL*, 62).

The wild child is eventually captured, however, by horsemen 'weaving in circles' (*IL*, 68). Horsemen riding in circles had previously failed, but one must note that the riders are now 'weaving'. This new usage connects the circle figure with another, perhaps equally important, figurative pattern: the woven structure, the web or net. Malouf is clearly aware of the derivation of the English word 'text' from the Latin *texere* (to weave); indeed, when Ovid suddenly recognises 'a kind of poetry' in the net-weaving of village fishermen, he also notes that he is thinking in terms of the 'old analogies' (*IL*, 64). By linking the successful quest for the Child with weaving action and thus with textuality, Malouf proposes text-making as a potential path to the apprehension of otherness. Certainly, this path associates itself with a certain violence, even violation: the terrified Child, captured by a weaving search, soon finds himself 'trussed like a pig'. However, the shaman's ritual singing, in an 'other, polar, voice' (*IL*, 69), calms the captive, thus suggesting that contact without violation may be enabled by the creation and use of an other voice, a new and distinct shared creation in the realm of language. In the quest for the other, it seems one must reach out into language in new ways. The other can be approached in the self-exteriorising yet potentially shared realm of the symbolic, by means of text-making. Access to the other, as to the linguistic symbol, entails uttering, outering, and the creation, through this outward venture, of new modes of being and of communication. It is a matter of discovering the 'spiders' language', the language of web-spinners, which Ovid fantastically imagines himself learning (*IL*, 21).

Ovid's first recognition of his own capacity to apprehend and, to a degree, master the strange world of Tomis is sparked by the sight of fishermen on the seaside cliffs hauling up nets filled with 'glittering surprises, their nameless catch' (*IL*, 27). The catch is not nameless, the poet implicitly understands, for those equipped with the right words, with adequate and appropriate language-nets. Very shortly after recording the sight of the fishermen at work, Ovid joyfully discovers and lays claim to a wild poppy, another glittering surprise within his world of desolation. His new impulse to assimilate and appropriate his world entails the exercise of linguistic, text-making powers. Starting from the words 'scarlet' and 'poppy', Ovid finds himself engaged in 'making' and 'work[ing] the spring' (*IL*, 31–2). In this way the poet is released out of his former life and into a new one. Even as the desolate world of Tomis had been, for Ovid, 'a state of mind, no place' (*IL*, 16), it now becomes a rich and engaging place by stimulating, through linguistic connections, a change of mind. This new working of the world, this poesis of spring, necessarily spurs re-creation and transformation of self – which Ovid at this very point of the narrative first acknowledges as needful.

Net-making soon returns to make more explicit its connection with textual practice. The village headman, the exile's host,
tells his grandson 'a story as he works away at a net' (*IL*, 38).
His voice 'weaves' even as the hands work the net; the old man is
'deeply absorbed' in both activities at once (*IL*, 39). Like the story-
teller himself, all listeners, even the uncomprehending poet, are
entirely caught up in the story, as in a net. These passages deftly
prepare for the consolidation of the text/net analogy when Ovid
learns to make nets himself and recognises the 'poetry' residing
in this new work (*IL*, 64). Not surprisingly, with the capture
of the Child, which occurs very shortly after the net-making
apprenticeship, Ovid embarks on a bilateral project of language
teaching and language learning: the poet teaches human speech
– significantly not Latin, but the newly acquired, other-language
of the Getae; the Child teaches the languages of nature. Both are
fishers, both are fish – mutually netted.

Clearly then, language, the realm of symbolic exchange,
presents one path of approach to the other, particularly when
language use is applied to the construction of complex, autotelic
patterns – as in text-making or poesis. However, Malouf's
narrative will make the turn toward its resolution by affirming
that the 'true language' is the 'speech of silence' (*IL*, 97), a
speech 'whose every syllable is a gesture of reconciliation' (*IL*,
98). The tone of these affirmations is so tinged with quiet joy
that one may take them as guarantees of the success of the
language-orientated quest. However, closer consideration of
this paradoxical 'speech of silence' must lead to at least a suspi-
cion of language's ultimate incapacity, its falling short. One does
not, finally, apprehend the other in language. Full reconciliation,
communion, atonement, at-one-ment, with the other, in the site
of the other – this experience is clearly beyond language, beyond
language as we know and understand it, beyond the differential
system of shared and conventionalised signs. This experience
of communion or full reconciliation with the other happens in
an other-than-linguistic place, in a realm of experience beyond
the scope of the symbol. Language, once again, is only a path of
approach. The silent speech of reconciliation is beyond speech,

and can be called a 'speech' only in so far as it is approached through language practice, through an extension beyond, a pushing out from, that practice.[16]

But language, moreover, is not the only path of approach. In the course of his novel's multifaceted quest for otherness, Malouf also extensively explores the path of identification, in relation to both imagination and dream. Identification, in psychoanalytic theory, is a self-constitutive initiative that first arises *before* a human subject's accession to language (the symbolic order), and one in which the pre-verbal child adopts a self-image located in an exterior mirroring of her or his body.[17] Thus, Malouf's close concern with identification gives some support to critical arguments affirming that *An Imaginary Life*'s deeper commitment is to pre-symbolic or, in Lacanian terms, imaginary modes of experience.[18]

Ovid, the aged exile, clearly identifies with the wild boy. He recognises, most significantly, that the wild boy is like him in 'having no other creature to share his mind' (*IL*, 52), in suffering extreme forms of personal isolation and exile. Yet identification does not entirely account for Ovid's response to the discovery of the wild boy, nor does the movement of identification specify the Child's eventual role within Ovid's self-transforming experience. Ovid, one must recall, has already been learning to identify, in various ways, with the Getae people of Tomis – a people he had initially considered unsettlingly unfamiliar and, from his metropolitan Roman perspective, irremediably barbarous. The wild boy, however, is more radically other, as Ovid quickly realises. He is not differently socialised; he is pre-social, uncultivated by human contact. The Child, although his importance is not exclusively a matter of identification, offers the most challenging focal point for identification and quite quickly takes prominent place in the poet's identification-orientated dreams and imaginings.

An Imaginary Life presents noteworthy instances of dream-mediated encounter with the other. Ovid has dreams of centaurs, which, like the wolf-men inhabiting the folkloric imaginings of Ovid's childhood, are key figures of radical otherness – the radical otherness of which the wild boy becomes the most important textual representative. In the first of the dreams, centaurs call out to the dreamer, staging what is quite clearly a version of the appeal (in the French sense of *l'appel*)[19] of the other: '*Let us into your world … Let us cross the river into your empire. Let us into your lives. Believe in us. Believe*' (*IL*, 24). Then, as one dream-centaur approaches the dreamer, some buried self rises up 'like a reflection rising to the surface of a mirror'. Ovid recounts, 'It was there, outside me, a stranger. And something in me that was its reflection had come up to meet it' (*IL*, 24–5). The mention of a mirror immediately alerts us to the theme of identification, the mirror being recognised, after Lacan, as identification's key figure. Malouf's scene stages, in dream form, an encounter with the other characterised by mutual recognition and mutual identification. And it includes the suggestion that the self already contains within it a version of the other, a reflection, a point of quite exact correspondence.

The first sighting of the wild boy provokes new dreams, which recall the earlier centaur dream and also submit it to a re-evaluative comparison: 'As in that earlier dream I am face to face with something that is not myself or of my own imagining, something that belongs to another order of being, and which I come out of the depths of myself to meet as at the surface of a glass' (*IL*, 52). The encounter with the wild boy is like the encounter with the dream-centaur, yet a significantly distinct experience, and one that modifies the interpretation of the earlier dream experience. Again, Ovid tries to maintain his sense that he contains in the depths of himself some corresponding version of the other. Yet he is equally clear in his recognition that the Child is indisputably other than anything the poet's self contains and is also more than anything he could imagine. Ovid finds it difficult to maintain his idea of reflective correspondence. Of his first brief face-to-face encounter with the wild boy, Ovid avers, 'it exceeds my imagining, that sharp little face with its black stare' (*IL*, 50). One catches here a suggestion that dream may go deeper into being than the faculty of imagination. Yet even dream experience, being self-generated, does not fully prepare or account for the confrontation with actual otherness, which cannot be thoroughly comprehended even by the deepest delved analogies of the self. Something in the depths of self answers sympatheti-cally to the other, as to an appeal, but no element of the self can correspond exactly to the enigmatic newness the other presents. Both imagination and dream are paths for approach to the other, but only for approach. The other as a real and distinct presence in the world is both unignorable and ungraspable; ultimately, the full apprehension of the other eludes both imagination and dreamwork. Ovid resolves his thinking about the wild child of the Tomis woods by affirming, 'He is the wild boy of my child-hood'; 'He is the Child' (*IL*, 54). However, informing this conclu-sion, founding it, is the recognition that the wild boy of Tomis, as the Child returned, is not merely a figure of imagination or dream, not a projection from out of the depths of self. The Child formerly and the Child now both manifest what one may call the category of the other; this precisely is what recreates the wild child as the Child. The Child is surely the Child because he surely manifests otherness, because he presents a reality that is not and can never be contained within the self.

A full apprehension of the other does not seem to be a possibility Malouf entertains – as least not as a living possi-bility. Right at the end of the novel, Ovid finally does correspond quite precisely with the site, the place, of other experience, of the experience of the other. One moves from the assertion, 'The Child is there' (exterior, not here, not me) to the final recognition 'I am there' (I am at last exterior to myself, other than myself, out there; I correspond finally with the not-I). But of course, the final 'I am there' marks the moment of death, the passage out of life and the lived experience of personal identity, the collapse of the border between self and alterity. And yet Malouf's text does strongly suggest that contact and exchange, communication and communion, can and do occur in life in some mysterious way – through face-to-face encounter and the previously mentioned speech of silence: 'Something, as we face one another in the darkness, has passed between us. We have spoken. I know it. In a language beyond tongues' (*IL*, 63). Ovid becomes convinced of desire on the part of the other; he comes to believe that the wild boy is inclined to seek the company of men. The belief in that desire combines with his conviction that contact and exchange have occurred and will occur again, and the effect on Ovid is profoundly regenerative. He is saved from the stultifying effects of exile, not by gaining a clear sense of who or what he is, but by focusing his attention and his desire on an embodiment of what he is not. His salvation does not arise from self-consolidation, but from a new sense of the self's radical contingency.

The energising of outward, other-directed vision transfigures Ovid's understanding of his world and himself. No longer a place of desolation, the Tomis world is now insistently full: 'full of tiny animals and insects, all of them worth observing ... full of strange fish, all beautiful in their way' (IL, 63). No longer a despairing exile, Ovid turns his thoughts to 'further selves ... contained within us, as the leaves and blossoms are in the tree' (IL, 64). Having encountered, recognised, acknowledged the other, Ovid is able to offer a resounding 'yes' to his world and to his own 'further' possibility for life. But 'further selves' and 'further being' are not to be understood as appropriations of the other; the other in Malouf is, and must remain, distinct and inviolable. 'Further being' is not taken from the other but called forth; it is self-generated enrichment awakening and arising in response to the other's appeal, even as the slumbering chrysalis yields new being to the call of spring: 'A membrane strains and strains, growing transparent, till the creature who is stirring and waking in there is visible in all its parts, forcing its own envelope of being towards the breaking point till with its folded wings already secure in the knowledge of flight, and of all the motions of the air, it flutters free' (IL, 147).

Self-regenerating, self-transfiguring benefits come only through effective contact and exchange between self and other. The other is not, is never, mastered, assimilated or appropriated. Some time after his Child-inspired transfiguration, Ovid still senses the Child as 'a separate center of energy' (IL, 79) – not as an addition to, or extension of, his own being. Still later in the narrative, when the relationship between poet and Child is much more developed, Ovid suffers, during a crisis moment, a terrifying 'vision of [the Child's] utter separateness' (*IL*, 106) – his utter separateness, his *outer* separateness. And very near the end of the novel, Ovid first affirms, 'He seems closer now than I ever thought possible', then continues, 'And yet for all his closeness, he seems more and more to belong to a world that lies utterly beyond me, and beyond my human imagining' (*IL*, 149).

An account of Malouf's engagement with alterity requires, however, a push beyond the realm of I-and-you, of individual instances of interpersonal contact and exchange. Encounter with the other occurs very differently in relation to larger social collectives. For the village community of Tomis, the Child is a wood-spirit or demon-possessed changeling. He is submitted to the same economy of fear and disavowal that gives its shape to the figure of the wolf. And not surprisingly, the crisis moment in the Child's relationship with the community does not follow upon a strong assertion of the Child's difference but upon a manifestation of unmistakable resemblance. When, in a delirium of fever, the Child utters his first human word, a word belonging to the collective, this action sets him apart rather than including him. Resemblance in the stranger proves more threatening, more insidious than his difference. Within the social body, individuals live contingently with their fellows, inflecting, deflecting, transmitting, transferring a great variety of social contents. However, the wild child, the outsider, the extreme form of the other, is not allowed to participate in this social economy. His potential contribution, once reshaped by paranoia, is understood as contamination – or more precisely demon-possession. It is only for Ovid, the individual in isolation, the exile, that the Child presents a force of revitalisation and regeneration. Running through much of Malouf's subsequent work is this sense that only the individual set apart, or standing apart, only the individual unbound from the demands of the collective, can appreciate the enlivening, creative power that encounter with the other may bestow.[20]

But one should recognise, also, that Malouf does not represent the human community as fluid and harmonious in its workings – and exclusionary or conflictual only in relation to the outsider. In Malouf's rendering of the social world, competition, conflict, division are already there, and the ostracism of the stranger is in fact energised not by a defensive reaction of social unity and harmony but by division and discord refocused on the figure of the outsider. In this light, it is possible to understand more clearly and more fully the potentially problematic role of the 'woman's world' within the novel (*IL*, 84). In a dark and dangerous way, the Child confronts, for the first time, what Ovid rediscovers – the power of women, and particularly the power of women over men. Gender competition within the novel turns around the character Rysak, the village headman and the exiled Ovid's host and protector. Rysak's headmanship and his more general masculine privilege are ultimately overmastered by 'the darker power of women' (*IL*, 100). Rysak's mother, a witchy old crone, gives a particularly unattractive, vindictive shape to this counter-world of women's power. And it may be that Malouf's portrayals of femininity and gender politics – marked by a close adherence to old-established, conventionalised mythopoeia – are inescapably problematic. Yet one still must note that even the most problematic figure, Rysak's mother, can be accounted for in relation to gender competition, gendered conflict – and not in relation to women's inherent wickedness. This old woman, who once, as mother of an infant child, was power absolute, wishes to reinstate herself. Although her son (himself an old man) is now in many respects her 'master', he 'was once a suckling, utterly in her power' (*IL*, 126). It is in her quest to renew her power and authority (in relation to one man, her son, and by extension, in relation to men in general) that the old woman turns against the outsiders, Ovid and the Child. Her action confirms that the forced exclusion of the outsider from the social body does not take shape, most compellingly, in defence of a pre-existing social harmony. Exclusion is spurred by the society's preceding dividedness, which manifests itself, in *An Imaginary Life*, most prominently as gender conflict. The outsider, in this way, is brought into focus as a threat by a displacement of pre-existing conflictual divisions within the social order.

Malouf's short novel thus manifests not misogyny but a thoughtful and specifically focused misanthropy, which one may describe as an abiding distrust of the human collective. A similar distrust marks the narration of Gemmy Fairley's experience in *Remembering Babylon* – to provide just one comparative example. However, in *An Imaginary Life* Malouf manifests his greatest optimism with respect to individual salvation – and perhaps his greatest pessimism with respect to the broader possibilities of social regeneration. (*Remembering Babylon* seems to hold out the possibility of the Australian nation's future regeneration-through-reconciliation; the novel concludes with a vision of the island continent luminously 'in touch now with its other life' (*RB*, 200).) The achievement of Ovid's imaginary history is in its strong affirmation of the redemptive effects of creative engagement with manifestations of alterity, and in its contingent presentation of exile as a potentially regenerative condition.

Although in *An Imaginary Life* Malouf most energetically and elaborately explores the question of self and other in relation to I-and-you, one-to-one relationships, his writing does not necessarily represent an individualistic and essentially anti-social Romanticism. Malouf manifests noteworthy interest in social formations, and if he shows these formations in an unfavourable light, as he very typically does, one should still maintain an awareness of continuity and integrity in his critique. Malouf represents an anxious society, a society that is uncertain and anxious about its own definition and constitution, and he takes it upon himself to portray the violence and rupture that follow upon intensifications of sociogenetic anxiety. It may be that many, or perhaps all, human collectives are anxious to some appreciable degree, but the settler society is more acutely, more inescapably so. The settler society, and all the problems that attend the settling and self-definition of such a society, are arguably among Malouf's concerns, although this more thoroughly social orientation becomes more apparent as his career develops. Already in *An Imaginary Life*, but more clearly in *Remembering Babylon*, the other and the outsider offer a creative (if too often misapprehended) challenge to social order as well as to individuality. Yet, one must still recall that Malouf's primary focus is, enduringly, on individualised, life-transforming experiences of encounter. Such experiences may be extraordinary, even wondrous – as when one confronts a birdlike, fence-hovering Gemmy framed by a molten Queensland sky, or a wild child, suddenly glimpsed, upon a forest's luminous margins. But even when the presentation is much less startling, when Jim meets Ashley in *Fly Away Peter* or when Digger meets Mac in *The Great World*, one senses that the author's main imaginative investment is in the articulation of I-and-you.

Child's Play

Turning from *An Imaginary Life* to *Child's Play*, one has the distinct impression of having stepped into an anti-work; taking up the enunciation of *Child's Play* itself, one may say it is a text that responds to its predecessor 'in an opposing spirit' and is yet its 'shadowy complement' (*CP*, 48). This marked character of auto-reflexivity is perhaps the clearest indication that Malouf has adopted a postmodern approach to his writing – more self-consciously and more methodically than in any other works preceding or following. The work's commentators certainly have been alert to its postmodern orientations and concerns. Woods, in a fairly representative reading, finds that the work is a 'metafictional' examination of 'the novel form'; its 'gaps' are intended to undermine 'the self-contained, complete world of the realist novel'.[21] In these reflections one can clearly discern the possibility of considering the novel as a kind of allegory in the postmodern manner.

Given the prominence of politically motivated violence, what is called 'terrorism', in the Italy of the 1970s (that is, in the years immediately preceding *Child's Play*'s first publication in 1981), it is odd to note that Malouf's Italian novel shows so little concern with real political questions. Indeed the terrorist's specific political orientation is a character element of which one learns next to nothing. This absence of real-world political theory and analysis lends credence to those critical readings of the text that conceive it as a postmodern allegory or metafiction, though attempts have been made to specify its serious political concerns. For Griffiths, terrorism in *Child's Play* functions as 'an act of aggression against the idea that stable authorized and universal values exist outside the social and political forces that underpin them'; terrorism's main work is 'an unmasking'.[22] This non-allegorical interpretation is certainly borne out by the text, but it brings us no closer to a historically referential account of political violence, nor does it give greater verisimilitude to certain curious aspects of the terrorists' experience – for example, their ritual nightclub-dancing excursions. Griffiths shows that the work is not purely or strictly an allegory, but without unsettling the notion that it is largely allegorical.

Dever reads the terrorist as 'an agent in the on-going construction of the writer',[23] and Malouf himself suggests, in interview, that it is 'from what I know of the writer' that the terrorist is made.[24] Thus, one may find in the terrorist novel, Malouf's third, a continuation of his meditations on authorship, on what an author is and how one becomes an author. Such concerns are very prominent in *Johnno*, and certainly not absent in *An Imaginary Life*, where the exiled Ovid learns to re-evaluate his previously established authorial status and undertakes to become, in new and challenging ways, the author of his own life. This sense of self-authoring, of the author as one who makes and remakes his life and himself, is unquestionably pertinent to the interpretation of *Child's Play*. Malouf's title occurs in his text as the title the ageing author has given to his 'Work in Progress' (*CP*, 79), which the approaching moment of assassination will convert into a progress never achieving self-definition; it will find its final shape as 'the unfinished masterpiece (yes, it will be unfinished)' (*CP*, 88). Yet part of the specific character of this work is that it 'defies' both death and the author's established life. In it, the author has 'remade himself in a form entirely unexpected and unpredictable' (*CP*, 89). And, of course, self-authoring is very much a part of the terrorist's project, even if he does not always evidence clear conscious awareness of this fact. The terrorist novel is ultimately darker in outlook than its predecessors. All writing, all authorial acts, are here envisioned as being toward death, toward future-perfect self-definition, toward all that one will have been and said. Nowhere else in Malouf does the lean-limbed, deathly-cool written symbol stand in such sharp contrast with the warm, living breath of common speech.

Accompanying, however, this concern with authorship and its attendant themes – finality, completeness, mastery, adult self-actualisation – are the play, the fantasy, the rituals of childhood, which inhabit the novel just as insistently. Indeed a key part of the project of interpreting the novel is sorting through the various writings of 'child's play' and sorting out what this play seems to mean for Malouf, how it takes shape in his imagination. Certainly, Malouf recognises that 'child's play' commonly figures an easy – perhaps too easy – and inconsequential undertaking. But it interests him much more that a child's play has to do with individualisation and socialisation, the two often being thematised in alternating movements. In one of the novel's more important instances of children's play, the terrorist comes upon a group of children playing tag (or touch), 'one of them always the outsider; the others always in flight from him' (*CP*, 116). The game moves its participants back and forth between the desperate exteriority of the third person ('it' or 'he') and the anxious (because unceasingly menaced) condition of group belonging, thus recapitulating the individual's fluctuating relationship with social life. The crucial point here is that the play is ongoing, ever unresolved; one does not, cannot, settle comfortably into either unbound individuality or an assured, albeit constrained, belonging. The child's play, then, is an enabling experimentation with a human life's more abiding and difficult tensions. It is not a charmingly naïve expression of *joie de vivre*, but a very mixed affair, in flux, fraught with contradiction and antagonism – like childhood itself, which the novel (or at least its narrator) characterises as 'the fresh, cruel, innocent, destructive beginnings' (*CP*, 89). The terrorist comes upon the game of tag as he is struggling with the news of Antonella/Graziella's violent death, and thus her definitive elimination from the group life of the terrorist cell and her definitive conversion, by the press, into the third person, the absolute outsider, of the established social world. Watching the play the young man feels 'intensely absorbed and happy' (*CP*, 116), as though the spectacle provides a ritual, symbolic relief of his distress.

If the author, as the terrorist affirms, is able to conjure 'out of children's games and boyish fantasies the whole horror of a generation's induction into the realities of war' (*CP*, 46), this achievement relies on the essential similarity or compatibility of the two realms of experience, childhood and war. The novel's repeated returns to the theme of children's play suggest that the human being never really graduates beyond the regulated yet experimental approaches to living that such play manifests. And this is not to say that the business of living never gets serious and consequential, but that it *is* so, and always on much the same terms, from the beginning. In the mixed character of a child's play one may discern the novel's ideal resolution of the tension it stages between fixity and flux (or fluidity), which finds form most pertinently in image patterns involving stone and water. These antithetical images may occur separately, in an alternating rhythm, or paired together, as when the author follows the path of 'five stepping stones over a stream' to return to key sites of youthful experience (*CP*, 120) or when the terrorist uneasily scans the rain-soaked stone structures of the place of assassination. The author, however, is more closely and sympathetically linked to water, which he uses as 'a regenerative symbol in his novels' (*CP*, 117). In the terrorist's account of his own life, stone is most prominent, beginning with the stone step of his newly purchased farmhouse, which, significantly, bears ancient inscriptions and may have been 'an Etruscan altar' (*CP*, 1). The terrorist's relation with water is often ambivalent, and late in the narrative, it is with horror that he dreams of himself in fog and among horses wading in the sea.

Admiring the achievement of his author-target, the terrorist observes, 'it is in the protean transformations and masquerades of this ego, its capacity to slip in and out of other forms, other lives, that he discovers that feeling for the oneness of things that both justifies his vision of himself as a phenomenon of nature and convinces us of its truth' (*CP*, 60). One suspects that the terrorist's private investment in his assigned task is here. The author's exceptional success in the modern human experiment, in the experiment of being modern and human, is in his graceful management of the oppositions and contradictions of experience. He is engaged and disengaged, connected to the life of things but also distanced. He has a uniquely fluid capacity 'to slip in and out'; whereas, the terrorist's alienation entails being somewhat 'in' and somewhat 'out' of the life of things, and never entirely occupying either position. His proposed assassination intends therefore to deny the possibility of *generalising from* the author's utopian disposition towards modern living. The young man can accept the life of modern alienated subjectivity; he even expects this acceptance, and the consequent return to life-as-it-is-lived, as the due reward of his act. His project takes place in 'a time outside [his] life'; his real life and work lie on 'the other side' of the great murderous event (*CP*, 94). But the acceptance and the hoped-for return to life hinge upon eliminating, striking out, the possibility the author manifests – his unceasingly resilient power of making and remaking his experience and himself. The terrorist is an Ovid who says 'no' to the challenge represented by the Child, a Dante who says 'no' to the challenge represented by Johnno. He hears the other's appeal, but refuses to acknowledge that the appeal is *to* him, *for* him; refuses the new version of himself that the other calls into being.

The terrorist-narrator quite consistently manifests 'fear' of 'the unpredictable',[25] yet he also stages 'the writer's refusal of himself as written: a refusal that can only be *writing*'.[26] This particular refusal of oneself as written, however, applies much more clearly to the author-target than to the terrorist. The terrorist's main project is in the service of fixity, finality, writtenness, and death; his assassination will convert the author from one who writes, one whose life and work are still fluidly in process, into one who is written, whose writing life is accomplished and defined. Writtenness and thus fixed self-definition contrast, of course, with the fluid, experimental, quest-orientated aspect of a child's play, for which the narrator feels, somewhat contradictorily, a marked admiration and appreciation. However, the narrator assumes the impossibility (for anyone except perhaps the author) of remaining in the state of creative process and play. This sense of impossibility leads to his commitment to fixity and to the deeply symbolic death-dealing act that will punctuate the author's unrelenting state of play.[27]

The child's play ultimately is the figure of life, just as writtenness figures death. Yet the terrorist professes the hope of finding life, of re-entering life, on the far side of an act of death, of murder. If this curious (and vain) hope is not to be taken simply as a piece of anxious, probability-eluding optimism, it may be the first indication that the novel is an allegory of modern alienation. The terrorist's quest, from this perspective, is to live alienation consciously, even analytically. He aims to achieve full self-consciousness in alienation, to know himself as alienated being, as an assembly of the effects of alienation. The novel's concern then is with modern alienated subjectivity, but also with a kind of (equally modern) heroism of alienation. In his ultimate character as an assassin, in the character he will bring to the 'event', the terrorist will be, he avers, 'composed of nothing but mind' (39), in a pure state of disembodied alienation. Such a notion of heroism sustains his assertion that 'The giants of our epoch are those lone figures whose real antagonist is themselves' (CP, 25), whose 'adventuring' is into the 'pure space' of solitude and self (CP, 26).

This sharpening of focus upon the problem of modern alienation turns attention to the incidentals of the terrorist's life, which criticism has tended in the main to skim over in pursuit of a tenable account of the protaganist's orientating project, his assigned assassination. The young man inhabits 'a rat's nest' of converted 'servants' quarters', along with innumerable others with whom he has no meaningful connection, but whose presence he often experiences as disquietingly proximate and intrusive – as footsteps, just centimetres distant, that seem

intent on walking 'into [his] skull'. Summarising his disorientation, he records, 'I have no clear picture of how the rooms and
passageways … are connected or where my room sits among
them' (*CP*, 5). Brokenness, fragmentation, and a general lack
of perceptible coherence characterise the physical structures he
inhabits, and by extension the cultural heritage these structures
manifest. Faceless anonymity is the rule: 'I am invisible. Just like
everyone' (*CP*, 9).

The work life, the life at the 'office' of the terrorists' cell,
conforms dishearteningly to the usual terms of modern bureau-
cratic employment. Atomised individuals pursue apparently
unconnected tasks. There is no exchange, not even during meals,
which are taken in common but in wordless denial of the most
basic facts of companionability. (The *companion*, one should
recall, is most fundamentally the person with whom one breaks
and shares bread.) The characters of the co-workers remain
unverifiable fantasy constructs. Social excursions with fellow
workers do occur, but without instituting any group dynamic;
everyone is as if alone. The dancing is in the mode of the late-
twentieth-century club, cruisingly errant, self-involved rather
than partner-orientated: 'you shift in and out of the crowd,
allowing the steps themselves to determine which of these
strangers will fall for a moment into partnership with you' (*CP*,
85). The terrorist/office-worker's preferred solitary entertain-
ment, the pornographic movie, represents another version of the
alienated sociability of the club. 'Two girls from nowhere' take
up with footballers on a road trip: 'Multiple sex on the bus while
the highway landscape streams past. More sex in the dressing-
room, among open lockers; in the showers; in a steam-room with
tiled walls' (*CP*, 98). In all this there are moments of almost-
connectedness, as when Carla gives the young man a quick but
startling make-over, or when Arturo shows up, by chance, at a
porno showing. But these moments of almost fellowship serve
mainly to pinpoint the terrorist's problem with modern life: he
is not quite 'in' and not quite 'out'; he knows fully neither the
warm recognition of belonging nor the cool self-sovereignty
of distance. Malouf's delineations of modern alienation do

not, admittedly, produce any of his more original or arresting passages. Such writing provides, however, a freight of modernity to lend greater substance to the terrorist's main project.

'The crimes we are to commit have no continuity with us', the terrorist asserts. 'Nothing in their geography, their politics, their psychology, leads back to what we are' (*CP*, 19). Such curious distinction makes the terrorists in training seem strangely like anti-authors – like authors only in that they are so exactly unlike them. They are also, one should note, anti-characters, defying with precision the usual realist logic of character development. Discontinuity, in the present case a discontinuity between identity and life, is a crucial concern in the terrorist's story of alienation, and its most prominent figure is the gap. Both experience and its representation are gapped, and both for this reason resist sythesising vision. The prospective site of the crime, as represented in an assembly of partial photographs, is marked by troubling gaps. But the terrorist-scholar is quite quick to recognise that the 'gaps' – also and more unsettlingly – 'are in myself' (*CP*, 29).

The most important figure of the gap is the mirror, which tantalises precisely because of the gap, never to be closed, that it opens between the gazing figure and the reflected image. Envisioning his task as analogous to heroic mountaineering, the terrorist speaks of 'the little mirrors in which the mountain's spirit is caught and reflected, the great antagonist' (*CP*, 26). He thinks of the 'event' he is preparing, and (not so consciously) of the great author-target, as similarly self-revealing and self-defining antagonists – to be mastered, in preparation, little by little. Late in the narrative, the terrorist reveals that he experiences the author's *oeuvre* as a 'vast mirror-world' (*CP*, 133). The most significant instances of mirrorings, however, are implicit. The mirroring of terrorist and author first suggests itself strongly when the former, in his preparation, reproduces the latter, 'his struggles at the desk, and the keen self-discipline they necessitate' (*CP*, 42). This reflexivity between the two becomes clearer when the terrorist observes that even as he has begun to gain an understanding of the author, the author has 'both understood and accounted for' the terrorist (*CP*, 54). Unquestionably, one finds both a mirroring and a prolepsis of the future assassination, when the terrorist concludes, 'in comprehending me he has also written me off' (*CP*, 56). The mirror-game is most chilling when the terrorist remarks of the author's life – 'Everything timed precisely' (*CP*, 77) – a little fragment of truth that applies with at least as pressing a pertinence to the proper fulfilment of the terrorist's labours. At no point, however, does the terrorist manifest a desire to become the author, nor does he believe that the author's abounding being might supply his own lack-of-being. His orientation is more in the tendency to become one with the object one scrutinises intensely – a murderous version of Keatsian 'negative capability'. He hopes finally to find himself and the other in the assassination. This ultimate act of connection, of union, will resolve the tension of identity and separation the mirror maddeningly maintains.

All the topics discussed thus far – authorship, fluidity and fixity, identity and distance, alienation, and the rest – come together in the novel's overarching concern with language and representation. The author's successful experimentation with the conditions of modern life is entirely language-bound; it arises from and manifests his textual mastery. Similarly, he presents himself to the terrorist as a textual problem, as a collection of documents that needs to be studied, analysed and interpreted. Even the photographs so prominent among the project documents, although not linguistic, are clearly materials for textual practice: the signifying elements need to be discerned and their interrelations examined. Terrorism, as the terrorist represents it, locates its true 'happening' in discourse, in the public language of report, in *'infamous crime, mindless violence, anarchy'*. Terrorism's real acts are 'language murders', and thus the great author is the most 'appropriate victim' of 'the war of words' (*CP*, 91). This war of words is not, of course, terrorism's exclusive field of action; it is the general state of the world, omnipresent and unrelenting. As Neilsen puts the case, the novel explores the thesis that 'we are … constructed by those who control language'.[28] Considered in this light, the terrorist's first self-identification shows itself to be startlingly apt: 'I am what the newspapers call a terrorist' (*CP*, 4). Newspapers are, for the terrorist, the principal site manifesting the discourse produced by 'those who control language'. This discourse, upon which acts of terrorism aim to have a disruptive and transformative impact, disconnects and kills; 'Far from catching life it disintegrates and distorts it' (*CP*, 113). And just here one arrives at terrorism's dilemma: 'We can only work through a medium that is itself the enemy and whose very nature is to deprive whatever it reports of life and power' (*CP*, 114). But is this 'medium' empowered public discourse, or is it language more generally? Neilsen does not say quite enough in affirming that the terrorist's real struggle is 'with language'.[29] The struggle is with a paradox marking our relationship with language. Verbal acts, our own and those of others, make our being and take it from us. We live and also die in language; or, to use the previously discussed terms, we write and we are written. The terrorist, unlike Ovid, can discover no transcendence, no beyond of language, nor can he effectively contest the terms of language's dominion. Inevitably, 'Language murder', which the terrorist discerns both in the power-ridden world and in his own project of resistance, must occur '*in* and *through* language', and 'it is also a murder *of* language'.[30] Yet one cannot succeed in the murder of language – only at best in the murder of the self that dwells in it, uneasily, and has no other dwelling-place. The terrorist's failure to find or make a valid place of being in language is tellingly revealed by the fact that the narrative of *Child's Play* completes itself after the death of its narrator. Language endures, it continues its work of unending articulation, in the absence of any given speaker. Language can sustain its paradoxical relationship with our being, though some speakers cannot; it can place us, at story's end, among apple trees 'heavy with fruit' and also, blithely, full of 'early blossoms' (*CP*, 145).

12 *Edmondstone Street*

In his postmodern novel of terrorism, Malouf strains the ordering power of the 'I' to the breaking point. His writing of the 'I' shows that this language element does not really enable individual being to enter and inhabit the world of words. Malouf does, however, take up the first-person voice in one more substantial publication, which is, significantly, an autobiography – that is, a genre that makes a strong convention-established demand for the first person. Malouf, however, has not given up his struggle with the 'I' and takes it up, as it were, only in a spirit of pacified resignation. In *12 Edmondstone Street*, he strives through language and memory to give the 'I' an original foundation that is spatial even more than linguistic.

Before exploring the childhood home as the primary location where self meets world, Malouf locates the house in relation to old Brisbane, and does so very curiously. He announces that Edmondstone Street 'was "mixed"' – but in what way, one must wonder? It mixes industrial and residential buildings, houses and factories, but it also borders Musgrave Park, 'a dark, uneven place, once an aboriginal graveyard', subsequently 'redeemed' (*ES*, 3). Thus, the 'mixed' aspect – Malouf's quotation marks are already suggestive – may also be cultural and temporal, and in ways that have very much to do with Australian colonisation. The use of 'dark' (which will recur in Malouf's text) is ambiguous and suggestive, but no more so than the 'uneven' that evokes irregularity, incongruence, inequality. And then South Brisbane, the house's location more largely considered, is characterised as 'already disreputable' (temporal mixing – both then and now), and it adds 'abos', 'swaggies and metho-drinkers' to the socio-cultural concoction of place (*ES*, 4). Malouf's grandfather – off kilter in relation to place and time – contributes a backyard 'Mediterranean garden' (*ES*, 5) and personal 'tales from the Arabian Nights' (*ES*, 7). Finally asserting his childhood home's centrality, Malouf concedes that it is 'at the very centre' of a dubious margin, of 'a low part of town in every sense, which is why immigrants settled there, and why abos, swaggies and metho-drinkers were about'. This alignment of immigrants (with which Malouf is linked) with more troublingly marginal social elements is confirmed when Malouf recalls *all* of South Brisbane being 'declared black' during the Second World War; however, he then denies this sense of all-in-the-same-boat, giving the house its final form as 'an island of light in the general blackout', as 'a little world of its own' (*ES*, 8). Is the house part of the troubling mix of South Brisbane, or is it not; does it participate in and reflect the ambient social world and its history, or does it not?

The house that emerges from Malouf's recollections certainly has trouble maintaining its distinction from the larger world beyond its boundaries. Like all first houses, it is not initially familiar, a place of 'dense affinities', but instead the first manifestation of the 'terrible otherness' of new-encoun-tered *'things'* (*ES*, 9). Moreover, Malouf's own particular first house, as soon as it begins to be specified, immediately wanders back toward that dark ambient world from which it has been isolated. A source of shame for the father (who has done much in the making of it), this first house is not 'modern', made of "merely local" material, uneasily 'native' and 'poor white'. It is a rudely 'reorganised forest' (*ES*, 10), whose inhabitants stand 'somewhere between bushie and brick-and-mortar man', or alternatively, 'just one step up from nomads' (*ES*, 11).

Malouf clearly understands that the first house makes the inhabiting 'I' much more than the 'I' makes it. He does not, however, explicitly acknowledge that the world, the social world, makes the house more than the inhabitant does. The house is not autonomous any more than those who dwell within it, a fact implicitly evident in Malouf's detailed record of the house's incapacity to establish and maintain inside/outside distinctions. This problem originates with a kind of structural deficiency: verandahs are 'open boundaries' (*ES*, 9), or again, 'no-man's land' (*ES*, 20), and in this they associate with the other main indeter-minate and undomesticated zone known as 'under-the-house'. Of course, the insecurely bounded house submits to nature's day-by-day assault, in the form of 'thick foliage' or 'possums and flying foxes' (*ES*, 10), but the social world's invasions of the

house, its house-breakings, have defining importance. Malouf
claims his memory cannot find images of legitimate visitors such
as his mother's friends, but he can clearly see the lower-class
pregnant woman, who smokes in the house where no one ever
smokes, then pronounces a disgruntled but casual 'fuck' (the
perfect word for her illegitimate congress with the household),
and in this way takes possession of one of the Front Verandah's
(amusingly named) 'squatter's chairs' – only briefly in fact and
yet, in memory, for all time. This woman's invasive force, which
cuts open 'the clear fabric of things', is a force from outside –
from 'a different world', spatially and socially, but also from that
very different time one calls 'the future' (ES, 16). 'Our Burglar'
– the titular capitals tell all – presents another case of defining
violation. Reflecting upon his intervention, Malouf writes, 'if my
parents' room remains a place of mysteries, it is because of its
intruders' (ES, 29). The 'Sorrowful Witness', Jesus of the Sacred
Heart, is another defining 'intrusion' from the outside (ES, 23);
'a celestial superintendent or voyeur' (ES, 24), he serves unflag-
gingly as the grandmother's proxy in the much-violated invio-
lateness of the parental bedroom.

The child Malouf identifies strongly with Our Burglar, and
even imaginatively colludes with him, which draws attention
to the fact that even the house's authorised occupants have
something of the interloper character about them. Cassie, though
closely associated with the mother and a constant presence, is
yet 'anomalous' (ES, 18); Cassie's father, an occasional visitor,
manifests the 'utterly foreign' and 'outlandish', giving clear
meaning to 'not family' (ES, 17). The child Malouf, resenting the
verandah sleep-out he shares with his sister, becomes a night-
wandering 'rebel nomad' (ES, 20) and thus resists the fate of
one who is 'cast out and then let in again' (ES, 21). Even the
parents, dominated by the designs of their parents, seem 'like
older children' rather than adult householders (ES, 25).

The house is not wholly possessed, nor is it possessed
whole. Malouf early affirms that the first house was originally
'undivided' and that its primary lesson was 'how one space opens
on to another' (ES, 12), but he then unfolds a quite complex

inventory of barriers. The first house includes, at least for the child, a number of places where one does not belong and cannot go – and where one invariably goes anyway, but surreptitiously. The house has, in other words, a number of taboo spaces. Appropriately, these spaces are protected by notional barriers. (One may also recall, more practically, that the house has few interior doors, and that even these are almost never closed.) The Front Room is a cold, class-affirming, symbolic space, which never receives any of the life of the house (with the exception of the child's on-the-sly shits, which are intended to warm and personalise it). Cassie's room is strictly off-limits to children – and predictably unyielding of its mysteries when its threshold is ritually approached and transgressed. The parents' room, approached and invaded in ritual mimicry of Our Burglar, is also disappointing: 'What's the matter? Do you want the lav?' (ES, 29). These quietly comic let-downs that attend transgressive ventures serve to make a more serious point: the barrier is not in place to protect and enshrine something precious and mysterious; it is, dishearteningly, an assertion of difference, of division, of separateness, of exclusion. Indyk first speaks of 'repression', and then more pointedly of repression's 'social path',[31] thus adopting a more overtly psychoanalytic thrust than the taboo-orientated reading presented here. Repression, certainly, accounts more thoroughly for the child's interiorisation of the constraints imposed by his material and social circumstances: commenting on his early 'training in perception', Malouf writes, 'You see what you are meant to see. You hear when you are called' (ES, 22). The pairing of sociogenetic restraints with occasional, venturesome transgressions ultimately serves to initiate the child into regulated desire – the standard under which we mournful moderns assemble – the desire not stifled, nor entirely controlled, but managed, first socially then personally.

In Malouf's early-childhood world, the barriers are permeable, at least on occasion, which may lead to the optimistic conclusion that a barrier is always also a point of passage. Barriers may be the unkind name for the 'odd, undisclosed connections' that abound, according to Malouf, in the first house and in the world (*ES*, 51). Yet one still does not in this way resolve the problem of the autobiographical subject's incapacity to securely house himself, to possess the whole house wholly. This abiding problem is probably the main inspiration for the fetishisation of the Brass Jardiniere, that magical holding-place for objects that have been rendered partial by separation from their meaning-assuring mates. One may recall also the thrill of under-the-house, the space that counters the social and material reality of the house proper (also the proper house), and thus affirms that the house is not, any more than its would-be possessor, entire unto itself, whole and coherent. Malouf's barriers, the barred thresholds of experience, may at times be passable, but one still has to contend with the edges of which Malouf's world is significantly composed (*ES*, 54, 62). At its edges the world contacts and marks the body, temporarily, with a bruise, or permanently, with a scar; the edge thus becomes a source of inscription, and a reminder that one's passage in the world is not always readily granted. Even the opened threshold is edged.

'And so', Malouf perhaps too blithely observes, 'at last we come down to it, the body – that small hot engine at the centre of all these records and recollections' (*ES*, 53). Deeper delvings now reach the core, but one gets also the sense that somehow the body has been a matter of avoidance, like the child's Front Room shits that are this body's immediately preceding metonyms. The body is the core space of habitation, but Malouf wishes to secure it, as much as possible, from the economy of divisions and constraints that so dauntingly mark the first house. The body distinguishes itself by its greater responsiveness to 'contacts' and its remarkable capacity for transformation, its 'unique, undeniable powers – of flight, of change, of eternal instant being. It is always in a state of becoming' (*ES*, 54). If the first house is ultimately too encoded, the body (Malouf hopes) is fluidly self-discovering. This body is put forward as the much sought-after site for personal agency, self-determination: 'For our bodies are inventions; we shape them to our views' (*ES*, 56). And yet 'The body has two lives as it has two sides, an outward and visible one and a dark, interior life that follows laws and processes we cannot always control' (*ES*, 61); the body is also divided, and cannot be securely known and embraced as one's very own. Its dark privacies correspond, moreover, to certain home spaces – notably 'lavatories' or 'dunnies' (*ES*, 61) – thus binding the body to the social and material structures from which one might hope to keep it free.

Malouf fills several pages striving toward an anthem to the body, repeatedly affirming the body's generative power and concentrated heat, the energy and heat of life. The anthem is modulated, however, by moments that contrast the body of the past with the 'contemporary body' (*ES*, 56), thus dividing the body in time and limiting the access of consciousness to the body's fullest reality. As so often previously, the autobiographer arrives finally at 'a limit', 'a threshold we cannot cross' (*ES*, 64), a 'wall we cannot go through' (*ES*, 65). The problem now is that one cannot find 'the experiencing mind-in-the-body' of one's various past selves (*ES*, 64). Each moment or phase of the past's embodied consciousness is lost in the ceaseless process of becoming. Recovery would require not only remembering but a concurrent and impossible '*un*-remembering', a disarticulation of the very experience by which the body makes and remakes itself and thus the consciousness of self.

And yet Malouf concludes by affirming the possibility of passage; indeed, the essay's last words are 'to pass through'. (One notes here a quieter instance of the transformational grammar that so powerfully shapes *An Imaginary Life*.) But to what does one pass through? To a clearer understanding of self, one suspects, although the passage is not made, only promised – and this promise is bolstered by a rather facile evocation of 'one last little blaze of magic'. Betting the bank on the 'actual body', the cumulative sum of all past bodies, Malouf affirms the 'door' resides within (*ES*, 66). But these final affirmative notes suffer from the typical weakness of a demonstration of faith: one does not *believe* because one is sure; one believes because one is not sure.

The title essay of the autobiographical collection does not succeed in founding the self (in a house without foundation). Malouf does not – and knows he does not – find his originating place, the true first structure of his particular being-in-the-world. He has considerable success, however – and perhaps not quite intentionally – with the project Edward Hills discerns: 'the mythologising of nascent and formative space into psychic maps that reveal the inner workings of the culture'.[32] One must wonder why Malouf finally looks toward – not at but toward – an ever-undisclosed place in the actual body. Why is he unwilling to concede that the secret of self may not be here in the body but there in the workings of culture; that one *is* precisely the *inner* workings of one's culture? (One may recall, with some puzzlement, the decidedly affirmative 'I am there' with which Ovid concludes.) In 'The Kyogle Line', which returns to formative experience following the adult errancies of two intervening essays, Malouf's faith in the body as the repository of the deeper truths of self is shaken by the recognition of the genealogy of ethnic difference to which the body testifies. Decidedly it means something to lay claim, as Malouf does in the poetry, to a grandfather's nose. The last essay fearfully acknowledges the question of ethnic difference, which is only nascent in the first. It manifests the fear that one's difference, rather than being self-generated and self-discovered, may be socially assigned; that one does not make one's own place but rather is put in one's place, in a place that may never quite feel like one's own.

'A Place in Tuscany' and 'A Foot in the Stream' lay claim to experiences of places very different from old Brisbane and the early childhood home. These texts attest to a more cosmopolitan multiplicity of perspectives upon the world. It is interesting, however, that both essays tend to represent the writer as being out of place, rather than in a new place. The Tuscan village of 'A Place in Tuscany' is acknowledged as 'its own world', and from the perspective of this specific and self-sufficient place, the writer's assigned cultural location is a matter of somewhat troubling vagaries. For his landlady, Malouf's 'Australia' is 'in some empty area of her experience between Poland … and New York' (*ES*, 78–9). Australia is where her tenant is when he is only 'in her thoughts' and not, for the present, 'in "her" house' (*ES*, 79). In 'A Foot in the Stream', as it moves toward its conclusion, one comes upon a pair of curiously belated announcements: 'India is full of temptations for the westerner' (*ES*, 118), and 'Western eyes' have trouble grasping certain aspects of Indian community (*ES*, 119). Once established, this differentiation between Indians and Western travellers (who are both bedazzled and puzzled by them) pursues its course by contrasting a newly constituted 'we' with 'India' (*ES*, 119). The experience of India, it seems, makes Malouf into a paid-up, card-carrying member of Western culture much more readily than Australia is ever able to do. Malouf is entirely at home in the West only once he is neither at home nor in the West. This has something to do with Australia's dubious status as an antipodal (and thus dislocated) outcropping of the Western world, but it also prepares, in an indirect way, for Malouf's acknowledgement, in 'The Kyogle Line', of the uneasiness marking his claim to Australian identity.

'The Kyogle Line', the last of the four texts making up *12 Edmondstone Street*, moves the autobiographical narrator out of the first home of his beginnings and into the larger world. Narrating his remembered self, Malouf writes, 'I was hungry for … some proof that the world was as varied as I wanted it to be; that somewhere, on the far side of what I knew, difference began' (*ES*, 127). Difference, however, has already asserted itself insistently and multifacetedly at 12 Edmondstone Street. And indeed, it is the difference inscribed in the place of familiarity, the home, that the new difference of unknown places is expected to resolve. The narrative quite quickly focuses on the father, a key element of the home world and yet not at all a well-known quantity. One reads first, 'My father's world was foreign to me', and then the narrator traces the father's foreignness genealogically: the father's 'people' are 'utterly ordinary' and yet, with quiet emphasis, '*not* Australian'; garlic-eaters who speak 'no English', they nonetheless 'had always been there' (*ES*, 129). This 'there' is at least as ambiguous as the adjective 'foreign' earlier applied to the father. One must ask, does 'there' place the father's family both in the boy's familial world and, more broadly, in Australia? And if so, what can it mean to be always there, in Australia among Australians, and yet to be, emphatically, *not* Australian?

These ambiguities rapidly yield strange fruit. During a waystation stroll, the boy first experiences an extraordinary and unprecedented togetherness with the father, a welcome feeling 'of our being together and at one' (ES, 130). Identification with the father and entry into the father's 'foreign' world, however, become a matter of liability. Coming back 'from the Men's' (ES, 130), that most assertively unambiguous of masculine spaces, father and son encounter the Japanese prisoners of war who provide the text's organising instance of abject, alienated difference: 'looking in at them was like looking in from our own minds, our own lives, on another species.' This vision is instantly estranging. In the brief space of a transition between sentences, the text sets the boy and the father apart from the group, the assembled Australian 'crowd'; it is suddenly a 'they' that perceives a 'vast gap of darkness' and a 'distance between people' (ES, 131). Of this 'isolating' movement, the narrator concisely observes: 'The moment you stepped out of the crowd and the shared sense of being part of it, you were alone' (ES, 131–2). The boy who feels himself set apart from the larger group does not, however, sense a tightening of the bond with his father. 'Our moment together was over' (ES, 132), the narrator constates, as the father retreats again into isolated incommunicability.

But this incommunicability may be the precise form of the paternal legacy: the narrator speculates, 'Was he thinking of a night, three years before, when the Commonwealth Police had arrested his father as an enemy alien?' (ES, 132). The grandfather's arrest has to do with war-provoked modifications in Australian immigration policy, which had formerly listed the Christian inhabitants of 'greater Syria' (then including Lebanon) as 'white', and thus as acceptable immigrants under the White Australia Policy initiated in 1901. Malouf brings this policy home – along with its treacherous shiftings: 'My father's right to be an Australian … was guaranteed by this purely notional view – that is, officially. The rest he had to establish for himself; most often with his fists' (ES, 132). One thus gains a whole new perspective on Malouf's father's remarkable skill at boxing – which in Johnno is admired merely as testament of a certain tough athleticism. This new writing about the fighting father shows that the father's wilfully acquired 'Australianness' must have encountered resistance in the social sphere – resistance as a form of social violence to be met with a countering violence. Malouf suggests that his father, on the occasion of his own father's sudden designation as an enemy alien, may have learned 'the colour of his own history' (*ES*, 133); in other words, both Malouf and his father may have been obliged to learn that their history has, in the eyes of some fellow Australians, a 'colour', and that this colour may be slightly, but significantly, other than white. Implicitly, the father's visible difference from the Anglo-Celtic majority is suggested, and one gains a clearer sense of the father's 'hidden deep hurts and humiliations' to which Malouf briefly and rather vaguely alludes (*ES*, 130) – but to which he is nonetheless the heir. Thus, Malouf moves toward the conclusion of his autobiographical volume, putting forward the most agonistic of all his representations of himself and his family within Australian society.

Malouf ends his narrative essay with his childhood self lost amid 'an inner argument or dialogue that was in a language I couldn't catch', and with the eerie sense of heading, in 'a different train' from the actual one, for 'a different, unnameable destination' (*ES*, 134). The boy thus falls into a self-estrangement from which the adult, presumably the 'unnameable destination' of the boy's uncertain becoming, has not entirely recovered. (Implicitly, the autobiography thus fails to arrive at its self-authorising signature; in place of author 'David Malouf' it finally inscribes the 'unnameable'.) Significantly, the boy's inner life now takes the form of a language he does not know, or does not quite know (cannot quite 'catch'). Among Malouf's final reflections on his father, on his father's silence, is the recognition that his father's first language must have been Arabic – a language the child Malouf has heard, spoken by his grandfather and his grandfather's friends, but does not understand. It is a language he has never heard his father speak, but the language that must nonetheless give its order to large portions of his father's memory and general psychic life. Arabic is the language of a fractured genealogy, the language of heritage the father split off from himself, in the course of his

Australian self-fashioning, and which he has tacitly refused to offer, as part of the paternal legacy, to his son. The boy is thus shut out from direct discursive knowledge of his grandfather, and from more than partial knowledge of his father. And with respect to the relationship between these two male predecessors, he is left for the most part to surmise and deduction.

The concluding passages of 'The Kyogle Line' return us (as so often happens in Malouf's writing) to the beginnings, in this case to the early, one may even call them the pre-thetic, passages of '12 Edmondstone Street'. Before Malouf presents his primary thesis – 'First houses are the grounds of our first experience', where we 'discover laws we will later apply to the world at large' (*ES*, 8) – he first makes mention of his father and grandfather and their relationship. He tells that his Arabic-speaking grandfather 'remained unknowable' (*ES*, 5); that his father 'betrayed' his grandfather by adapting too thoroughly to life in Australia; that there is 'no link' between them (even though, paradoxically, the father is also 'deeply imbued ... with Old World notions of filial piety'); that the father 'never expressed' his feelings, and the son, therefore, does not know them (*ES*, 7). The fractured genealogy is all here, in short form, before the elaboration of the thesis-governed text, which is in fact a substitute construction attempting to mend and restore, in the spatial idiom of 'home', what is genealogically irreparable and irrecoverable.

One recognises, thus, the full import of Malouf's revelation of 'the inner workings of the culture'.[33] It is the pressure of the social world, of the cultural context, that fractures genealogies. The sense of 'personal exclusion or distance' so frequent in *12 Edmondstone Street* is to be understood, in large part, as an effect 'of migration and the loss of language'.[34] Attar suggests that the persona of 'The Kyogle Line' suffers a too-personal glimpse into 'the life experience of the alien'; he then argues that Malouf has a migrant identity that is 'submerged' or 'severed' in relation to the acknowledged self, but which shows itself, in veiled form, in his writings.[35] For Huggan, 'The Kyogle Line' develops into 'an impressionistically illustrated debate on the nature of cultural difference',[36] a reading that is true enough but rather too gentle in its terms. The point is surely that the *social negotiation* of cultural difference can have highly disruptive, even violating effects on those designated as different. For this reason, Malouf is 'bound to place' but also 'aware of placelessness'; for this reason, Malouf resists notions of '"fixed" location or identity'.[37] Malouf's deeply felt drive to confront difference, to seek self-transforming encounter with otherness, does not reflect a self-possession that is venturesome because secure, nor is it joy-born in its entirety. It arises also from the ordeals of his initiation into Australian social life.

12 Edmondstone Street, Malouf's last substantial publication to use first-person narration throughout, arrives late: four years after *Child's Play* (already a somewhat problematic first-person performance) and following two major publications, *Fly Away Peter* and *Harland's Half Acre*, that are not ordered upon the first person. (*Harland's Half Acre* makes use of first-person narration, but it is carefully framed and contextualised. The first person alternates with third person in the articulation of the novel's six parts, and spontaneous first-person narratives by characters take place within dialogical situations.) Significantly, the autobiographical volume diversifies the first person, breaking its association with continuity of experience. Its four texts situate the 'I' in distinct times and different places. These various articulations of 'I' do not cohere into a well-worked portrait of 'David Malouf', nor are they meant so to cohere. One senses that Malouf, in composing the texts of *12 Edmondstone Street*, was exploring, and thus also tracing, the limits of the first-person perspective. Particularly in the first and last of the four texts, the 'I' is strongly driven to know and discover, but strikes, repeatedly, against the barriers that mark what the 'I' does not know and cannot discover. Individual subjectivity, at least in Malouf's experience of it, seems too fragile and too fraught to stand as a stable site of encounter with the world – full and multifaceted as Malouf's version of the world invariably is. The stories of the 'I' give way, as Malouf's career develops, to narratives that look into the views provided by various 'I' eyes, or make use of various 'I' voices, variously situated.

4
Multiple worlds

Fly Away Peter

The analysis of *Fly Away Peter* and *Harland's Half Acre* will bring Malouf into focus as a writer of multiple-worlds fictions. This new emphasis makes itself felt early, in *Fly Away Peter*'s opening passages, which establish Jim Saddler as an inhabitant of 'two worlds', an up-close, minutely detailed world at ground-level and a mapped world, territorialised, and always envisioned from above, from the bird's-eye view (*FAP*, 2). Ashley Crowther, as soon as he is introduced, is shown to be composed by two very distinct places, by two modes of self-location: he is an Australian landowner (with considerable holdings) and yet one who 'had been away to school in England and then at Cambridge' (*FAP* 3). Birds, one soon learns, are messengers from other worlds: the dollar bird comes 'down from the Mollucas', the 'Sacred Kingfisher' from Borneo (*FAP*, 14, 29); sandpipers carry knowledge of 'northern Asia or Scandanavia' (*FAP*, 19) – and of England, and of Australia (*FAP*, 25). Places of being are spectacularly multiple and discover their relationship through migrations, transfers – innumerable movements to and fro.

'World' for Malouf is a place of being that is composed of a diverse heterogeneity of elements, marked by tensions but also manifesting a high degree of internal coherence – a place of being entire unto itself and yet marked by multiple contingencies. Worlds are geographical and experiential, and in some cases individual consciousness is understood and presented as a version of 'world'. Thus, one may perceive a subtle but significant shift in the author's vision: the world-making power of an 'I', to which an earlier work like *An Imaginary Life* so strongly attests, gives way now to an understanding of consciousnesses as sites where worlds manifest and elaborate their meanings.

In *Fly Away Peter*, the pluralisation of the fictional world gives rise to a new emphasis on insight as an often literal 'looking into,' as a way of contacting and discovering an alternative world of experience, a distinct place of being. The clearest enactment of this theme is probably in the use of field glasses to gain intimate access to the worlds of birds. It is as Jim is '[h]olding one of them in the glasses' that he begins to enter birds' experience, imagining first a 'heart beat' and a 'flutter' of struggling wing, then the immensities the 'tiny quick eye' has seen (*FAP*, 3). Malouf's portrayal of vision, of the vision that looks into the specificities of other worlds, is noteworthily technical. Field-glasses come first, but are then followed by camera lenses and darkroom productions – and eventually a biplane ride provides the aerial view. Vision, real vision, typically entails some kind of prosthesis. The human being seemingly does not see well with the unaided or 'naked' eye. Real seeing requires an augmentation of the acuity of the gaze; it is also pertinently a matter of praxis, a deployment of acquired skills. Therefore Jim's wonderment in response to the sandpiper photograph – '*This is it; this is the moment when we see into the creature's unique life*' (*FAP*, 27) – is preceded, one may say necessarily, by his matter-of-fact but still gratifying recognition of Miss Harcourt's personal savoir faire. Jim appreciates 'the apparatus of a hobby, or trade'; he enjoys 'the order, the professionalism, the grasp all this special equipment suggested of a competence' (*FAP*, 26). The photograph is thus understood to achieve Jim's own project by a distinct but related path. Imogen Harcourt's work is also a seeing-into the life and world of the other – of birds, of this living bird now photographed. And of course the photograph is also a seeing-into the life of the photographer, Miss Harcourt, whose values, sensibilities, and particular understanding of the world are captured in the photograph at least as much as the bird's living image.

All the 'trans' words, very much in evidence in *An Imaginary Life*, reassert themselves in *Fly Away Peter*, as do the concept-themes – transfiguration, translation, transformation, transition – signalled by such dictional choices. In the earlier novel, transformation and passage are insistently in an upward direction, toward presumably higher states of being. Now Malouf sees the movement across and through to be essential, in and of itself, to our fuller humanity. Passage itself, the action of moving across and between, becomes the object of the self-actualising quest. Birds therefore take shape as focal figures of this novel: birds are conceived as eternal migrants, whose very life is a 'passage through its own brief huddle of heat and energy' (*FAP*, 27).

Encounter with the other, not surprisingly, offers in almost all cases the promise of passage. Thus Jim's sense of himself and of his place in the world is so thoroughly transformed by his encounter with Ashley that the character feels he has been 'made free of his own life' (*FAP*, 5). And Jim soon reveals himself to Ashley as the guide to new ways of seeing which effectively recreate the world's form and order and even open up worlds never before glimpsed. At their first encounter, Jim points out a dollar bird, invisible for Ashley. Twice he repeats the question that is also a kind of appeal – 'See?' – and finally brings out Ashley's joyful 'I can see it!' (*FAP*, 15). Following Jim's 'gaze' Ashley comes for the first time to a sense that his world, his land, is 'crowded and alive'. As his land 'shift[s] into a clearer focus', Ashley becomes 'intensely aware for a moment how much life there might be in any square yard of it' (*FAP*, 16) – or, one may say, how many smaller worlds are contained within the larger one, a composite, that he claims as his own. Discovery therefore is presented as a reconfiguration of encounter. Ashley, one learns, 'discovered Jim' who in turn 'discovered Miss Harcourt' (*FAP*, 19). Through an other-activated power of passage, one discovers newness in – and thus renews – oneself and one's world.

As soon as the narrative establishes its fine contingencies of multiple worlds and its carefully balanced schemes of passage, discovery, and transformation, history enters the text as rupture. *Fly Away Peter* remains a narrative of multiple worlds, and it continues to pursue its delineated themes. But relocation becomes now dislocation; the impulse to communion yields to forces of disintegration. Malouf's themes are, as it were, at war with themselves, struggling to maintain their life-affirming thrust in relation to a new and hostile context, the world of war. Like many thousand others – 'from places back home' and whose lives are 'similar' to his own – Jim finds that his initiation into war in Europe places him in a 'world … unlike anything he had ever known or imagined' (*FAP*, 58). Newness is here certainly, but no longer a newness one can readily and creatively assimilate.

The war is history and rupture, but just as pertinently it is culture – or at least a site upon which culture has worked. In the second half of his novel, Malouf engages, as he must, with Anzac mythology; his efforts have met with divided evaluation. Gelder and Salzman express dissatisfaction with the novel, finding that it 'overrides its historical mode … with depoliticized polemic' and ultimately renders 'history as myth'.[1] Karin Hansson, much more generous in her assessment, claims that Malouf's work is 'always thrusting aside purely political and social issues in the exploration of new spatial, linguistic and imaginative domains'.[2] Nettelbeck seems to find a carefully measured place between the two poles of for-and-against. Malouf, she finds, strives to create a 'communal space' of culture 'through the re-evaluation and re-imagining of national mythologies'. Yet she detects a troubling 'tension' between 'an imperative to reconceive' and 'a desire to recuperate', a tension that may lead to reinscription or remythologising of the very national character one wishes to contest and change. Malouf's 'compromise' resides for Nettelbeck in the fact that his 'ideal of reconciliation' necessarily depends on 'what it represses or excludes'.[3] Andrew Taylor states a similar case rather more starkly when he claims that Malouf's 'Great War is a reawakening to the horrifying abuses of humanity from which white Australia emerged'. Malouf's presentation of history is, in Taylor's view, a quite disturbingly ambiguous 'matter of detour and return'.[4]

What both Nettelbeck and Taylor are pointing to may be conceived as a rather disheartening problem of cultural change rather than a problem in Malouf. Perhaps cultures change by way of detours and returns, by refigurings of problematic histories of repression and abuse – or this at least may be, in summary form, Malouf's sense of the process of cultural change. Certainly, one can find in his novel various narrative details that show an alternative, critical perspective upon Anzac mythologies – even though Malouf, at the same time, makes use of the stock of themes and images these mythologies provide. The process of Jim's enlistment is elucidating in this respect. Jim's receipt of his send-off gift (the sexual enjoyment of a young woman) *precedes* his real decision to enlist, yet effectively tips the balance of Jim's mind in favour of enlistment. Jim enlists in part because he has accepted the gift-reward for enlistment; that is, he enacts the ritual and mythology of the war before he actually engages to serve. Malouf's point, in so structuring the process of Jim's enlistment, is that one inscribes oneself first in war's mythology and only subsequently in the hard facts. Indeed, it seems that one may be always already inscribed in war's ideology or mythology; maybe one always already 'knows the drill'.

Although Jim's seduction occurs within the play of quite conventional, recognisable war ritual, it is punctuated, significantly, by a troubling irruption of repressed knowledge or counter-memory[5] – which Malouf details assiduously. As Jim arrives with his young woman at the door of her rooming-house, as he stands on the very threshold of his initiation, the evening's 'stillness' is ruptured by 'a vicious burst of sound' from a neighbouring park, then a woman's shriek, then the curses of various men. 'Abos!' says the young woman dismissively. Then follows 'an explosion. Breaking glass' and, staggering into the light, 'a black silhouette that became a white-shirted man with his hands over his face and blood between them'. Then, strangely, the wounded man executes a 'graceful dance', before a renewed attack, its 'thumps', and a 'woman's raucous laughter' (*FAP*, 39). 'Abos', again, is Jim's companion's only comment, again dismissive, 'as if the rituals being enacted, however violent, and in whatever degenerate form, were ordinary and not to be taken note of' (*FAP*, 39–40).

The mention of 'rituals' in relation to the witnessed violence strongly suggests that Malouf intends the 'Abo' uproar as a counter-staging both of war's enactments and of the male/female relations war encodes. An 'explosion' first indicates the scene's mapping in relation to war. Spilled blood and a thumping violence (as of booming guns) further shape the scene as a sort of burlesque of battle. At the same time, it is clear that the female contribution is no longer supportive and compliant; a woman's voice comments on masculine struggle first with a shriek and finally with rude, apparently derisive laughter.

Crucially, the spilled blood is Aboriginal blood. Its spilling, although a matter of ritual, and thus profoundly symbolic, is *declared* unimportant, not to be attended to, not to be remembered. The victim of this violence is appropriately ill defined, coded as 'black' but seen only as a 'silhouette', not as a fully delineated face. Indeed, the face is covered by hands and blood; it is covered because it has been wounded. The face, the key to an identity, has been the main target of violence, a violence that seems almost deliberately identity-effacing. The black figure of a man, thus defaced, is revealed to be, just as pertinently, 'white-shirted'. This black figure is invested, covered and dressed, by 'white' meanings and intentions. Thus, the precise details of Malouf's brief staging of Aboriginality and violence demonstrate that the author sees white Australia's engagement with war in Europe as an unconscious negotiation with the nation's troubled history, a history that includes most pressingly the abuses committed against Aboriginal peoples. Malouf's novel does not, then, perform unthinking variations upon conventional Anzac themes. It does make use of these themes, these mythologies, but it also articulates – at least in some instances – the return of Australian culture's repressed.

The key scene of violence in Australia is also the first suggestion that violence, the foundational constituent of war, enacts and thus confirms certain forms of masculine identity (as war mythology so commonly suggests it will). This idea returns later, again in a grim and unsettling manner, during Jim's war experience, in the hate-driven relationship with Whizzer. One learns that the two immediately 'got to the bottom of each other', and that 'Enemies, like friends, told you who you were.' Jim's new and surprising knowledge, however, is of 'the black anger he was possessed by and the dull savagery he sensed in the other man' (*FAP*, 63). This coding of seemingly instinctive hatred and violence as black and savage recalls the earlier staging of violence in relation to Aboriginality. The two young white Australians have clearly interiorised a cultural paradigm, whereby hatred and violence link metonymically with the (black and savage) 'Aboriginal' and thus give an other and 'surprising' shape to buried, unacknowledged constituents of self. So, to clarify the core idea, one may say that war's violence reveals and confirms certain forms of Australian masculine identity, or, speaking more broadly, certain forms of masculinity bred by the unresolved, disavowed antagonisms of a race-divided society.

Australian culture, then, is already in the war – or at least coordinated with the war – well before Australian armed forces are. Malouf is careful to show how a culture is recruited to war, even to an ostensibly distant war. He portrays the war's insinuation of itself into the Australian scene in the more obvious ways – for example, through the mass gatherings and manifestations of newly enlisted men, which Jim observes while briefly in Brisbane. But war in Europe also inscribes itself upon smaller, ineluctably personal, everyday-life situations. Miss Harcourt greets the first arrivals of the new season's bird migrations as '*refugees*', a new and strange word for Jim (*FAP*, 43). During his first ride in Bert's biplane, Jim cannot elude the realisation that such flying machines, previously recreational, 'had changed their nature and become weapons' (*FAP*, 51). Jim's father makes a malicious mention of 'white feathers' (*FAP*, 54), the traditional symbols for the supposed cowardice of those who fail to enlist. The world of war is one of the novel's larger and more significant world-structures, and like other such structures it is both autonomous and contingent. It connects with, impinges upon, a multitude of other worlds, great and small.

Yet, the world of war, once one is inside it, reveals certain cruel specificities in its structure and organisation, which set it

apart from other worlds represented in the novel. Neilsen strives
to counter the force of Malouf's representation of the war world's
horrific specificity, its radical difference from the novel's other
worlds, arguing that the war is 'contained by, and ultimately part
of, natural processes', that nature thus has a 'framing function'
in relation to historical horrors.[6] Certainly, Malouf is careful to
show that natural process continues all around the world of war.
Nature's representatives (again, most notably birds) move across,
and in and out of, the war's territories, and Jim is able to continue
his observation of birds while fulfilling, in other moments, the
responsibilities of the active soldier. Yet Jim, as must be emphasised, arrives at a crisis moment in which he concludes that his
pre-war nature-focused activities, and his efforts to continue
them while at war, are meaningless – and desperately so. Even
though he is ongoingly confronted with the 'whole history of
divergent lives' that nature so insistently manifests, Jim falls
into deep doubt on the question of value: 'Worth recording all
this? He no longer thought so. Nothing counted.' Nature's status
as the source and foundation of value is mined unremittingly by
war's 'disintegrating power' (*FAP*, 104).

   In one of Jim's clearest moments of thoughtfulness, he
reflects, 'It would go on forever. The war, or something like it
with a different name, would go on growing out from here till the
whole earth was involved; the immense and murderous machine
… would require more men to work it, more and more blood to
keep it running; it was no longer in control' (*FAP*, 102). Jim's
fearful intuition is paralleled, moreover, by Ashley's response
to war experience, which is more searchingly analytical and
perhaps more alarming in its final shape. Ashley, an intellectual
and an officer, sees in modern war 'the emergence of a new set
of conditions'. Modern war, he concludes, has become 'a branch
of industry', and 'industry from now on, maybe all life, would
be organised like war' (*FAP*, 112). Jim's and Ashley's convictions
about war's expansive, world-reforming thrust challenge nature's
supposed power to accommodate and contain.

   In his assiduous detailing of war experience, Malouf portrays
war as anti-life. War does not appear as a massive manifestation

of life force temporarily turned against itself; war's action is against life and life's action is against war – in both cases, relentlessly. Water, age-old symbol of life energy, is 'the real enemy': 'It rotted and dislodged A-frames, it made the trench a muddy trough. They fought the water that made their feet rot, and the earth that refused to keep its shape or stay still' (*FAP*, 81). Water works to dissolve all structures of the world of war, even that most basic unit of structure, the body of the fighting man. And among the novel's darker ironies is the fact that the warriors are eternally unwashed, evidently having no access to water's redemptive, cleansing power (a power Malouf decisively evokes in later works, *Remembering Babylon* and *The Conversations at Curlow Creek*). Life also opposes war's will to exterminate through the agency of living beings that infiltrate and inhabit the anti-life world of war, exerting their apparently boundless energies against the living warrior. Lice breed teemingly on the filthy soldiers. Rats not only steal 'the very crusts from under your nose', they bring to each war death a nightmarish appearance of fecundity, of irrepressible superabundant life: 'The rats were fat because they fed on corpses, burrowing right into a man's guts or tumbling about in dozens in the bellies of horses' (*FAP*, 81).

War, then, is the anti-world within the assembly of living worlds. In its disintegrating force is its integrated character. Its autonomy does not correspond with the autonomy of other worlds; it is antithetical. It is not the case, however, that war contains no elements shared with other human or natural worlds. As Jim recognises, violence is, always was, a part – a deeply disturbing part – of his back-home worlds. But in his former life, he was able to perceive (albeit naïvely) the violence as 'extraordinary' (*FAP*, 105). War's production of extreme, multiform, ubiquitous and unrelenting violence ultimately makes violence obviously and sickeningly ordinary – the ordering logic of war's overall complex structure.

War's impact upon its human agents is at least predictable, perhaps ineluctable. Jim and Whizzer must discover mutual hatred, although allied – and this hatred must be more meaningful to both than any adversarial feeling about any German soldier. Still more pertinently, an old man engaged in 'winter sowing' (a basic act of coordination between the living human being and the living world) can only be 'crazy' (*FAP*, 106); in relation to war and from the perspective of war, no other conclusion can be drawn. The single most compelling demonstration of war's impact upon its participants is in the conclusion of the friend-ship between Jim and Clancy Parkett. A shell blasts Clancy 'out of existence', blasts him not even into bits but into 'strange slime' (*FAP*, 84). This slime of blood and body grease covers Jim from head to toe, thus providing Jim's war baptism. The themes developed in relation to Jim's friendship with Clancy – contact, intimacy, communion – thus receive the precisely grotesque consecration that the world of war ordains.

It is strange – and for some readers, no doubt, unsatisfying – that Malouf resolves his narrative in relation to a measured optimism. The novel makes its first strong move toward its resolution through the clear recognition and reaffirmation of the world's enduring multiplicity. Ashley, the narrative's learner perhaps even more than Jim, reflects, 'There were so many worlds. They were all continuous with one another and went on simul-taneously.' He understands, moreover, the specifically human form of multiple worlds, appreciates that he constitutes 'his own world' and that all of the men around him represent 'their worlds, each one, about which he could only guess' (*FAP*, 110). Although Ashley's darkest reflections, his previously discussed conception of an emerging total-war world, follow a few paragraphs after his multiple-worlds affirmation, the brighter theme ultimately dominates – but in relation to Jim. Thus, the novel returns to the early symbiosis between these two characters, in which (most typically) Jim enacts Ashley's envisionings.

Jim finally achieves a synoptic view of his war experi-ence, thus reaffirming the capacity to create effective, accurate mental maps that has characterised him throughout the course of narrative development. Crucially, however, the newest and latest mental map is 'immensely expanded': it includes Jim, his fellows, and his adversaries, enacting present-moment battle actions; it also shows, simultaneously, 'the long view of all their lives, including his own', and including the lives of natural living beings – from 'woodlice' to 'wheateaters' – here and elsewhere, past and present (*FAP*, 117). Although Ashley intuitively glimpses, it is for Jim – only Jim – to fully *envision* the multiplicity and interconnectedness of worlds. Jim thus demonstrates what one may call the worlding power of the human imagination, and does so most importantly in relation to the world of war. He marks a human victory over war's disintegrating power, over its paradoxical deployment of disintegration as an integrated system. War, as anti-world and expansive destroyer of other world orders, now finds its place within the temporal and spatial economy of worlds. It is, quite simply, there too, with its own scope and duration. It is not contained and framed by nature, as Neilsen too optimistically puts the case, but included, like nature, in the broader cosmic order of things. One should note, too, that Jim sees from above, from the air, and thus achieves his passage into the place and perspective of the other – in Jim's case, the place and perspective of the bird. Jim thus joins other Malouf characters, such as the earlier Ovid, who arrive at a transcendent and encompassing vision through a devoted, even devout, response to the appeal of the other.

Jim's final 'digging in', once again led by Ashley (or more accurately in this case, by Jim's dying dream-vision of Ashley), complements the achievement of the synoptic view. It is a return from the sky to the earth, to encounter and engagement with the earth. Vision, redirected and reshaped, becomes contact, intouch-ness, at-one-ment. The newly discovered earth is clearly sanctified, smelling 'so good' and so entirely purged of the stench of war-tainted ground. It is the holy bread of communion that is ever in the making, a 'doughy' richness that Jim and his multitude of fellows will 'knead' together. Thus, digging in, a signal, self-orienting act of the modern soldier – and particularly of the Australian soldier or 'digger' – finds ritual and symbolic form as an ontogenetic quest. It is an end of things, a digging of one's own grave, but also a return to 'the beginning of things' (*FAP*, 126). For Jim and his mates, this place of beginning is Australia, the ironically rendered 'other side' of the earth and final goal of the digging quest. And of course, two large-scale worlds, Europe and Australia, have been forging their relationship throughout the novel's duration. Here, at last, in the moment of final digging in, the writing affirms the importance of bringing an Australian perspective to Europe. This too is part of Jim's role, to see things from a European perspective but through Australian eyes: 'Overhead, all upside down as was proper in these parts, were the stars' (*FAP*, 123). In this seeing is yet another of the novel's affirmative returns. A similarly generous appraisal marks Ashley's much earlier evaluation of Australia, when he sees clearly that Australia is not, and never will be, England, but accepts, indeed values, the difference he perceives.

As Neilsen notes, however, Malouf accords considerable, perhaps decisive, importance to the 'theme of individual uniqueness'.[7] By electing Imogen Harcourt as the final bearer of Jim's remembrance, Malouf keeps in play the theme of human community, which places emphasis not so much on the individual's uniqueness but on her or his connectedness and interdependence. Yet Imogen's remembrance focuses on concentrated moments of Jim's 'intense being' (*FAP*, 131), on his birdlike character, 'alert, unique, utterly present'. Indeed, her final sense-making arrives at the conclusion, 'That is what life meant, a unique presence' (*FAP*, 132). The enunciation of Imogen's intractable grief therefore recalls Lear's lament for dead Cordelia, the lament enshrining the notion of the irreplaceable individual, who will never – five times never – come again. This unstinting valorisation of the individual and of individual relationships, so characteristic of Malouf's fiction, credibly emerges from the conditions of Ovid's exile; in *Fly Away Peter*, it is uneasily at odds with the preceding staging of war experience and the logic of war. It must strain, at least to some degree, a reader's sense of the novel's overall coherence.

Although it cannot perhaps make all odds even, Malouf could not do better, for the clear and compelling statement of his case, than the final image of the surfer. 'Hanging delicately balanced … with arms raised' (*FAP*, 132), his pose birdlike, like a bird 'sharply outlined against the sky' (*FAP*, 133), this surfer lightly bears the weight of momentous individual life, and affords individuality its greatest power of affirmation. One may readily concur with Neilsen's sense that, in the surfer image, nature and culture finally discover 'a complementary balance',[8] or with Taylor's closely related idea that the surfer provides the final confirmation of 'a harmony of the human and the natural'.[9] The surfer rides on water as a bird rides air currents, moving along and through them, using a minimum of individual will, concentrating entirely upon the graceful acceptance of being moved – the world being already and always very thoroughly energised. Distinctly post-imperial in perspective – indeed, going against the dominant imperial ethos of wilful intervention in other worlds – Malouf presents the human project, in the final surfer image, as a matter of attuning oneself to pre-established patterns and flows. The image is of self-fulfilling self-relinquishment, of giving oneself to life in the very flux of its unfurling.

Harland's Half Acre

Patrick White's *The Vivisector*, *Harland's Half Acre*'s most important predecessor, may have a more intense and deeper delved understanding of art and the artist. (White's vision is neatly summarised by the cool and studious cruelty of his title.) However, Malouf's novel has much more to say about what it might mean to be an *Australian* artist. It is the first and last of Malouf's novels to pursue its course entirely within Australian contexts – although Europe remains an important point of reference and European experience receives some narration, notably through the character Knack.

The sharpening of focus on Australian concerns does not, however, alter Malouf's imaginative orientation in relation to multiple worlds; indeed, the Australia presented, and Frank Harland's artistic formation within it, strongly suggest that Australia's multiplicity is being affirmed. Early in the 1984 novel, one learns that Frank's nascent vision sees that 'The light was inside things', that each of the worlds within the world contain within them their own particular truth, or light. Landscape, in the same early moment of the narration, takes shape as 'granite outcrops and enormous stone eggs' (*HHA*, 14), thus suggesting that various portions of the land aspire to be worlds unto themselves, each containing within them, like eggs, a full portion of rich potentiality. The use of the egg as little globe or little world occurs a few times in the narrative: Knack's skull, a vessel crammed with a strange wealth of experience, is first called an 'impenetrable hemisphere' and then a 'monstrous egg' (*HHA*, 119); Uncle Ashes (more grandly, Sir Charles) daily confronts 'the world … in the shape of an egg in a china cup' (*HHA*, 198), which he taps, cracks, and spoons into his mouth, with the easy assurance of a powerful man-of-the-world. Ashes is, like Knack, originally an import from continental Europe. Indeed, transported and translated European elements, which have been incorporated into the Australian scene, are prominent in various ways. Killarney (or at least the idea of Killarney, half-remembered and half-imagined) organises the Harlands' sense of family legacy. Knack, an established South Brisbane inhabitant, is as meaningful an element of the Australian scene as any other character, despite his enduringly foreign accent and his burden of European memories.

As the application of the egg-as-little-world image to individual characters already suggests, the novel's representations of multiple worlds have as much to do with human and social worlds as with natural ones. Malouf treats 'families and households as organic or ecological entities'; each household is a 'micro-version' of the larger, ambient world.[10] These families need however to be understood not as collections of sameness but as uneasily assembled sites of incongruity and cross-purposes. The novel's principal characters first encounter the variousness of the world, and the stark differences it contains, in relation to family experience. The family, according to this novel, is 'that close, disorderly unit' characterised by 'conflict' but also by the cohesive forces of 'affection', 'dependence', and shared 'habits' (*HHA*, 97). The disintegrating forces of difference are more prominently evident, however, than those of cohesion, and some problem cases are dramatically and summarily resolved: Gerald refuses the role of heir by committing suicide; Pearsall, after straining against family expectations, disappears without discoverable trace into the lower depths of Australian social life. Malouf's families' incapacity to sustain themselves in relation to conventional alliances and dependencies gives rise, as Neilsen notes, to various 'substitutes', but these are compensatory substitutions and none are 'happy'.[11] Family patterns of relationship never seem adequate to the needs and demands of individual personalities, although almost all characters seemingly would wish to find within the family frame a meaningful foundation for their sense of self. Malouf is evidently using family relations to stage the individual's difficulty in inhabiting social structures (a difficulty that typically preoccupies the author). Interestingly, he understands family, and by extension society, as an assembly of differences. In this view, we are not social fundamentally in relation to similarity; our society is composed of those with whom we are obliged to negotiate differences.

Clem Harland, head of the Harland family, provides the best focal point for the seemingly inevitable difficulty and disruption in the unfolding of family life. As the novel makes its first moves toward its conclusion, Clem reappears triumphantly as a product of 'years of pampering and self-regard', a personality firmly founded on 'a belief in his own centrality' (*HHA*, 167). This is the father who has turned one of his younger sons into his house-keeper/ caretaker (a role from which Tam will never again be able to free himself). His portrayal as a kind of insidious Anchises who rides on, and rides out, the strength of his sons, gains force at the novel's conclusion when a 'magnificent Clem Harland', at his artist-son's retrospective exhibition and funeral gathering, unexpectedly emerges as the star of the show – perversely, a kind of child-star, with his 'baby-like features that life does not touch' (*HHA*, 226). Clem's almost oneiric self-involvement is passively antisocial, a refusal of social role and responsibility that excuses itself by being blithe, unthinking, guileless. But Clem, very clearly, has enjoyed his portion of power, which is socially accorded: he is a father and the head of a family. And he is a key representative of both family and society, and more crucially a key representative of the problems that may inhere in family and in society. Injustice certainly exists in the social world as Malouf represents it, and perhaps it is sustained in large part by those, like Clem, who exploit unjust systems of power and priority with the sole alibi of not being the originators of the order whose benefits they enjoy. Malouf's treatment of families reveals a consistent concern with 'notions of succession',[12] but these patterns of succession – especially masculine succession, from father to son – are notably troubled. This suggests first that the convention of masculine priority may well be at the core of social and familial problems, and also that Australian society, in Malouf's view, is troubled in relation to succession. Established distributions of power and patterns of relation may inhibit the society's progress, its renewal of itself, its capacity to see itself succeeded by a new and perhaps better order.

In *Harland's Half Acre* families are at the centre of the author's social vision, but Malouf is careful to extend out from the centre toward margins, and to show the relations that obtain between more central and more marginal social elements. Households have thresholds and border areas, liminal spaces, that manifest their ambiguous relations with extra-familial space. The main setting being Brisbane, one finds again, as in '12 Edmondstone Street', the 'verandah sleepout, neither inside or out' (*HHA*, 55), which orders Phil's impression of that more outlandish place, Frank's improvised studio in the ruined frame of Pier Pictures cinema. And it is in relation to these two similarly liminal spaces that Phil first wonders where, in what place, 'we and the multiplicity of things are in touch' (*HHA*, 55). First spied through a hole in a front verandah's floor, the liminal space under-the-house is represented in more detail, and more troublingly. For Phil, this space remains a bit 'uncanny' (*HHA*, 144) – one thinks immediately of Freud's *unheimlich*, or 'unhomelike' – but its longstanding presence leads him to the more comfortable notion that it is 'darkness domesticated', a matter of 'local reality' if also part of 'the underside of things'.

However, for Gerald, who is not a native Queenslander, the place is 'full of threat' (*HHA*, 145). Under-the-house is the preferred space for anti-familial acts. Gerald chooses the under-the-house space for his suicide, and he is discovered by Tam, who goes there to pursue his characteristic anti-familial gesture, sulking.

The extra-familial world's disruptive force is in liminal spaces and also in certain characters who are 'not family'. Knack, for whom one of the novel's central chapters is named, is undoubtedly the most important of the characters who are not – as most are – part of the complex web of family affiliations. He climbs, as if grotesquely resurrected, out of a Holocaust body-disposal ditch, and proceeds from that horrific European point-of-origin toward his Australian life. As in the texts of *Johnno*, *Child's Play*, and *Fly Away Peter*, *Harland's Half Acre* powerfully associates modern Europe with terror and violence. In accounting for the place and role of Europe in Malouf's Australian *Kunstlerroman*, critics have quite consistently emphasised Knack's final acts of murder and suicide and the blood-spattered Harland painting these acts produce. Ross first affirms that, from Knack, Harland learns 'that to be Australian is to be an innocent, to be divested of history'. Yet, he goes on to say that the blood on the painting may 'symbolize the unyielding demands placed on the artist' or again 'the unlimited possibilities of art'.[13] Ross's final understanding seems too exclusively aesthetic, especially when considered in the light of criticism that gives more emphasis to Knack's association with the grim trials of modern European experience. For Leer, the blood marking of the Australian artist's painting announces that 'The sufferings of European history have come within the ambit of Australian experience'.[14] Neilsen, who finds that the novel tends generally to link the ordeals of 'violence' with 'greater awareness', argues that after Knack's suicide – and only then – Frank finds in Australia 'the savagery and passion he had previously associated with Europe'.[15]

Knack's role in the novel is best captured by Edna, his Australian 'missus or whatever she was' (*HHA*, 125), and his eventual death-pact partner. '[W]ithout Knack', Edna affirms,

I'd never have known even the half of what I am, I'd have
missed myself – walked right past myself in the dark. It
was like being turned round and seeing yourself for the
first time, what he could show me. Like there were things
in me – not all good things even – I mean not *nice* but me;
and the same things in him as well, and when we came
together they could flow out of me … People think I'm
sunny. I'm not. Not always. Not deep down. There's a lot
of darkness in us. (*HHA*, 121)

Knack's value begins with his difference, a darkly marked
European difference, but one that is elucidating, especially for
a notably home-grown Australian like Edna. The notion, to be
found elsewhere in Malouf, is that one can only really see oneself
from an exterior, other perspective. More interesting however
is Edna's sense that one can arrive, through the perspective of
difference, at a sense of correspondence, a sense that one has in
oneself versions – not identical but corresponding – of the other's
traits. In this recognition, according to Edna, one can discover a
release from self-entombment, from a deadening containment in
buried aspects of the self. Yet the most interesting development
in Edna's confession is her final arrival at the first person plural,
her speech about the dark that is in 'us'. This 'us' could be read
merely as the coupling of Knack with Edna's 'I', but that would
make her final statement on darkness rather redundant: she has
already stated that she and Knack share the not-all-good, not-
nice things. The final 'us' more likely aims to extend to fellow
Australians (such as Phil, to whom she is confiding), or even to
fellow human beings, of whom Edna believes she has learned
something fundamental.

But the enlivening, self-revelatory aspect of the other's
intimate proximity has its dangers as well as its satisfactions,
contains a death as well as a life. The relationship Edna wishes
to characterise so favourably ends in the violent effacement
of both partners. One may say, however, that the final truth
of the relationship passes to Frank, through the blood-marked
painting, as a kind of legacy. His initial reaction – 'Such reds!
What painter would have dared?' (*HHA*, 126) – may seem, on

first consideration, rather too narrowly aesthetic. But one must recognise that Frank is discovering in life levels of intensity and passion that art cannot perhaps approach. In other words, one may conclude that that blood-marking of his painting protects Frank from becoming airily aesthetic, from placing his art apart from and above life. But more crucial is what Frank eventually does with the Knack/Edna legacy in his art. There is 'Untitled 14', the harrowing painting in red, which is both a 'tribute' and a 'sharing' of Knack and Edna's 'fate' (HHA, 224). A later painting of Edna reasserts Frank's 'power to affirm'.[16] Colour relations here are reversed: a red ground is feathered over with blue, instead of blue ground being feathered over with red blood splatter. Thus, the awareness of blue – firmamental and richly fluid, the blue of sea or sky so crucial to landscape – takes shape, not in naïve innocence but in relation to stark, concrete knowledge of the suffering and violence in the human world. Knack's legacy is violating, yet ultimately productive, and in this it contrasts with the subtly oppressive experience of familial bonds, by which one tends to be pent in rather than opened up to the world.

Knack, during his Australian life, is noteworthily an antique-dealer, a minor merchant of the 'fragments of broken house-holds', proprietor of a dust and shadow realm where 'elements of several rooms, from different periods and levels of society, had been thrown together'. The curio-world of his shop presents 'a parody of settled existence', disturbingly affirms 'some final break in the logic of things' (HHA, 105). Knack, then, is not simply marginal to familial centrality; he is contrapuntal, a kind of antithesis to which the thesis of family-and-household gives rise. Frank Harland first discovers Knack, already in company with Edna, in a wine shop 'squashed in among the half-caste women and long-faced drunks' (HHA, 104–5). He lives and does business in South Brisbane, a darkly encoded city zone. As one learns in '12 Edmondstone Street', South Brisbane was declared 'black' during wartime – for reasons of security. Thus, Knack's deployment in the novel, which does much to elaborate Austra-lia's relationship with its European legacies, also links signifi-cantly with larger questions of marginality, ethnicity and race.

Gelder and Salzman complain that in *Harland's Half Acre* Aborigines are 'barely noticeable'. As in their criticism of other Malouf works, they denounce a confusion of history with myth, finding that the writing is 'keen to mythologize' and thus implicitly to celebrate 'the fact of white possession'.[17] Certainly, among the novel's characters' most pressing concerns is that of taking possession or laying claim to some portion of the world, to some place within the world. But to code this drive to possess as 'white' is questionable. Early in the novel, Aborigines are acknowledged as the 'first creators'. Young Frank and his brothers undertake fingertip 'retracing' of the lines of their images, or impromptu, childish excavations that seek to restore the Aboriginal carvings to their original clarity. Even these early scenes from childhood begin to communicate the sense that the Australian artist must strive to find a way into preceding lives, preceding imaginings – that is, necessarily, into Aboriginal lives and images. The Aboriginal images are the first things in Frank's world that do the job of art; they create, by the force of their own being, 'a meeting-place for separate lines of existence' (*HHA*, 23). Taking possession then is most pertinently a repossession, a second possession, an act of retrieval that lays claim to a world that has previously belonged to others. Frank and his brothers, following Pearsall's lead, learn to see that Aboriginal 'spirits of the place' may be, through their deep union with the land, 'more enduring in time' than any of their white ancestors, the later-arriving Irish immigrants. Frank's early images therefore serve both as 'reminder and inventory'; their production is also 'a first act of repossession' (*HHA*, 31). He wishes to repossess for his living family what his ancestral family has lost, but his project crucially includes the recognition of the still earlier possession of the land by those whose abiding presence is documented in artful and enduring inscriptions upon the land.

Aborigines and Aboriginality are not among the novel's most salient concerns, but they may represent the novel's most important hinge-topics, the topics upon which other more substantial treatments turn. And *Harland's Half Acre* gives more attention to Aboriginality than any of the other novel-length works before *Remembering Babylon*. Gelder's and Salzman's objection may originate therefore in the character of Malouf's representation. Following the novel's early, favourable acknowledgement of Aboriginal art and its place-claiming, place-defining function, Aboriginality is disturbingly associated with the abject, and begins to function as the organising core of Malouf's more broad-based portrayal of abjection.

The Aborigine first takes shape as modern Australia's abjected element (that is, the element rendered abject by social and historical forces) during Frank's Depression-era wanderings, in the episode that concludes the novel's first section, 'Killarney'. Frank seeks shelter in the grimmest of all sites symbolising modernity's failures, an auto junkyard, or in Malouf's words, a 'graveyard of journeys'. Frank's first choice is 'limousine' accommodation – the irony is rather corrosive – but he is repelled by the 'blood curdling cry' of 'a black devil, all blue-black hair and breathing fire'. Frank immediately concedes the 'prior right' and 'fierce dark possession' the shadowy tenant asserts, then shortly after sees – or dreams he sees – that all the cars contain 'watchers', whom he perceives as 'stately figures, also black' (*HHA*, 47). Frank somewhat deliriously but aptly concludes: 'The place was haunted by spirits older than the ghosts of cars and their owners. He had disturbed a rite, or interrupted an assembly of the dispossessed' (*HHA*, 47–8).

At the conclusion of the junkyard episode, the wanderer faints dead away, thus making the land itself his bed, and awakens rejuvenated, purged of illness, but puzzling over 'what pact he had made with his native earth' (*HHA*, 48). The use of 'native' at this precise moment of the narrative clearly confirms the understanding previously suggested in the narration of Frank's childhood experience: Frank Harland's native land (the land of his birth) is also, inescapably, native earth – that is, Aboriginal land. Just a few pages before the junkyard episode, Frank half-discovers, half-forges his sense of belonging within the human world, but it is 'with those who were outside' that he identifies and seeks his place (*HHA*, 43). He aspires, one may say, to a kind of togetherness in difference, but understands that his chosen path of identification must place him outside the social body as it is conventionally understood.

Aboriginality's abjection is not extremely obvious in the junkyard episode – the black watchers, for instance, are 'stately' – but a few key points are well made. Clearly, the Aborigine of modern Australia inhabits the abandoned sites of white society and white identity – these ruined cars that were once among the key loci of identity, so crucial to their owners' sense of self. Thus, the places of Aboriginal being are precisely those that are no longer a part of the society as it presently defines itself, and indeed the abandoned places are non-places, sites where disavowal ('this wretched *thing* was never mine') must struggle with uneasy, unwilling movements of memory and recognition. It is not yet entirely clear that the abjection of the Aboriginal spirits entails acts of ejection, of casting out, and that this casting out is a matter of systemic social violence – although the passage does finally name the spirits as 'the dispossessed'.

A little later in his story, Malouf begins to clarify the violent and systemic aspects of abjection, presenting a 'young half-caste' boxer, the pride of an 'abject' white father in 'dirty singlet'. This young man finds in boxing the only way 'of saving himself for a time from the inevitable round of drink, then jail, then more drink; of keeping off … the shadow and the sour stink, and angry sick despair, of fellows three or four years older than himself' (*HHA*, 53). The cruellest element in this characterisation is of course the phrase 'for a time'. The young man can only really defer his descent into the abject zones of Australian society; his 'half-caste' status implicitly assures him, and others, of his eventual defeat. Even the young man's training space, an under-the-house space with the aspect of a grimy cage, forecasts a dismal future against which his vivid struggle will prove vain. Interestingly, his refusal – even if it is only temporary – to disappear into the outlands of abjection seems to mark him as a nemesis figure. Reflecting upon the father's boast that the youth is 'a killer', the narrator, Phil, confides: 'I thought it was his father – that nearest of all white men – he might decide to kill' (*HHA*, 53). Metonymically, this fated youth will return to the story, in its later developments, recalling the inescapable doom and also this doom's potential disruption of established social order. The metonymic return takes place in a miserable jail cell containing 'derelicts, *drunks* and *half-caste youths* in *boxer*-shorts and torn and *bloodied singlets*' (*HHA*, 193, emphasis added). The blood-marked singlet may be the most significant element here, as it represents the violently transmuted legacy of the white father, who had earlier been imaged in a dirty singlet. The young half-caste boxer also returns, more directly, as the subject of a Frank Harland series, thus confirming Frank's committed affiliation with the abject shadow elements of Australian society.

Degradation through violence will come to the young boxer through the white father, but the white progenitor does not thus elude the violence of which he too is potentially the object. Following upon the young boxer's metonymic return, during a jailhouse riot, a man is injured: 'He was howling and holding his hands over his face; they were covered with blood.' This recalls the very similar scene in *Fly Away Peter*, in which Jim briefly sees an Aboriginal man holding bloodied hands to his injured face. However, in this case, the sufferer is 'a young policeman' (*HHA*, 214), which suggests that Malouf aims to show that white authority ultimately must suffer the violence and abjection imposed upon the society's outcast elements.

Julia Kristeva has argued that the abjection, the making abject, of certain constituents of the individual's body and of the social body is foundational to the formation of the human subject and society. The 'I' constitutes and recognises itself, and the social world constitutes and configures itself, only by ejecting and alienating elements that originate within, and are thus parts and products of the self, or of the society. Excrement, for the individual subject, is the most obvious case of a self-constituting abjected element: although my excrement originates in me, is my product, it is something with which I disidentify; it is the not-me/not-mine that allows me to define and assert, in a primary way, what I am (or more accurately, what I wish to understand myself as being). Corpses, such as Malouf's car-corpses, also provide key examples of the abject, which is typically something disinvested, something life has abandoned. As Kristeva puts the case, the repudiated yet self-constituting abject is the crucial instance of originating shadow or ambiguity; it is a haunting presence, the benighted form of 'something rejected from which one does not part'.[18] Abjection, however, is social in origin and destination: it arises in response to social demand (to be complete and clean), and it borders and defines the path by which one becomes social.

Malouf's representation of abjection is quite in keeping with Kristeva's theoretical account, particularly in the amorphousness he ascribes to abject elements. It appears that the abject cannot be named or specified, only vaguely indicated; it does not find clear definition in perception or in language – that fundamental socialising medium. The abject is (necessarily) unrecognisable or less than entirely recognisable. As Kristeva stresses, the abject's most characterising feature is 'ambiguity'.[19] Thus, in the pursuit of Pearsall, the fallen brother of the Harland family, one encounters the inhabitants of Australian society's lower depths as 'foul-mouthed, foul-smelling bundles' whose distance from more fortunate members of their society is like a 'gap between species' (HHA, 192); or again, one confronts 'a figure, all teeth and hair' arising suddenly out of 'a mound of rags' (HHA, 213) – this last figure recalling the 'black devil, all blue-black hair' of Frank's junkyard experience.

Abjection's most intense and disturbing portrayal occurs upon the discovery of the Brisbane slave camp. Phil, the narrator/witness, provides a carefully detailed account of the social insider's response to the spectacle of the abject. From a holding cell, where some of the (ostensibly) rescued slaves have been collected together, comes an 'eerie howling' (HHA, 213). Phil compares the cell to 'a whole kennel of dogs' and anxiously avers that he sees 'nothing human in it' (HHA, 214). Shortly after, the word 'abjectness' enters Malouf's text, and Phil reveals, through his own reactions, the common psychic and social dynamics pertaining to encounter with the abject. Phil does not feel 'compassion' but rather 'shame, panic, a sense of deep unclean-ness'. He adds, very tellingly, 'What I wanted to re-establish was my own cleanliness, and I felt ashamed of that too' (*HHA*, 215). The problem, for Phil and for other observers situated within the society's clean, orderly, acknowledged ranks, is that 'all the men were alike in their filth'; they show themselves to socialised eyes only as 'ragged, indistinguishable bodies' (*HHA*, 215). The men of the slave camp cannot really be accepted back into, reintegrated with, the social body, because humanity and meaningful individuality can be understood only in relation to these men's exclusion. To take back these abject elements could only be to confirm oneself and one's society as abject, a possibility Malouf briefly portrays: succumbing to a 'contagious and terrible' force, the crowd of observers momentarily takes up the 'howling' of the abject men (*HHA*, 214).

Abjection has to do with the borders of the social world, with where and how they are drawn, and also with their disturbing tenuousness. The border of the abject, initially drawn in relation to Aboriginality, reveals itself as smudged and unclear with the slave camp discovery: none of the slaves is represented in relation to race or ethnicity; all are simply bodies, or at best, and just barely, men. In the depths of abjection, race and ethnicity are ultimately non-signifying. Abjection can be, and often is, the white man's lot, and it can refer to Europe as well as to Aboriginal Australia. The novel records that Australians, learning of the slave camp's existence, are shocked by the appearance of 'a monstrosity' in a 'quiet suburb where everybody minded his business'. 'Backyards', one learns, 'ran down into the gully where these men had been chained and beaten. No one had heard or seen anything. Nothing had been reported' (*HHA*, 212). This passage's formulation clearly alludes to Holocaust situations: the monstrous camp's proximity to everyday, orderly society combines uncannily with the society's strange incapacity to see and acknowledge what is happening. Thus, something like Knack's experience of the European Holocaust is not only possible in Australia, it is actual. What is not clear is whether this inscription of horrific modern situations in the Australian social scene manifests a change in Australia or a change in the ways in which Australia is perceived and understood. Kerr suggests that Malouf's fictions, and *Harland's Half Acre* most specifically, represent a 'forced coming into consciousness of the Australian people'.[20] This emphasis on consciousness rather than actuality is probably well judged. In his Great War novel, *Fly Away Peter*, Malouf had some use for Australian innocence; in *Harland's Half Acre*, Australia is made to know itself and its own diversity, which includes some home-made horrors. As Phil realises, in confrontation with the slave camp's discovery, 'We were all involved, there was no escape from it' (*HHA*, 212).

It is very interesting therefore to recognise that Frank Harland, ultimately the great Australian artist of the novel's resolution, is to be listed among the novel's abject elements. Commenting on Frank's late-career lionisation, Phil remarks that the art works 'could be seen now to proclaim a people's newly-discovered identity in a place it scarcely knew existed, and whose actual presence, like the old coot who had created it, might in the natural state have evoked a fastidious pooh!' (*HHA*, 189). Similarly, Phil's disappointment with the too-neat organisation of Frank's retrospective exhibition leads to this conclusion: 'Mess, that was what was missing, and it was essential' (*HHA*, 224). Frank makes an early pact with the images of the Aborigine, the touchstone instance of abjection, and subsequently confirms this bonding in the auto junkyard. The details of his working body, his materials and his use of them, all speak of that deep and troubling ambiguity associated with the abject; Phil's sense of essential mess includes 'a clawlike hand ... with frayed and grubby cuffs', working amid 'untidy scrub' and with materials 'sopped up out of tins' and 'smeared on' or 'allowed to drip and puddle' (*HHA*, 224). Frank, the great Australian artist, is abjection misrecognised, but misrecognised because redeemed. His creative working of his material shows that this material (of which he himself is a part) is not, was never, alien, though it had been alienated.

Frank creates not a collection of works but a place, 'Harland's half acre', and this place, like the man, is abjected – 'pooh!' – evoking for members of polite society (if they could see it for what it is, which they cannot). Frank's place, however, is

Australia condensed, concentrated, and thus it is the Australian land itself (with which the Aborigine is so closely associated) that a dominant strain of the national imagination has submitted to abjection. Landscape in *Harland's Half Acre* is most typically 'open and discontinuous', revealing 'gaps, ruptures, and alternative histories'.[21] This is the landscape, so resistant to monological national imagining, to which Frank's art gives voice, or rather voices. His work does not deny the gaps and ruptures, nor does it seek to fill them in; it cultivates them.

Neilsen argues that Frank 'draws closer to the Natural by means of a cultural practice',[22] an assessment that is largely true but in some need of qualification. As Frank's career develops, one gets a sense that he tends to experience the human elements in his world as impedimenta he must work through to achieve his most meaningful perceptual and creative relationship with the land. And indeed, Frank's troubled relationship with his family, his primary connection to the social world, manifests itself early on. The artist's earliest sense of his personal mission concerns 'the question of how he came to be Frank Harland and how he had got into the world – at what point in time and place and through what bright hole in reality' (*HHA*, 22). This notion of entering the world through a 'bright hole' denies, or at least eludes, the common reality of emerging out of a mother's womb and into the core of a family. One also senses that Frank's slightly later, but still youthful, conclusion about his life's unfolding – that 'his life was meant to go cross-wise and be led in defiance of his nature rather than in the easy expression of it' (*HHA*, 44) – arises more out of his problem with fitting in with his familial world than out of any native difficulties in his personality. Having entered his personal and artistic maturity, Frank produces a Cubistic work in which the figure presents itself 'simultaneously in many planes'; 'it was a self-portrait, the face all fragments. A force from "out there" that was irresistible but might not, in the end, be destructive, had struck it to splinters' (*HHA*, 149). This work is one of several life-studies of human figures, and it comes after the harsh lesson of Knack's and Edna's violent deaths, so one may conclude that the 'out there' exerting the splintering force is the human and social world. Thus, the fracturing or fragmenting of the human personality is a social effect – not a natural inadequacy of human structure, nor a liability entailed by the mind's confrontation with the natural world. It is rather that one resolves, to the degree that this is possible, the fragmentation of self and the self's perspectives through creative interaction with space, with the more benign 'out there' of nature and landscape (a distinctly Romantic understanding, one should note). Frank Harland (like his author) harbours a deep belief that nature coheres, though the human being and the primary human experience of nature do not. Frank's late career is tellingly marked by the dream-vision of a quilt, a life-affirming quilt 'green beyond green, an island continent in the dark of his sleep', but composed 'of fragments gathered and laid side by side' (HHA, 178). Fragmentedness is the primitive shape of experience that creative imagination must remake as multifacetedness. Self, and the space the self apprehends, are fragmented by a multiplicity of perspectives, but can yet be ordered, and rendered beautiful by that ordering.

Ultimately, Frank Harland, as artist, fully adopts the role of medium – not so much a creator any more, but the means of the world's expression. In the final productive phase of his career, on his island, each new painting comes into being as 'a newly emergent form out of the island itself'. Frank now produces an art in which 'each made object had to be judged first against the natural objects it rose from and among which he now set it down' (HHA, 187). The novel's arrival at this particular *telos* of artistic becoming strongly suggests that Frank has been following (though perhaps only semiconsciously) the orientation of Aboriginal creations he had discovered in his nonage. In his maturity, he does not seek to impose or inscribe himself on the face of the world but rather (like the Aboriginal traces and images that marked his childhood home) to find himself a part of the world's manifestation of itself, to find himself as one of many voicings of the Australian land.

The Great World

Although it carries on with the multiple-worlds orientation, *The Great World* is more thoroughly a novel of transactions. In *Harland's Half Acre* the lines of impact and influence are at times unidirectional: one learns in appreciable detail the effect Knack has on Edna or Frank, but the narration remains silent about how either of these characters impacts upon Knack. The 1990 novel is more scrupulous in demonstrating that change, in the human world, is nearly always a matter of *ex*change. Australian identity, both individual and national, is shown to emerge through continuous negotiation between connectedness and separation (or loss). Australia, as modern nation and potential homeland, comes into being through transactional movements – between past and present, between Australia and Asia, Australia and America, between public and private life, between individuals and their communities. Most particularly, the novel aims to show how contemporary Australia has been formed by participation in the Second World War. Much of the novel narrates the post-war decades, right up to the mid-1980s – that is, up to a time that precedes only by a few years the novel's publication year. The war experience, however, remains the organising referent throughout, particularly with respect to the development of characters, their sense of themselves, their relationships and interactions, their sense of community and their participation in that broader sphere of experience that one may call national consciousness. At the core of Malouf's meditation on the meaning of the war experience is the conviction that contemporary Australia takes shape in response to trauma. Working from Lacanian psychoanalytic theory, one may say that trauma, the trauma of war, constitutes Australian identity – what it means to be Australian – but *only* retrospectively; this peculiarly modern identity is an imaginary coherence that is constituted, that comes into being, through the experience of its disruption and loss.[1]

The Australian war experience begins as a frenzy of transportation and exchange. It is 'the movement, from one continent to another, of a million articles of no great worth or use' – but a million articles that rapidly discover their status as invested objects, as the previously unrecognised underpinnings of identity. Malouf reflects, 'Transactions. Deals. They took up so much energy, engendered so much feeling, you might have thought they were the one true essential of a fighting man's life, of tenacious, disorderly *civilian* life inside the official military one' (*GW*, 43). Once transported to Southeast Asia, the Australian soldiers become a 'cargo cult'; these men carry upon their bodies, and also inevitably, inside their heads and hearts, 'relics, the accumulated paraphernalia … of a world that had exploded in fragments around them, and would have now, in the spirit of improvisation, to be reconstructed elsewhere … But they were experts at that. They were Australians' (*GW*, 44). Australianness is here understood as an expertise in improvisational self-fashioning, as a capacity to reconstruct a new world 'elsewhere'. And this is a forging of community that recapitulates, albeit in idealised form, the work of nineteenth-century European colonists in Australia. Yet, as we must note, the idea of Australianness asserts itself only in response to 'a world' – the world of Australian civil life – which has been 'exploded in fragments'. Moreover, the accumulation and circulation of objects and signs, of objects as signs, falls rapidly into dispersal, a scattering – what Malouf calls a 'a general stripping' (*GW*, 45). Following the surrender of the Australian forces to the Japanese, the harem-scarum *bricolage* of Australian self-fashioning is cast upon foreign roadsides – 'spare sweaters and socks, cheap watches …, propelling pencils, fly-swats, bronze Buddhas, bolts of shantung and Thai silk, inkwells, packs of cards, flasks of Johnny Walker Red Label whiskey' – all this and much more is lost almost as soon as acquired (*GW*, 44).

But this loss of the 'miscellaneous oddments, the detachable parts and symbols of civilised life', this loss of the objects the men had used 'to reassure themselves of where they had come from and what they were' (*GW*, 44), is not of course the final reduction of individual and group identity. The Australian prisoners of war endure a protracted experience of deprivation, and its attendant humiliations, which culminates in the loss of bodies – the loss of fellow bodies, to execution, starvation, or disease, and the loss of one's own body. Imaging the dissolution of identity in relation to the POWs' most ineluctable plagues, diarrhoea, and dysentery, Malouf writes, 'Their insides went liquid. Everything they ate turned to slime' (*GW*, 111). This internal dissolution, at once physical and psychological, is accompanied by equally disastrous, defamiliarising effects on the body's visible form and structure: 'fellows turn inside out'; 'the skin of a man's face grow[s] thick as elephant hide'; 'thin boys' swell monstrously, with testicles like 'footballs', penises 'eight inches round', 'ankles thick as tree trunks', and 'feet like balloons'. Summing up the case, Malouf writes, 'Their bodies had gone berserk and were dragging them back to a time before they had organised themselves in human form and come in from chaos' (*GW*, 142). Thus, it is through the rediscovery of the body as volatile, as horrifyingly fugitive and changeful, that the Australian POWs arrive at the degree zero of individual and group identity. With the loss of a secure grasp of the body one loses, necessarily, the locus of personal identity and the indispensable anchor for social participation.

Malouf's post-war Australia is indelibly marked by the war experience. It is impossible for the war generation to return to the imaginary nation, the nation constituted retrospectively, by the rupture and rapture of trauma. This national 'home' is the place one recognises only after being torn away from it. But just as importantly, post-war Australia is no longer (if it ever was) an autonomous modern nation. It is, as the demobilised soldiers soon discover, a transnational entity, a place of transnational transactions. One of the war's primary effects on the homeland, it seems, is to open it fully to the world, to the world's multifarious and decentring influences. Both the world of war and the post-war home have a peculiarly postmodern allure. In Southeast Asia, the first camp of the Australian prisoners of war is established 'in the abandoned booths and tea-gardens of the Great World, an amusement park where' – in the days before the surrender – the Australian soldiers 'had gone to drink Chinese beer, dance with taxi-dancers and have their pictures taken' (GW, 118). Upon return to post-war Australia, the former soldiers strike upon 'the Cross', Sydney's famously infamous haven of decadence and bohemianism. Here Malouf evokes 'a crowded place with the atmosphere of a playground' (GW, 175), a place where all nations and classes encounter each other daily and nightly, buying and selling everything imaginable, and, more often than not, tumbling precipitously into the violence of the zone's innumerable 'savage episodes' (GW, 176). The Cross in Sydney, by the play of resemblance, recreates the wartime Asian amusement park, the Great World, as a compelling rather than merely derisory analogy for the late-twentieth-century world, transnational in culture and economy, heteroclytic yet syncretic, mixed, migratory, multidimensional. Thus, the coherent imaginary nation of Australia is doubly lost – lost in the trauma of its inception and lost again in the nation-dissolving effects of cultural and economic globalisation.[2]

To the question Malouf's novel now poses – how does one live in the new world of post-war Australia? – there are two principal responses, which are embodied, almost typologically, in the book's two principal characters, Digger and Vic. Digger remembers and contemplates; Vic forgets and acts.[3] Of these two figures, it is clearly Vic who represents the predominant spirit of the post-war decades. A man whose public persona is 'all energy and unbounded confidence', Vic represents the late-twentieth-century tycoon, who understands wealth as hyperextension rather than accumulation. 'A millionaire isn't a man who's *got* a million', he declares. 'He's a man who *owes* a million, and if he owes ten million, all the better' (GW, 256).

Vic's financial empire, moreover, is thoroughly transnational, a delicately balanced web of speculative investments, agreements, and alliances extending to America, Europe, East Asia, and the Pacific Rim. Vic's death, in the novel's final pages, coincides exactly with the world-wide financial crash of the mid-1980s, thus confirming him as the representative of the Australian urge to look beyond the nation, to look away from history, the past, and toward seemingly unbounded future potentialities. Of course, Vic's death also signals the failure of his version of post-war Australian self-fashioning. Digger, Vic's counterpoise within the novel, recognises at last the limitation of Vic's wilful, instrumental disposition: having chosen against memory, against history, 'Vic did not entirely *believe* in the world. His capacity to deal with it had to do with his conviction that it was there only insofar as he could act on it' (*GW*, 297).[4]

Digger, *The Great World*'s rememberer, first takes on his role in wartime, when he becomes the keeper of the list and maintains in his memory, ever unwritten, the few hundred names of his fellow Australian POWs, in scrupulous alphabetical order and attended by abundant details of each individual's biography, before, during, and after wartime. (One has here a mnemonic version of the synoptic view Jim Saddler achieves toward the end of *Fly Away Peter*.) In post-war Australia, Digger becomes the living memory of the war and its legacies, a flesh-and-blood archive. Possessed of a vivid, detailed sense of history, he embodies what the enterprising Vic cannot afford and yet cannot quite live without. Even as Vic extends and expends, Digger accumulates and retains. His ethic of memory, which has the commanding simplicity of prayer, is a communion with all that has been in time: 'He wanted nothing to be forgotten and cast into the flames. Not a soul. Not a pin' (*GW*, 179). This idea of an ethic of memory, of memory as ethical and ultimately communal, marks a crucial development in Malouf's novelistic career. The valorisation of the role of memory in projects of self-fashioning, for individuals and for collectivities, is clearly inaugurated in *The Great World*, though more fully developed in its successor, 1993's *Remembering Babylon*. It also anticipates its successor by linking questions of memory to the genealogy of the nation.

In so far as history may be conceived as the social, and socially authorised, form of memory (a conception that is clearly central to Malouf's thinking), one may ask by what paths does memory become history, and also what kind of history it becomes. Nettelbeck credits Malouf with elaborating a responsible discourse of history, one that 'acknowleges its own intention and process of construction'. For her, the novel succeeds, at least partially, in negotiating the troubled ground of national history. Yet Nettelbeck also stresses that to assert one version of national history is to leave aside, to exclude, other, competing narratives of the nation. She argues that Malouf chooses a plural presentation of 'multiple and flexible "threads"' – threads of memory – and thus demonstrates his concern with avoiding any singular, authoritative narrative of history.[5]

Yet there remains the question of just what kind of history – what historical stuff or substance – Malouf's novel strives to render. Neilsen suggests that Malouf's main focus is upon 'history that does not pretend to be empirically verifiable'.[6] Elaborating itself in large part by collecting together the human events that remain below the threshold awareness of historiographers, the novel affirms, according to Buckridge, 'the ineffable value of "ordinariness" in all its forms';[7] for Rodgers, it aims to capture capture that 'unrecorded life' which is a great part of the 'fabric' of our lives.[8] Knox-Shaw pushes further with this line of thinking, arguing that the novel aims to undermine the grand designs of national myths (which impress themselves so strongly on the historical sense) by portraying 'the plain grind of everyday living' and producing a world of 'irreducible quiddity'.[9] Andrew Taylor, however, has expressed serious reservations about the value Malouf's distinctly different historiography, which may be 'the denial of History in the name of the Unhistorical',[10] which may be an 'other' history that is also 'the other of history'.[11] One may add that *The Great World*, perhaps problematically, does not include substantial renderings of what one might call others' histories. The novel's fictional world is saliently masculine in composition, as Malouf's imagined worlds quite typically are. Despite their noteworthy differences, Vic and Digger (and also Digger's father) manifest, as Indyk remarks, 'an essentially masculine desire to reach out to encompass the world as a whole'.[12] Neilsen goes further in his consideration of gender, recognising that the novel's men are mobile, its women for the most part 'confined', but adding that Malouf shows that this confinement is culturally enforced.[13] Considering gender representation from this perspective, one may say that Malouf represents a masculine bias in modern Australian culture, but does not advocate this bias and maintains, moreover, a critical perspective upon it.

If *The Great World* is open to questioning with respect to gender representation, it is still more so in relation to cultural and racial difference. The novel is for the most part a meditation upon the formation, in recent history, of post-European Australia, the nation that comes after Europe, turns away from and yet derives from Europe. This post-European, predominently Anglo-Celtic Australia is represented by Keens, Currans, and Warrenders, and by the numerous exclusively Anglo-Celtic names making up Digger's list. This version of Australia only really discovers itself, it is true, through dislocation and estrangement in southeast Asia, but the difference represented by Aboriginal Australia is not a very prominent concern.

As in *Fly Away Peter*, however, the place of the Aboriginal, if not prominent, is nonetheless significant. It serves to circumscribe the novel's overall project, and to cast it, fairly much from the outset, in an autocritical light. Digger, uniquely the great rememberer, also sets himself apart by being the only character in the 1990 novel to form close, personally transformative relations with black Australia, during eighteen months of his early manhood, when he lives and works with a travelling carnival troupe that includes several Aboriginal members. 'Living with the blacks', one learns, 'had made him see things in another way: from the side and a bit skew, but with a humorous scepticism, as they did. He wasn't one of them, he knew that; but after a time they were as open with him as if he was' (*GW*, 57).[14] Two concerns, liminally evident here, are pursued in detail and in depth in *Remembering Babylon*: what is, what has been, the role of Aboriginal peoples in the formation of the modern Australian nation; also, what is, what has been, the impact of black Australia upon white (or post-European) Australia?

Digger, like the earlier Jim Saddler, confronts Aboriginality, and its potentially troubling presence in Australian society, in the period of his life that immediately precedes his going off to war. The significance of this confrontation enters very thoroughly into Digger's consciousness of himself and of his world, and in this he differs from Jim. For Digger, the structuring of white violence in relation to the Aboriginal presence is a clear and recognisable fact of Australian life; indeed, this structuring gives definition to the representational game in which he knowingly participates. The carnival troupe's main attraction is the opportunity it provides to fight with black boxers, to pit oneself 'against forces that had to be pushed back now and then, flattened and shown their place'. A plain 'hatred of flash niggers' motivates the challenger, along with the socially oriented 'wish to impress the girl he was with or his mates'. But of course the challenger is a dupe, a 'mug', who does not recognise that the fighting is spectacle not contest, that it is a 'put-up job' (*GW*, 55). It is a carefully ordered staging of real social conflict, which mobilises, for the troupe's profit, real hatred, real fear, and fascination. Digger, though he begins as just another cocky white 'mug' who goes up and gets decked, subsequently joins the troupe as a co-conspirator. Unlike Jim, he comes to see clearly that white Australian masculinity is deeply invested in an arrogant yet anxious, adversarial attitude to the Aborigine – or rather to *the figure* of the Aborigine, to the Aborigine as psychosocial construct.[15]

Yet Digger fails to generalise from his knowledge, or fails to generalise effectively enough. Recognising the provisional nature of his acceptance by his Aboriginal cohorts, and also his failure really to understand them in depth, he opts for a return to white masculine fellowship and makes enlistment the consolidating gesture of his renewed commitment. He knows his Aboriginal mates will see war recruitment as a white Australian put-up job. He sheepishly confesses to being a 'mug', but does not rethink his decision even when faced with carnival-boxer Slinger's terse, ineluctable comment: 'An' I thought we'd learned you something' (*GW*, 59). Unlike Jim, Digger can see the violent game that structures Australian interracial relations, but despite his greater clarity he cannot extricate himself from the game. The best he manages is to play the game, for a time, on the other side, before becoming a fighting man in more conventional and more dangerous terms. But Digger's experience still serves to register the Australian Aboriginal presence in Malouf's 'other' history of World War II. This war, like the preceding one, is a notably white, masculine venture, and one that, once again, carries the psychic charge of conflictual black/white relations in the home country. Ironically, Digger and his mates will enter the war much as they once entered the boxing ring, engaging their masculinity and belligerent race-pride in a game so structured as to leave them beaten before they are well started – and by representatives of a hostile, alien race.

Yet Malouf, significantly, does not dwell upon race-hatred and race-orientated anxiety as central aspects of the Australian experience of war in south-east Asia. One gets a strong sense that the problem of being worked like 'coolies' has to do with the POWs' belief in their own higher racial status (*GW*, 119, 152), as does the fear of going 'black' due to tropical infections of the blood (*GW*, 141). A similar register of racialist thinking is evident when a POW worries over whether the unvarying rice diet will make eyes 'go slanty' (*GW*, 142). But for the most part Malouf focuses attention elsewhere – once he has put the element of race conflict in place, in the Australian setting, in relation to Digger's carnival career. Malouf renders the actual experience of the war as a kind of existential crisis – a deep challenge to basic humanity, basic human value – and, perhaps more interestingly, as an identity-shattering displacement. One of the novel's main themes – that the human being's sense of self is strongly attached to place – receives much of its primary development in relation to the myriad personal displacements the war effort entails.

When Vic sees a young fellow soldier, formerly cocky and game, accept a sudden, indisputable death sentence, the narrative is quite clearly in the realm of existential crisis. Both Vic and the fellow soldier see the white stool – sure sign of the cholera victim – the latter produces. As the condemned man's expression moves, in just seconds, from 'panicky recognition' to 'dumb patience', Vic is made to face, vicariously, 'the hard facts of existence' (*GW*, 41). Vic, in his pre-war youth, had already seen evidence, in Australia, of his existing 'in a world in which forces were at work that took no account of ordinary lives' (*GW*, 105). But the war experience manifests such a world in much more extreme forms.

Malouf's concerns are quite distinctly different, however, when Vic strikes on a cure for Digger's rotting leg. The infection is certainly life-threatening, and it first takes shape for Digger as existential crisis, as the 'illuminating darkness of an ultimate wisdom', as both 'genesis' and 'truth' (*GW*, 155). Vic's response is of another order; he has learned the lesson (although perhaps unconsciously) that one can only live – or in the POW's case, survive – in relation to place, in relation to the specific traits and qualities of a particular place. This relation, moreover, shows itself to be transactional. For all its horrifying, seemingly inimical strangeness, Vic and Digger's south-east Asian non-place – one of the dozens of work-camps between 'the Malay and the Burmese borders' (*GW*, 130) – includes a river, and thus a fluent assertion of ongoing life. By immersing his rotting leg in this river, on Vic's instigation, Digger delivers himself over to a life-giving predation, a force of life that feeds on death and yields renewed hope of life. As tiny fish – Vic's 'tiddlers' – feed on the dead flesh of his leg, Digger recognises that 'All the stink and ooze of it was being taken back into the world, away from him, into the mouths of the living and turned back into life there.' Digger feeds his filth and disease and death to the greedy mouthed spirits of place and receives in return 'cleanness' and life. This is his wartime 'baptism', as he rightly intuits, but it is just as clearly another of the novel's many transactions, and one that accords with life-as-it-must-be-lived in the places of the war (*GW*, 161). Nor is Digger's healing at the river a singular instance of the transaction of life-giving predation; something very similar occurs when Vic institutes the practice of eating his sick friend's rice ration. By this theft, the sick man's care-giver sustains and fortifies himself.

It is of some interest that Vic outstrips Digger in his readiness to recognise the transactional potential of their wartime places. Digger seems clearly to have, of the two of them, the richer, more sensitive response to life and the world; Vic is typically represented as 'all locked up in himself' (*GW*, 95), or as one who has a smothering 'membrane between him and the world' (*GW*, 123). But Digger, crucially, is the one who has previously established an identity-founding relationship with place. Digger Keen's sense of self is enduringly bound to Keen's Crossing, and even in the 'worst times in Thailand, this connection would sustain Digger and help keep him sane' (*GW*, 199). Vic has no pre-war place of belonging. His failure throughout the course of the novel to find any self-confirming place or situation does much, in fact, to elucidate the psychological content of his restless financial ambitions and the dispersed, abstracted, essentially placeless business empire he eventually builds for himself. Possessing no proper place, Vic is not so disposed to resist the terms of association and assimilation put forward by new and unfamiliar places. As for Digger, being place-connected urges him toward the affection and admiration he feels for Mac, whose virtue, in Digger's eyes, is precisely 'Self-possession'. Digger finds the world so 'full of interest' that he gets 'lost in it' (*GW*, 116); it enchants him out of himself, but seemingly does not present itself in the practical terms discernible to Vic's 'hard-headed wisdom' (*GW*, 133). Although a worldly place may found his sense of himself, Digger's outward orientation makes place, even his self-founding place, the very portal of an experiential errancy. But as one sees clearly in Malouf's work, at least from *An Imaginary Life* forward, if not already in *Johnno*, the real business of the human being is not identity-consolidation but the adventure of the other, the not-I.

Naming is the act that inaugurates the transactional relationship with otherness, with the great world and all things in it. It is a writing of the world upon the world, a putting in place and a confirming of place. Digger's lists have this function. Indeed, Digger represents, generally speaking, the intuition of perfect fit between names and the world's constituents, an orientation recalling the old idea of medieval scholarship, the belief in a natural essence-grasping, essence-inscribing language originating with Adam. Old Adam's self- and world-defining acts are not, of course, a new interest for Malouf: Ovid makes the spring by recovering the name for 'poppy' and for its colour, 'scarlet'; Jim Saddler effectively creates a sanctuary world for birds by assigning names appropriately. Digger does much the same work with his 'magic formulations' of place: 'You spoke them … and there they were: *Lake Balaton, Valparaiso, Zanzibar*, the *Bay of Whales*' (*GW*, 197). For Malouf, as for Paul Carter, space does not pre-exist the cultural process of its making and naming.[16] Naming establishes the relationship between human consciousness and the world, giving both a fuller reality, as 'Keen's Crossing' most aptly demonstrates. This key place is, significantly, a crossing, a place of intersection between the individual identity and the world.

The quiet importance of Hugh Warrender, the hidden poet, the poet unrecognised by any of his familiars, resides just here, in naming, in the power of language to complete reality, to give fuller being to aspects of experience that exist already but which are not recognised until they find their true shape in words. The wedding-gift of verse the poet offers his daughter speaks in this vein, asserting that 'The animal in us knows/ The truth' but is 'dumb' and unwaveringly 'In love with what is always out of reach'. What is out of reach is the 'Word beyond word that breathes through mortal speech' (*GW*, 236), but on occasion, in the act of wedding or in a poem, the language that is more than just language can for a moment be found and held: one speaks one's feeling and thus makes it both word and act; one engages in performative speech that speaks and acts in the same moment, that unites speech and action. The 'still invisible presences' are in this way discovered, in a moment and yet for all time, by being given shape in words, in the poet's words and (he hopes) in wedding vows. The epithalamium goes on to characterise the 'occasion' of human communion and community as 'the precarious gift' and 'the mixed blessing' (*GW*, 237) – these being the phrases Digger the rememberer will later recall for Iris (*GW*, 266). Poetic speech creates and inaugurates, but then shares what it has made, as Ellie, the bride, clearly shows by following the enunciation of the poem 'with her lips', by knowing it already 'word for word' (*GW*, 237). The 'mixed' aspect of the proffered blessing is not only in the mixed aspect of wedding vows (the joy and sorrow, sickness and health), but also in the nature of the spoken gift or blessing, which always presents itself as a mixing place, a place of coming together. The critical commentary upon Warrender's poetry, which occupies a pivotal position in the novel's unfolding, also dwells upon the character of poetic speech, of speech as a bringing into being – *poesis* is a making – and a bringing together. The university man who offers a kind of critical elegy for Warrender coins the phrase '*other* history', which he first characterises as that which poetry speaks for, and then, more concretely, as 'all those unique and repeatable events, the little sacraments of daily existence' and as the too-often 'unseen' and 'unspoken' experience that 'binds us all' (*GW*, 283–4).

This 'other history' is not yet the novel's master key, though the notion has been much taken up in its criticism and interpretation. As one can see already in *Fly Away Peter*, historical events in their usual guise too often rupture the progress of human time, and this character of history – or perhaps History – is also prominently a part of *The Great World*. Pons finds that the novel is structured by an 'interplay between continuity and discontinuity',[17] and thus by the two opposing versions of history. 'Other history' clearly does much to organise the themes of synthesis, community, and continuity. Crucially, it is closely linked to common speech, and to poetry understood as the exalted form of common speech. It depends on enunciation for its very being, of which it has none without enunciation. (Significantly, Digger's life of 'other history' with Iris originates with a legacy of letters.) History as rupture, on the other hand, manifests itself most clearly as a rending of the human fabric woven of time and language; it shows itself when the Australian POWs are 'hurled into a place where anything could be done and was done, in animal fury and darkness, in blood, din and a thick-throated roaring before words' (*GW*, 122).

Continuity and also the human will to continuity are figured in the novel's many lines or threads, which give a spatial representation to concerns that are most pertinently temporal: 'Even the least event had lines, all tangled, going back into the past, and beyond that into the unknown past, and other lines leading out, also tangled, into the future' (*GW*, 296). The lines are tangled, and thus difficult to trace and to sort out, but one gets a strong sense that a human life is *in* the tangling of lines of continuity and connection, and also in the endless work of disentangling – of ordering and interpreting. Relationships in *The Great World* emerge in the transactions of entangling and disentangling oneself. They do not necessarily arise out of sympathetic affection or compatibility; they are facts of sociability rather than achievements of the heart. Imperfect sympathy, incomprehension, and even hostility mark the novel's relationships, even the closest ones, but they are not failed relationships for all of that. Digger responds with affection to the difference he perceives in Mac, but he initially detests Vic, with whom he will eventually develop abiding ties and yet for whom he will never feel much more than a sense of responsibility coloured by a bemused tolerance. The point of relationship seems to be that one is acted upon, definitively, and that one proceeds, as a result, with altered perception and an altered approach to life. Relationships therefore ramify, extend new lines, directing Digger toward his decades-long post-war love affair with Iris, Mac's widowed sister-in-law; destining tycoon Vic to die in the woods around Keen's Crossing, in the arms of Digger's deranged sister Jenny. A new relational entanglement is typically a preceding relationship's disentangling – that is, both a way of letting go and of remaining engaged, both an extension of the enigma of the other and, at least partially, a clarification. For Digger, Vic and Iris both serve in the working out of what Mac meant, and what he still means. One may concur, therefore, with Nettelbeck, who argues that the novel's lines include 'lines of meaning', which 'are the *border-lines* between known limits and unknown space'.[18] Lives, as envisioned in Malouf's transactional terms, are 'all crossing, and interconnecting or exerting pressure on one another' (*GW*, 296). But of course there are frequent failures, where a life or a life-line fails to maintain connection and continuity. Pons usefully notes that both Digger and Vic (and later also Greg) represent 'discontinuity in the family line',[19] thus manifesting Malouf's typifying preoccupation with problems of genealogy.

The novel resolves itself upon the image of the child Vic preoccupied with threading a needle, a task 'he knows is simple yet finds so difficult' (*GW*, 329). Here, Malouf's now familiar figure of thread or line is clearly ordered in relation to the theme of passage, of making a passage. Malouf forecasts and also summarises Vic's lifelong difficulty in making passages, from his desperate solitude into community, from one phase of his life into another. A grimly ironic allusion orders the scene: one recalls Christ's assertion, in the gospel of Matthew, that a camel can pass more readily through the eye of a needle than a rich man (like tycoon-to-be Vic) can enter the heavenly kingdom. This biblical allusion combines, moreover, with an internal reference: the child's thread looks forward to (but also in textual terms recalls) the loop of thread that serves as Vic's wartime survival-charm. The child's thread, like the soldier's, begins as white thread but becomes increasingly 'grubby' (*GW*, 329), begrimed through protracted contact with Vic's body, with Vic's life. In Singapore, the recently demobbed Vic is reminded what a commonplace commodity his precious thread is, and thus has 'a vision suddenly of how small it was, all that had happened to him' (*GW*, 171). This is the vision of the eye of history, and it reveals the paltriness of individual experience, however testing and intense. But beneath this pessimism is also the optimism that bides its time. It is contained in the author's commitment to recording the little moments of 'other history'. Although the needle's eye is but a tiny portion of the human world, the child Vic 'can see the sky through it', and then 'a whole house' (*GW*, 329), and then again a slightly older boy (a representative of his own near future) triumphantly mastering the task of bike-riding, and finally an increasingly 'smoky' darkness (*GW*, 330). He can see, in other words, a whole world and a whole life. One can, it seems, see more than one can do, envision more than one can accomplish. The novel ends by offering the exact measure of its optimism, and its pessimism. With night coming on Vic's thread still has not made its passage through the needle's eye, but his conviction is unwavering: 'Soon it will' (*GW*, 330). Considering the case in the light of Vic's overall history of successful and unsuccessful negotiations of passage, one may say that a more accurate resolution would be: it will not soon and it may not ever. But Malouf seems committed to the notion that there is something of human value even in the faith or belief that will not be justified, will not be fulfilled.

6

Remembering Babylon

In addition to being the cornerstone of Malouf's reputation, *Remembering Babylon* brings into focus the specifically postcolonial aspects of the author's vision and thus provides an important perspective on the work that precedes it. The previously established elements of Malouf's vision are now organised around questions of postcoloniality and nationhood: what is a nation, and how is it constituted; more particularly, what is Australia, and how did this erstwhile collection of settler colonies remake itself as a modern nation? Both *Harland's Half Acre* and *The Great World* offer multiple-perspective, wide-angle imaging of Australian modernity; *Remembering Babylon* distinguishes itself through the intensity of its genealogical concerns. As the title suggests, the book strives to initiate a remembering, an ethical and instrumental process of memory and also a re-collecting of that which has been dismembered. The work opens upon the acknowledgement that the formation of the national body has entailed the cutting off, the exclusion, of elements real and present, yet disavowed by the dominant forces informing the nation's self-imagining. If Australia is to be experienced coherently as a modern *and postcolonial* homeland, the excluded elements must be rediscovered and restored – this in brief is Malouf's position. One must make peace, through remembrance, with the nation's history of dismemberment. *Remembering Babylon*'s epigraphs orientate the theme of remembrance, first providing alternative versions of the present world – is it 'Jerusalem or Babylon', the sanctified, promised place or the place of exile – then moving on to apocalyptic imagery that poses the unsettlingly personal question 'Wilt thou remember me'? Who is it then that worries about being remembered? Who is in danger of being forgotten? Should Australians or, more broadly, the various communities of the modern, increasingly globalised world – should we remember the colonial past, and how should we remember it?

As the novel's narrative unfolds, it becomes clear that, in Malouf's view, Australian dismembering and disavowal have been exercised principally upon Aboriginal peoples. However, it is precisely on the question of Aboriginality and its represen-tation that the work has faced its most intense opposition. A critical controversy marks *Remembering Babylon*'s immediate reception in 1993, its publication year – also, pertinently, the International Year of Indigenous Peoples, and the year following *Mabo v. Queensland*. In early November of 1993, Germaine Greer publishes a review challenging Malouf's representation of indigeneity and denouncing the principal character, Gemmy Fairley, first as the enabling centrepiece of Malouf's 'supremacist fantasy' and then more simply as his 'fake black'.[1] Peter Craven promptly rebuts Greer, denouncing what he sees as her 'Philis-tinism' and affirming that Greer's hostility merely reflects her 'own post-colonial condescension towards her former country'.[2] The gloves now off, further debate ensues. Peter Otto, in an article-length review, seems to align himself with the detrac-tors when he asserts that the novel performs an 'erasure of the political'. However, Otto engages thoughtfully with the figure of Gemmy – the character Greer treats so dismissively – and finds in Gemmy a revelatory 'locus or catalyst for certain kinds of disorientation intrinsic to the colonial experience'.[3] In the following year, Veronica Brady publishes in an American journal: *Remembering Babylon*, in her view, responds productively to the challenge of *Mabo* and aligns itself with *Mabo*'s demon-stration that the argument of *terra nullius* 'has no standing'.[4] The debate within Australian publications seems to culminate, however, with the appearance of a full-length scholarly article by Suvendrini Perera, the most fully elaborated of the novel's early-appearing adversarial critiques. Perera's argument, in brief, is that Malouf misappropriates 'the indigenous body' and mobilises it within 'the discourse of happy hybridism'. In so doing, Malouf produces a 'transubstantiated' version of indigeneity, which then allows for the 'evacuation' of the space of the indigenous and 'the substitution of colonising for colonised bodies'. The overall outcome is 'a Providentialist narrative of colonisation'.[5]

After 1994, the voices in favour of Malouf's novel seem to outnumber and overpower those that speak against it. *Remembering Babylon*, which had been short-listed for the Booker Prize (but without ultimate success), is honoured in 1996 with the inaugural International IMPAC Dublin Literary Award. Upon the announcement of this award, Gia Metherell publishes a strong statement in the novel's favour, recognising and validating its expressed will to reconciliation of Australian society's divided elements: *Remembering Babylon* 'presents the story of white colonialism as inextricable from the story of black Australians', and this acknowledgement of 'a shared history' coincides with the position adopted by the Council for Aboriginal Reconciliation.[6] In the broader international context, some critics express reservations about the work, but these are more modestly presented and embedded in largely favourable appraisals. So, Sheila Whittick, publishing in France, suggests that it is 'difficult to identify' Malouf's final position with respect to the Eurocentrism of his principal settler characters;[7] in Belgium, Marc Delrez and Paulette Michel-Michot publish their finding that the novel represents 'a renewed, dual, dialectical sense of identity proper to Australians', but that it perhaps 'only furthers native dispossession'.[8] Other commentators affirm the novel's value in terms that suggest awareness of the early denunciations, but without confronting them directly and explicitly. Thus, Michael Mitchell credits Malouf with undertaking a 'perilous but necessary transgression' of conventionally understood cultural boundaries;[9] Carolyn Bliss asserts that the envisioning of Gemmy as a bridge-between must be understood as failed myth.[10] However, these later publications do not counter so much as skirt the early arguments against the book; the challenges are left largely unanswered.

The contestatory criticism, from Greer through to Perera, unites in its will to defend cultural and racial borders. The contemporary world is understood as an assembly of cultural territories, all of them representing and defending their borders and constituencies with greater or lesser degrees of success. This critical perspective is acutely problematic with respect to Malouf, because his work so insistently involves the testing and questioning of borders, boundaries, and boundedness – already in *An Imaginary Life* and in the subsequent fictions up to *Remembering Babylon* and beyond. Malouf's creative wager is that one can cross interpersonal and intercultural borders imaginatively; his ethical belief is that one should try to do so. In Malouf, boundedness exists to be surpassed. Self-overcoming, through responsiveness to the appeal of the other, is one of his principle themes. Indeed, a common motivation for Malouf characters, albeit often unconscious, is the quest to find the perspective of the other – to see the self from the other's perspective. Clearly, orientations such as Malouf's may open an author to the charge of cross-cultural transgression – to the charge of venturing into realms of representation in which the author has no valid claim – but one should ask then if Malouf's imaginings duly recognise and respect real-world issues of cultural difference.[11]

In a manner that recalls but is significantly distinct from *The Great World*'s pairing of history (as rupture) and communal 'other history', *Remembering Babylon* sets up, immediately, a divided presentation of time. The first sentence positions events 'in the middle of the nineteenth century, when settlement in Queensland had advanced little more than halfway up the coast'. Yet this same sentence, and thus the entire narrative, opens with 'One day', a phrase not very far from the 'once upon a time' of a traditional fairytale, and concludes with an evocation of children at play who suddenly see 'something extraordinary'. The prose proceeds with mentions of 'forest' and 'wolves' – familiar sites of European folk tales – but then specifies the source of the 'make believe' game as 'a story in the fourth grade Reader' (*RB*, 1). A book, a schoolbook, embedded in specific historical context, thus feeds folkloric imagination. Yet it becomes clear that the folkloric imagination, once fed, dominates the understanding of time's unfoldings. Gemmy's advent is first submitted to childhood's imaginative regime – 'the tales they told one another, all spells and curses' – then becomes a product of 'a world over there', which then becomes 'the abode of everything savage and fearsome', and finally assumes its definitively undefined status as 'Absolute Dark' (*RB*, 2–3). This development manifests, of course, the ways in which the children *have learned* to understand their ambient world; the children's understanding is obviously and inescapably socio-genetic. In these ways the novel offers two versions of time – the time of history and the time of the folk imagination and folk memory – which will subsequently pursue their somewhat strained but curiously coordinated relationship.

The problems that inhere in the Queensland settler community's situation, and that are intensified by Gemmy's arrival, are not only of a temporal order. Alice Brittan argues that the novel brings into focus 'the problem of material equivalence posed by the meeting of heterogeneous cultural systems' whose 'understandings of value' are 'incommensurable' – a situation that makes acts of naming 'extraordinarily urgent'. In colonial situations, Brittan continues, 'imported goods' take shape as 'insecure, besieged objects'. But, at the same time, imported objects, by their very arrival and ongoing presence, signify, one may say assert, 'the rights of territorial possession'.[12] Considered in this light, Gemmy's initial self-designation as a British 'object' proposes him as a particularly troubling version of the unstable imported object and a highly disruptive reframing of the terms of territorial possession. Not surprisingly, then, he also strains the urgent need to find and assign stable names. In the first few pages concerned with portraying him – or rather, settler perceptions of him – Gemmy is variously 'a scarecrow', a 'creature', a 'prisoner', a 'specimen of – of what?', a 'man', a 'half-caste or runaway', a 'straw-topped half-naked savage', a 'simpleton', again a 'man', 'an odd unsettled fellow', 'a pathetic muddy-eyed, misshapen fellow', again a 'man' (albeit much damaged), and 'a mongrel' (*RB*, 3–8).[13]

The evaluation of Malouf's cross-cultural vision must turn upon the figure of Gemmy Fairley, the novel's 'black white man', or again, its 'white black man' – Malouf uses both phrases (*RB*, 10, 69). In preceding novels, Malouf had mainly explored the dynamic, mutually articulating relationship of self and other in relation to pairings of intimately bound but contrasting characters: Ovid and the Child, Jim Saddler and Ashley Crowther, Digger Keen and Vic Curran. In the 1993 novel, Gemmy stands as the principal instance of difference, of otherness, for all other major characters. And of all the characters, Gemmy is most clearly presented as a site for the reconfiguration of postcolonial subjectivity and identification. If such reconfiguration – or transfiguration – is a problem in Malouf's text, the problem must centre on Gemmy.

Gemmy's cultural performance, to begin with, needs to be recognised as productive rather than merely reproductive. Gemmy stages questions of cross-cultural perception, puts into performance an exploratory reading that aims to cross the bounds of difference. Such perception, such reading, which aims not at appropriation but at recognition, enables rather than impedes effective, productive cross-cultural negotiations. The question Gemmy poses within the text is not primarily – what is Aboriginal identity? His advent raises much more pressingly a series of differently focused questions: what is European settler identity; how (and to what degree) is this identity predicated upon conceptions of Aboriginal difference; how does the case of Gemmy perturb and challenge these conceptions; how does Gemmy represent in himself, and stimulate in others, a work of re-evaluation and rereading?

Gemmy's character-specific capacity to raise questions about cultural identity and cross-cultural interpretation is clearly signalled in Malouf's canny handling of first encounter, of Gemmy's first confrontation with a North Queensland settler community. Ivor Indyk's argument that Malouf's fiction tends toward 'emblematic' representations[14] is nowhere more splendidly confirmed than in the imaging of Gemmy on the boundary fence, precariously balanced, flapping his arms, birdlike, and backgrounded by the 'warp and glare' of molten gold sky and 'blazing earth' (*RB*, 2–3). Emblematically, indeed, the image seems to capture with immediate clarity Gemmy's peculiar this-ness and to captivate also the imagination of the witnesses – especially Janet – who will subsequently return to it repeatedly in memory. In emblematic presentation, image is immediately discursive; imaging *is* meaning. Gemmy's image, within the tremulous haze of heatwaves, manifests all the ambiguity of the abject object. He is perched on a fence, awkwardly and uneasily between worlds, and although he is birdlike he cannot quite manage to take flight; his is an unending failure to achieve transcendence.

The emblematic clarity of Gemmy's first appearance (which includes his being clearly ambiguous) does not continue into his encounter with the larger settler community, where the regime of perception and interpretation is significantly different. One needs now to recognise what Paul Carter characterises as 'the theatrical nature of cross-cultural relations',[15] which are especially theatrical in situations of encounter. Historical actors perform, and events are staged, in accord with pre-established (albeit often unconscious or unacknowledged) scriptings. One may note here, too, Carter's suggestion that historical writing often presumes to stage for the first time what it can only restage. However Malouf (an erstwhile collaborator of Carter's) is alert to both the pitfalls and the possible advantages pertaining to the theatrical character of cross-cultural encounter; he plays upon the pre-established elements of encounter scenarios, inscribing critical difference upon a familiar territory.

Gemmy's advent provokes a spontaneous acting-out of the terms of settler sociability and community. The settler society manifests itself as a shifting hierarchy, organised by competition and marked by instances of conflict. In negotiating Gemmy's possible inclusion, the society renegotiates itself. It enters briefly into a state of 'noisy carnival' (*RB*, 10) – a kind of interregnum, a moment of established authority's suspension and a consequent experimentation with rules and roles. Degrees of inclusion or belonging become evident, as well as degrees of confidence – or anxiety – with respect to individuals' sense of their own inclusion. Thus, the guessing-game arising in response to Gemmy's cryptic pantomimes rapidly becomes an informal contest in which ineffective contributions may be harshly received: 'Don't be daft, Jack, that couldn't be it. What a noodle! Hark at the ninny!' Some of the young men anxiously perceive the strange new situation as 'a test', and when this test takes a bad turn for one of them, Hec Gosper, he turns definitively against Gemmy. Small children (who understandably experience their social inclusion as tenuous) are 'astonished' and thrown into uncertainty about the social codes that it is their job to learn (*RB*, 11). Liminal Lachlan (neither a small child nor a young man) participates with exceptional success and thus enjoys newfound social recognition and a consequent 'power' (*RB*, 12). Janet, although Lachlan's senior, confronts the relative disqualification that accords with her femininity. As with the Child's arrival in the village of Tomis, Gemmy's advent presents an unintended challenge to pre-existing social order. Gemmy's goal (albeit only semi-conscious) is recognition and at least a provisional acceptance in the community; however, his bid for entry calls into question the very terms and conditions of community.

While portraying Gemmy's first attempts at self-representation, Malouf focuses attention on 'the rag' with which the newcomer covers himself – or perhaps one should say, the rag with which he doesn't quite manage to cover himself. The rag's ineffectiveness as a covering adds a comic element to the text, but also carries the suggestion that the rag is not, most crucially, a covering. This rag is Gemmy's only piece of clothing when he first encounters the novel's Anglo-Celtic settler community. While being examined, sized up, by the settlers, Gemmy removes the rag from his waist and presents it for examination. He then becomes anxious as he watches it passed from hand to hand and mutely communicates his will to have it back. The basic terms of this encounter scene are familiar enough: naked savagery confronts clothed civility. Yet Malouf, in his narrative detailing, works carefully to defamiliarise the episode; the easy, recognisable oppositions are not allowed to determine its development or resolution.

The rag that Gemmy proffers then reclaims is not savage garb, is not Aboriginal clothing – though the settler community clearly misreads it as such until it is presented for closer examination. The rag, once examined, proves to be 'the remains of a jacket', begrimed but originally 'blue, perhaps royal blue' (*RB*, 12), a child's sea-jacket of European, and almost certainly British, origin. Gemmy evidently retains it not as covering but as sign; it intends to show much more than it hides. As this jacket-rag confirms, Gemmy presents himself to the settlers not as a reassuring transfiguration of the other but as a troubling transfiguration of self. Malouf's reworking of the scene of colonial encounter does not offer Gemmy as an assimilable stand-in for the absent and unassimilable Aborigine; it does not presume to render Aboriginal otherness as naked fact, nor to consolidate a fantasy-inspired misrecognition of the other. Gemmy's rag is unmistakably an uncanny object that synecdochically confirms Gemmy in his status as the familiar defamiliarised.

The presentation of the jacket-rag is Gemmy's first assertion of his peculiar claim to inclusion in the white settler community, but it is also the initiation of his production, within this community, as a 'mixture of monstrous strangeness and unwelcome likeness' (*RB*, 43). This notion of 'mixture' strongly suggests a hybrid status, but one that is, crucially, a matter of settler perception; the settlers begin, now, upon presentation of the rag, to think of Gemmy in terms of mixture or hybridity. Readers concerned with Malouf's treatment of cross-cultural negotiation may find this outcome rather too easy, but one should note that Malouf's concern is with *perceived* hybridity, and that the author does not undertake to confirm the rightness of settler perception. Moreover, this perception of cultural mixing disturbs the settlers rather than reassuring them. It does not resolve for them the problem of cultural difference; mixture is, on the contrary, the most anxious and unsettling possibility that difference suggests to Anglo-Celtic settler minds. The novel's focal character has no Aboriginal bloodline though he has received appreciable Aboriginal cultivation. Through his use of Gemmy, Malouf demonstrates that it is not the Aboriginal presence but the possibility of cultural in-betweenness that most challenges white Australia's aspiration to form a coherent sense of itself. The novel's small community of Scottish settlers has already formed an exclusionary, us-and-them stance with respect to Aboriginal peoples. The Aborigine, in other words, is the representative of 'Absolute Dark' (RB, 3) – the other, the outsider, in simplified, stereotyped form. The discovery of Gemmy, however, presents the Aborigine in a new and disruptive way, as one who can exert a transformative influence upon the relocated European.

Settler perception of Gemmy, moreover, is arguably multi-ple, not simply in the sense that he means different things to different observers, but also that he potentially evokes different ideas and memories in each individual observing mind. But Gemmy most disturbs the Queensland settlers by symbolising an 'abject' version of the self.[16] A kind of shadow-identification with Gemmy precedes and resists settler interpretations oriented by notions of montrous mixture and contamination. Malouf's presentation of Gemmy's early life, what Whittick characterises as his 'bleak, dehumanized, Dickensian childhood in "civilized" Britain',[17] thus becomes more thoroughly inter-pretable, particularly when one re-examines settler memories of home, or 'hame'. Ellen McIvor's early life, though better than Gemmy's, is certainly not without its abject aspects. Young Ellen had witnessed her coalminer brothers' degradation through life in the pit: 'She had watched them grow up, each one, from eager, affectionate little lads into coarse fellows who pushed down and extinguished everything that was fine in them' (RB, 54). Their whiteness, that last bastion of race-pride, is recalled as 'the dead marble whiteness' produced by a 'sunless world'. For all Ellen's occasional fondness for the idea of 'hame', this lost place is ultimately 'the dismal world she had grown up in' (RB, 74). The settlers' relocation to Queensland does not appear, then, as a descent from grandeur. Some at least among them may well be susceptible to experiencing Gemmy as an 'abjectifying' mirror rather more than as an alien and degenerate hybrid.[18]

But putting the complications of settler perception aside, is it accurate for Malouf's readers to interpret Gemmy as a hybrid? Certainly he fails to manifest the quite pronounced degree of syncretism, the intermingling of two or more cultural formations, which one would typically associate with hybrid status. Gemmy is never able to integrate his personal history. His English childhood remains split off from his subsequent Aboriginal acculturation, asserting itself, always disruptively, in stammering English speech, in unwelcome memories, and in nightmares. Indeed, Gemmy's characteristic stammer does not manifest a loss of former language powers but rather a return to an old inability to lay secure claim to the world through the mediation of *English* words: the return to English brings the return of the stammer. Gemmy's alienated relationship with English language and culture shows itself symbolically in his first encounter with transported European culture. He surreptitiously witnesses a scene of wood-chopping, which conjures up the inaugural word of his rediscovered relationship with English: 'The word flew into his head as fast and clear as the flash and whistle of its breath. *Axe. Axe*' (*RB*, 30). But the axe, of course, is a cleaving instrument: it does not bind; it splits apart. A similar use of symbol attends the definitive end of Gemmy's participation in the settler community. When Andy McKillup begins to work toward Gemmy's ostracism, Gemmy is using a hammer, an instrument for construction, for fastening things together, for building – even, one may say, for nation-building. Gemmy's ringing hammer blows recall Pete Seeger's hammer, with which one hammers morning and evening 'all over this land'. Andy, as it were, takes the nation-building hammer from Gemmy and gives instead the imaginary Aboriginal stone, which soon becomes the totem of Gemmy's exclusion.[19]

It is precisely the violence – indeed, the deep personal violation – marking Gemmy's experience of English culture that makes his English identity unassimilable. This violence he meets with in the settler community consolidates the constitutive breach in his personality rather than mending it; English and Anglo-Celtic forms of culture first provoke and subsequently maintain the splitting of Gemmy's mind. The character's only hope of happiness lies not in a successful syncretism but in the symbolic, almost ritualised dissolution of the script of his English colonial identity. This dissolution, under purging rain, into 'bits all disconnected' (RB, 181), is the necessary precursor to Gemmy's final acceptance of the Aboriginal gift of 'the land up there' (RB, 118) – his only possible place for validated being-in-the-world. Moreover, the identity-documenting script that Gemmy has reclaimed from the schoolmaster Abbot is mistakenly reclaimed; it is not, of course, Gemmy's own story. This error, however, is as perfect in its way as Gemmy's inaugural slip of the tongue, his substitution of 'object' for 'subject' in his first characterisation of himself. The script of English colonial identity is an imposition by an alien and alienating power, a consecration of dispossession. This misrepresenting script, and Gemmy's ineluctably mistaken relationship with it, together demonstrate that imperial culture bars Gemmy from the path of syncretic biculturality. Gemmy can never reclaim, own, and incorporate his legacy of 'English-ness'; only symbolically can he play out his relationship with it – and even then, not by a production or reproduction of symbols but by a purging of the unincorporable script.

One character in Malouf's novel, the minister Mr Frazer, does nonetheless put forward a thoughtful envisioning of Gemmy as a hybrid and, all told, as a successful one. In the writings that later become his 'report', Fraser represents Gemmy as one who has felicitously 'crossed the boundaries of his given nature', and thus, as a 'forerunner' and 'exemplum' of the future develop-ment of Australian cultural identity (RB, 132). Such utopian optimism no doubt accounts for a certain tendency among critics to read Frazer as the representative, within the fiction, of Malouf's own thinking: Perera names Frazer as *Remem-bering Babylon*'s 'recording conscience';[20] Neilsen asserts that Malouf 'leaves us in no doubt' as to 'the correctness' of Frazer's 'insight'.[21] Although it would be foolish to deny a significant utopian strain in Malouf's work, the understanding of Frazer's vision as Malouf's very much needs to be questioned.

Malouf's narrative *represents* the writing of Frazer's utopian text; that is, one does not simply see what the character writes, one witnesses a very noteworthy portion of the character's writing

process. While penning his utopian vision, and more particularly, Gemmy's place within it, Frazer falters and interrupts
his composition. Just after Frazer writes of Gemmy as a hybrid
exemplum, Malouf makes a shift into the immediacy of present
tense, and writes, '[Fraser] breaks off, his hand pausing above the
inkwell. He has come to a knotty place in his reflections, feeling
a lapse of the high emotion that has carried him on' (*RB*, 132).
Clearly, this breaking off has among its textual functions that
of alerting readers to the need for some thoughtful circumspection. Frazer's vision is not to be gobbled up or swallowed whole.
His writing needs to be read and interpreted in accord with its
process – with some thoughtful interruptions rather than a too
free-flowing ease.

Frazer, one should recall, first plays an authoring role when
composing the 'Colonial fairytale' of Gemmy's life (*RB*, 19).
Indeed, the episode of the first documentation of Gemmy's life is
thoroughly compromised in relation to truth-claim and conforms
unsettlingly with the rule of writing, of writing technology, put
forward in the writing lesson of Lévi-Strauss's *Tristes Tropiques*.
For Lévi-Strauss, writing is not about memory or truth so much
as it is about power, the power of those who write over those who
do not write – and who, as a seemingly ineluctable consequence,
are written. So, in Malouf's first scene of writing, Lachlan, who
has demonstrated himself to be the ablest interpreter, is excluded
from the writing process, and he experiences this exclusion as a
humiliation and thus a loss of power. Frazer, self-elected to the
role of author-biographer, proceeds through a series of 'wrong
guesses', producing 'whole phrases' out of Gemmy's 'odd bursts
of sound' and 'half-meanings' (*RB*, 17). George Abbot, the scribe,
seems however to intuit the special power that he accrues as
the producer of the material inscription. Resenting his role as
'a mere clerk' (he is an 'abbot' after all), the scribe first impro-
vises 'a phrase or two of his own' then moves on to 'alteration
of fact'. These acts are 'an assertion of personality, of indepen-
dence' (*RB*, 18–19), a partial appropriation of the writing event
– a claiming of power, of the power that is more in writing than
in truth. Oddly, it is only Gemmy who fully understands the

writing exercise as a power ritual that works to disenfranchise and dominate him. Having sniffed the fresh ink, he correctly surmises that it holds 'the smell of his life, his spirit, the black blood they had drained from him' (RB, 21). Significantly, the blood the writing has drained from him is not merely dark but 'black'; Gemmy seems to intuit that the writing seeks to isolate and expropriate the portion of Aboriginality in him.

Accounting for Gemmy takes shape as a historicisation, as his inscription in history. Gemmy's life, his story, must be written down. Yet what ensues also participates in that other, less stable rendering of human time, folk tale or 'fairytale', and it bears this rendering's typical marks, being community-authored by oral exchange. This perturbation of historiography is perhaps inevitable. Gemmy's memory, a fully human memory, is a partial holding distributed by desires and fears; Gemmy wants to remember some things, and not others. Quite understandably, he does not enjoy a full and secure possession of the story of self he is called upon to provide, nor is he secure in the language, English, in which he must now speak himself.[22] Gemmy cannot author-ise his story, but nor can the authority that questions him. The community's minister, who dialogues with Gemmy, cannot really understand the stranger, although he very much wants to. Therefore, without realising it, the minister works from colonial preconceptions about what Gemmy's experience must be, and what it must mean. Moreover, the primary author's incapacity allows, even invites, the schoolteacher-scribe to impose himself, his power, his desire, upon the making of history. The misfortune of the situation resides in the ineluctable fact that historiography emerges from an interactive production of social actors, of individuals who are invested in history, who have a self-interested desire to take place in history and to shape it in a certain way. A certain project of community is always already at work in the making of history. Historiography, which one may understand as the social consolidation of memory, is written *towards* the future as well as *from* the past. The community producing it is working with a pre-established sense of itself, its meaning, and with a will to consolidate a particular framework for its future development. As for Gemmy, who presents an anomalous and disruptive case, it is clear that writing him into Australian history is also, necessarily, a way of writing him out of it. The text of settler-colony Australia requires that he disappear even in the moment of his appearance.

Writing enters Malouf's narrative very problematically. But the solution to the problems involved in writing can only be more writing. Writing enacts power, a world-changing power, and thus a power that cannot be ignored or circumvented. Considered as a whole, *Remembering Babylon* asks to be considered as an instance of supplementary and corrective writing, a contribution to the broad-based, diversified project of setting the record straight. The text stages, moreover, within its narrative, a version of supplementary, corrective writing. Mr Frazer is once again in the role of text producer, of writer. Once again, he works closely with Gemmy, but the way he works with Gemmy is significantly changed. What the minister seeks now is not Gemmy's knowledge of self but his knowledge of place, of the land they both inhabit. Frazer calls the project 'botanising'; it entails seeing, studying, and recording what is there, in the place, in the land. It is a modest project – 'Small, creeping leguminous plant … *Kardolo* in the native tongue, with a blue flower like cultivated tea' (*RB*, 128) – but it leads Frazer to some important recognitions. He learns to see his new antipodal place as a land of plenty, no longer the 'hostile and infelicitous' place he and his fellow settlers had previously imagined. The minister also recognises that he has adopted this new vision from Gemmy and that Gemmy has adopted it from Aboriginal peoples. 'We must', Frazer writes, 'humble ourselves and learn from them'; 'We must clear our minds of what we are looking for to see what is there' (*RB*, 130), thus 'changing ourselves' instead of the place. In his new text, Frazer explicitly elects Gemmy as 'the exemplum', the defining figure, for the building of a place-orientated community consciousness. '[I]n allowing himself to be at home here', Frazer affirms, Gemmy 'has crossed beyond the boundaries of his given nature' (*RB*, 132). Thus, European settlement of Australia is reconstrued as a project of self-overcoming, as a movement beyond the self and toward the other – toward a new sense of identity and community that is explicitly associated with Aboriginal Australia.

Certainly, Frazer's 'report' is not so tellingly undermined in its truth-claim as his first composition is, but the elaborately narrated first writing must cast some doubt upon the later document. The 'report' pays greater respect to Gemmy as a site of knowledge, and it is focused on the land more than on Gemmy, who is recast as an Australian spirit of place. Certainly, Frazer has learned to see Gemmy's reality and value more clearly, but perhaps not yet clearly enough. During the later botanising excursions with Gemmy, which constitute the minister's quite limited initiation to cross-cultural knowledge gathering, Frazer does not reveal himself as a particularly quick and able learner. Indeed, his bumbling efforts in this regard yield some of the novel's better comic moments: his mispronunciation of the Aboriginal words for his botanical discoveries renders one of them as 'an old man's testicle', another as 'a turd' (RB, 67). Generally speaking, the character is notably bound up in his own thoughts, his own private projects, and enjoys at best a sort of respected marginality in relation to his community. An utterly sincere, but all too frequently inept sympathy characterises his relations with Gemmy. And when Frazer attempts, on Gemmy's behalf, to communicate his vision to the powers – that is, to the colonial government – he fails utterly. To sum up the case, Frazer and the Romantic, providentialist utopianism he represents have their place in Malouf's novel, and it is a carefully circumscribed place.[23]

Gemmy is not easily subsumed by the term hybrid, nor certainly can one discern in him the cleanly limned exemplum for modern Australian self-fashioning which Frazer too optimistically, too idealistically portrays. One may yet ask, is Gemmy presented as a version of Aboriginality? Does Gemmy in moments manifest himself as a fake black man or a transubstantiated indigene? Certainly, his learning to live with an Aboriginal tribe has transformed him. Between transubstantiation and transformation, however, there is an appreciable conceptual distance. One should note, also, that if Gemmy were not transformed – deeply transformed – Malouf's imagination would be paying little respect to the specificity and coherence of Aboriginal forms of culture. But in any case, the instances of transformation, or perceived transformation, are several, and they deserve some consideration. There is 'the whole cast of [Gemmy's] face' – which is analysed, it should be noted, as an understandable effect of a particular non-European acculturation: 'his teeth had been worn down … from eating the native food'; 'his jaw, over the years, had adapted itself' to produce 'the new sounds' of Aboriginal languages (*RB*, 40). Gemmy's movements are unsettlingly silent; in this too he signals Aboriginality for the settlers. More crucially, he has a deep and detailed knowledge of the land: he understands it in Aboriginal terms and interacts with it in accord with Aboriginal codes. All these details serve as readily understandable, modestly concrete manifestations of a sixteen-year process of cultural initiation.

Malouf ventures into more difficult and delicate areas of representation when he ascribes particular forms of intuitive knowledge to Gemmy. A brief and not very daring example of this occurs when Gemmy feels 'the hair on the back of his neck stiffen' at the approach of unseen, unheard black visitors (*RB*, 93). A more extensive, more imaginatively venturesome instance of such intuitive knowledge occurs elsewhere, however, in relation to Gemmy's botanising excursions with Frazer. The presence of Aborigines – always unnoticed by Frazer – receives this handling:

> As for what the blacks would be seeing, Gemmy knew what that was. He himself would have a clear light around him like the line that contained Mr Frazer's drawings. It came from the energy set off where his spirit touched the spirits he was moving through.
>
> All they would see of Mr Frazer was what the land itself saw: a shape, thin, featureless, that interposed itself a moment, like a mist or cloud, before the land blazed out in it full strength again and the shadow was gone. (*RB*, 68)

In accounting for this passage, one must focus first upon the assertion 'Gemmy knew'. Malouf typically locates knowledge in the consciousness of a specific character, as he does here. Malouf thus registers the experience or feeling of knowing, something that is more akin to what is called conviction than to objective knowledge. Gemmy does not feel his thought as belief; he feels it as knowledge. He is in the midst of what one may call an acculturated sense of the known and the true. Malouf does not put forward an assertion of his own true knowledge of Aboriginal experience but rather a credible portrayal of his character's inner life and world-view. He shows what his character has learned to believe, and in so doing demonstrates that individual knowledge needs always to be evaluated in relation to cultural contexts.

Yet one should also note that Gemmy's mind immediately likens Aboriginal perception to something pertaining to his other world, his other life: in Aboriginal eyes he, Gemmy, will have a 'clear light' around him, 'like the line' he has seen in Frazer's drawings. Thus, Gemmy's consciousness, even in this quite adventurous moment of its imagining, does not ape or mimic or fake black consciousness. Again one has a sense of this mind's specificity: it is a mind divided between two distinct cultural worlds – and a mind ever hungry to make associations between them, because, as a general rule, the two do not fit together at all well. Gemmy's imagination does evidently incline toward the work of integration, of synthesis – the more active, agential pursuit of hybrid self-fashioning. This work ultimately fails, unfortunately. One finds in Gemmy a desire for hybridity, though not its well-resolved actualisation.[24]

But the most engaging and suggestive aspect of the passage in question is its delineation of the problem impeding effective cross-cultural encounter. Encounter between white and black, settler and Aboriginal, does not occur during the botanising excursions. It does not occur because of limited visibility, which Malouf understands, quite unusually, as a bilateral problem – not simply as a problem of the white colonist's vision. Frazer's ways of seeing do not discern the Aboriginal watchers; but the watchers cannot clearly see Frazer either. A difference of degree is noteworthily registered: the Aborigines' capacity to see Frazer is limited, but Frazer sees 'nothing at all', even when the Aboriginal watchers are 'meant to be seen' (*RB*, 68). However, Gemmy's importance, as the witness of failed encounter, is not so much that he has – or believes he has – access to black vision but that his particular position, both in between and divided between, allows him a unique comprehension of the problem of cross-cultural gazing.

Gemmy's textual role, then, is quite clearly to raise rather than resolve questions of identity and difference. Most acutely, this character problematises the understanding of hybridisation as an easy resolution of cultural difference and the antagonisms that may attend it. There remains, however, the possibility of electing another character, Janet McIvor, to fulfil the role of hybrid exemplum for a utopian Australia-in-the-making. Janet's experience of bee-swarming, her ravishment by bees, most strongly suggests this interpretative possibility. Indeed, the swarming incident is right at the core of Perera's denunciation of Malouf's supposedly facile and irresponsible deployment of hybridism. According to this reading, 'hybridised European bees' claim Janet as a bride, and thus consecrate her privileged (and pointedly non-native) hybrid status;[25] hybridised spirits of place – of a land already colonised and hybridised – elect and by the same gesture create a duly hybrid (but nonetheless white and European) preferred inhabitant for the land. The notion of the ravishing bees' hybridity is not, however, Malouf's. Janet, it is true, will become in later life a hybridiser of bees, a creator of new strains, but the swarming incident has to do with Mrs Hutchence's bees. Mrs Hutchence, as one learns, keeps 'stingless native bees' and also 'imported ones' (*RB*, 139). The bees that swarm upon Janet are 'armed angels' (*RB*, 143); they carry the threat of the sting. So, the swarmers are imported, it would seem, and likely as not Europeans, but their hybrid character is neither stated nor suggested. Whatever its relation to the theme of hybridity may be, Malouf's bee swarm clearly intends to manifest unassimilable otherness, an order of knowledge and being that is beyond the human, a superhuman ravishing force.

(One recalls the transfigured Zeus's claiming of Leda, or better still Danae, when the divine transfiguration takes the form of a shower of gold, and imagistically is not unlike a bee swarm.) In this moment, the text strains toward realms of experience outside the human intersubjective realm – beyond society, culture, and ideology. One may not favour such a fictive move, and one may question its validity or its success, but Malouf's imagining nonetheless maintains, upon examination, its integrity; the writing's real details resist its reconstruction as a neocolonial allegory of cross-cultural encounter.[26]

Determining the degree and character of Janet's hybrid status is a matter of quite substantial critical and interpretative consequence, because Janet is, indisputably, the ordering consciousness for the novel's resolution. This mature Janet, however, is a nun and a scholar-scientist. Both of these roles discourage the reading of Janet as somehow representative, as some broadly applicable model for modern Australian self-fashioning. Far from manifesting an empowered hybridity, Janet occupies a marginal place within her social world, willfully apart from this world though inescapably drawn into its ongoing legacies of violence. Janet, now Sister Monica, inhabits a convent 'deeded' to her sisterhood by the widow of an 'old ruffian' who made his fortune 'blackbirding for the sugar interests up north' (RB, 184); the deceased benefactor is, in balder terms, a kind of slave-trader, and the deeding is a history-cleansing bid for respectability in which Sister Monica is inescapably complicit. Even her life-orientating science, her study of bees, cannot avoid being seized by the worldly powers, scrutinised and (mis)interpreted. Janet, then, can hardly represent a point of resolution for the strains, conflicts, and contradictions of modern Australian social life; she is much more recognisably a point of focus, a stress point where the strain of history is brought to bear, rendingly, upon the individual.

Janet's final role, as the narrative's orientating consciousness, is most pertinently to situate prayer at the novel's resolution, to establish prayer as its final defining gesture. Prayer, of course, manifests aspiration rather than achievement. Janet aspires to

discover and inhabit a world in which the borders, the thresholds, are radiant – as with the sudden, briefly luminous, shoreline
meeting of continent and ocean in the novel's final moments.
Yet this blessed reconciliation is crucially a matter of 'approach'
(*RB*, 200). Within the world of experience the novel records,
difference rubs roughly, or is roughly rubbed; the border, the
margin or edge, is a site of contact and learning, but also of
lesion, of wounding, even scarring – as is quite typically the
case in Malouf.[27]

How then does *Remembering Babylon* take its place in our
contemporary world of cultural and racial borders? How does
it participate in negotiations, often conflictual, of Australian
cultural actuality? The preceding analysis strongly suggests that
Malouf is a tester or questioner of borders and not an inatten-
tive or irresponsible transgressor. His novel reveals an acute and
thoughtful knowledge of where the borders stand, how they
have been drawn and how sustained. It represents the difficulty
of entering and effectively inhabiting new cultural territory,
and despite its clear commitment to reconciliation, it maintains
a measured circumspection with respect to the resolution of
difference presented by hybridisation. Malouf recognises that
the border that presents the possibility of contact and exchange
is also, at least potentially, a barrier.[28] His writing arises out of
a confrontation with the nettled questions of how to represent
difference and the encounter with difference, of how – in what
ways and on what terms – one may represent the cultural other.
Malouf's Frazer stumbles upon such questions, and so, one
surmises, has Malouf. As Spinks acknowledges, Malouf does not
resolve 'the intractable problem of representing but not speaking
"for" the "other"',[29] but he is clearly aware of the problem and
self-consciously wrestling with it. He offers a 'writing that is
struggling, of necessity only partly successfully' to reshape the
world in and by which it is shaped.[30] Authenticity of voice cannot
be ratified by bloodlines nor by the demonstration of appropriate
ethnic indices – not least because no writer, whether pertaining
to a relatively empowered or disenfranchised group, can lay
claim to freedom from the power systems of the social world.

The writer's responsibility, then, cannot be to resolve her or his relationship with power and violence – their history and their actuality. The writer must register conflict and contradiction, in the world and in the self, and must struggle. Gemmy Fairley – already established as a complex, multivalent figure – may also serve as a textual embodiment of this necessary struggle.

The provocatively titled collection *De-scribing Empire* was published in 1994, the year after *Remembering Babylon*'s appearance. In the concluding text of that collection, noteworthily titled 'Reading Difference', editors Tiffin and Lawson laud 'the resilience and ingenuity of textuality in eluding forms of constraint and control'.[31] This statement affirms implicitly the existence of a diversified body of contemporary texts, in which each text in its own way counters, eludes, and thus counters, the representational limitations imposed by the power systems of its social world. It may be that by reading differently, by reading for difference differently, one could ascribe to *Remembering Babylon* a portion of the resilience and ingenuity Tiffin and Lawson so hearteningly evoke. In this way Malouf's own creative endeavour would align itself with his principal theme, self-overcoming. For the individual – including the individual author – for the community, even for the nation, self-overcoming finds, perhaps even creates, a new place of being and also a new time of life. Malouf's principal commitment to his ethics of memory is just here. But one must note quickly that ethically driven memory does not restore an imaginary selfhood, an imaginary homeland. Memory's creative role is to unsettle, to unbalance. Memory, whether individual or collective, does not restore us, reassuringly, to what we were; it challenges us with disarming recognitions of what we have not quite been but might still become.

The Conversations at Curlow Creek

The Conversations at Curlow Creek clearly follows from its distinguished predecessor, opening upon the question, 'What is it in us, what is it in *me*, that we should be so divided against ourselves, wanting our life and at the same time afraid of it?' (*CCC*, 3). However, *Remembering Babylon* is principally focused upon the problem of apprehending, then learning to value, difference or otherness within the processes of self-fashioning; whereas *Conversations* organises itself much more around defamiliarising the familiar, showing the gaps of darkness and strangeness that inform relationships of assumed intimacy and examining the ensuing problem of self-knowledge. The novel treats its opening question seriously and accepts that a human life, that human lives, must be ordered in relation to the question's ultimate insolubility: we are 'divided against ourselves' (that is, against oneself and against one's fellows), and this abiding division is marked by opposing movements, alternating or simultaneous, of desire and fear. Thus, the new novel reproblematises the concerns of *Remembering Babylon*, resolving itself upon the cleansing, which is also an inaugural baptism, of the unceasingly divided human animal.[1]

Working from Stephen Slemon's assertion that, particularly in the context of settler societies, 'literary writing is about internalized conflict', Borg Barthet argues that Malouf's 1996 novel represents 'the entanglement of anti-colonial resistance with imperial power'.[2] This entanglement and its perturbatory consequences are most immediately evident in relation to the experience and representation of gender. Masculine gender identity, its uncertainty and instability, becomes a more pressing concern than ever previously in Malouf. Langhurst is early revealed as a blusher and, what is perhaps worse, a bleeder. His possession of an orifice that bleeds – his nose specifically – strikes him as rather less than manly. His main mate, Garrety, clearly finds something dubious in Langhurst's generally anxious concern with his body and its vulnerabilities. But Langhurst's gender uncertainty manifests itself most clearly around the topic of his twin sister and his dog. His close resemblance to a female has been, particularly in childhood, 'a great torment to him – the only one he had ever known' (CCC, 19). His significantly female shaggy dog Nellie is his erstwhile constant companion, part familiar spirit and part lover – it is absent Nellie to whom he calls in his sleep. His attachment to this female dog 'whose spirit, he believed, was somehow continuous with his own' (CCC, 22), is at least partly compensatory – a way of dealing with the female twin whose place in his sense of self he cannot quite assign. Although the troopers require of themselves a hard and unambiguous masculinity, Langhurst's case is not entirely peculiar. The metaphors by which the troopers account for their fond alliances are spousal, as one sees when Kersey describes himself and Snelling as 'a couple of old married men' or Langhurst and Garrety as 'an old married couple' (CCC, 118).

Adair also has his place in the assembly of ambiguities Malouf builds around gender identity. Adair is Fergus's mother throughout the younger boy's early childhood. As if to underscore this troubling of conventional assumptions about gender identity, Malouf ascribes to Virgilia a nervy squeamishness about the plain and dirty facts of childcare. Faced with an infant Fergus in need of changing Virgilia is first 'aggrieved' and withdraws to 'a safe distance'; she subsequently shows 'a mild disgust' and only at last some small portions of 'curiosity' and 'envy'. Adair, meanwhile, pursues not only the actions but the thoughts and feelings of a mother, taking pleasure in 'these moments of intimacy' and revelling in the idea of 'How completely, while he worked, Fergus was his' (CCC, 83). And one should note finally that Virgilia, who is not naturally and immediately inclined to motherhood, is on the other hand the 'prime mover' and the 'authority' in her relationship with Adair (*CCC*, 86) – and this same Adair will eventually pursue the ostensibly ultra-masculine career of a military man.

This new register of gender uncertainty and ambiguity – effectively a breakdown of gender conventions – coincides with a much increased emphasis on the body as the main site of human experience. The body is the unstable locus of identity, but it is also the only real, continuous locus identity can find. Adair loves and yet resists the body's 'secret dedication to disorder' (*CCC*, 145). His body consistently confounds his will to be civilised and self-sovereign, but he cannot get round his sense that this same body is 'his way into the world' (*CCC*, 145). The sexual drive is the aspect of bodily life that he feels most acutely – and Malouf presents sex as very much a bodily expression, an embodied arousal responding to an other's embodied calling-into-relationship. Adair repeatedly attempts, and repeatedly fails, to elude or resist the body's exigencies. Such struggles leave him in a state of perplexed desire, an eminently civilised state of being in which desire's object is neither accepted nor relinquished, achieved nor repudiated. (Ironically, Adair is most civilised in his sense of his failure to be civilised.) The young Adair inhabits a body 'all turmoil, all disorder, blind lust'. It is not, however, the intensity of his drives but his failure to be at one with them that specifies his character. Adair contrasts with Fergus, a high-born child of nature who enjoys easy-going physicality and sexuality, but still more sharply with the nature-aligned character who is not born to privilege, the trooper Garrety. Garrety's sense of heterosexuality is simplicity itself: of women, he knows only that it is 'a grand thing, any chance you got, to fuck them' (*CCC*, 13). All but untouched by civilised demands for physical and sexual self-restraint, Garrety has little or no sexual imagination – of which Adair is abundantly possessed.

Adair's adolescent desire for the serving girl he sees cleaning a staircase is Malouf's most graphic portrayal of male hetero-sexual desire. It produces a sexual intoxication without direct fulfilment; it focuses exclusively on carnal details, but collects these as a stock of invested images: 'her dirty footsoles', 'the light of her thighs', 'her raised rump' and (due to her headcold) the 'moist sound of mucus in her nose' (*CCC*, 143). The last of these details is the most exquisite, as its allure is so clearly a work of imagination: the young man must associate metonymically the moistness in the nose with the moistness he would hope to find between the luminous thighs. The crucial aspect of the rendering of the desired object, however, is that it is remembered; the images have not been acted upon but stored up. These then obtrude upon – this is their role, and the body's role – the process of the young man's civilisation. While Eamon Fitzgibbon discourses on the creation of a 'just world of perfect reason and order' (*CCC*, 144), young Adair is beset by 'the need to relieve himself savagely of the vision of that girl's thighs'. Striking upon an image that is physical and yet unformed (the image of a lump), he sees himself as 'lumpishly untransformed' (*CCC*, 145).

Adair's troubled history of desire is variously detailed, including his confused passion for Virgilia and also his experience of Mama Aimee's impetuous, desperate huggings, which are 'dreaded', but also 'hotly longed for' (*CCC*, 51). In Malouf, close encounters with women are quite frequently unsettling for male psychologies.[3] And yet, in *Conversations*, one may say that this unsettling power is more crucially an aspect of bodies. The press of Aimee's body disturbingly blends the smells of tears and liquor. But one should also note that Carney's unignorable bodily presence disturbs Adair at least as much as Aimee's disturbed the child he once was. Moreover, the embodied turbulence of adolescence is not restricted to Adair, the main male case, but extended in an important scene to Virgilia, whose desire for Fergus is legible, for Adair, as an assembly of bodily signs. She stares at the sleeping Fergus with 'a dreamlike fixity': 'Her lips were parted. Her teeth glistened. She looked, Adair thought, as if she were drugged' (*CCC*, 100).

Conversations sets up an early division between 'nature' and 'the law' (*CCC*, 7), which extends itself subsequently to a division between eros and civilisation. Consistently, the life of the body, and its preponderant impact upon the general shape of human experience, are unambiguously aligned with nature and eros, but one finds also that civilisation and the law seek to lay claim to the body's life, to curb, contain, and govern. Of the two configurations of social force, the law is certainly the grimmer antagonist: it is unjustly selective in its applications; it meets the body's insubordination with physical force that restrains or violates, and claims ultimately the right to extinguish the body's life. Ultimately, the 'other condition' of the human being, which contrasts with and opposes the holy fullness of embodied life, will be the 'insufficient law' (*CCC*, 219).

Civilisation, however, presents a more ambiguous case. Adair is 'always aware of limits'; whereas Virgilia, perhaps even more than Adair a product of enlightened civilising education, 'accept[s] no limits' (*CCC*, 72). This is surely more Virgilia's concept of herself than a plain, true statement of her character. One may recall the scene at the Park (the novel's ideal seat of civilisation), in which the two boys, Adair and Fergus, wade deeply in the slimy, fish-teeming water of the lake, while Virgilia's deportment is curiously divided between freedom and restraint: she is 'bare-legged, with her skirt daintily lifted', but she does not venture beyond 'the shallows along the shore' (*CCC*, 86). Virgilia's lies, however, her tales of chance-met wonders with which she confounds Adair, arise from the young girl's 'spirit of idealism' (*CCC*, 75). They show that her temperament, her deeper will, and her values are against limits, though she does in many instances conform to the civilised codes of femininity. Yet limit is not simply constriction and confinement; it is also a matter of measure and proportion, and thus links favourably with Enlightenment values, such as those that yield the valorisation of 'Clockwork' (*CCC*, 80). The civilised ethic represented by Eamon Fitzgibbon seems to be to use measure and proportion, ultimately to 'use time well', so well as to surpass limits and enter into the hallowed realm of 'Freedom and Joy' (*CCC*, 82).

Returning then to the cases of Adair and Virgilia, and one could add Fergus to the mix, it seems that civilisation need not be, in all cases, the repressive modern apparatus that it seems to be, in the main, for Adair. The law is invariably against embodied life, but the law and civilisation are not congruent. Civilisation seems never directly to oppose bodily life, though bodily life frequently resists or opposes civilisation. The notably civilised, post-Enlightenment understanding of the body as an organic machine or engine is powerfully present again in *Conversations*, as it is in '12 Edmondstone Street'. The body, in an early mention, is occupied with 'its business of pumping blood, pouring out heat, supplying sap' (*CCC*, 5). It is elsewhere presented as a dumbly patient, tirelessly labouring, essentially admirable animal. But the body in nature is different from and more attractive than the somewhat lumpy organism the perspective of civilisation reveals – and at times, rather treacherously disparages. While watching ants swarming on an oak's trunk in preparation for a rainstorm, Adair becomes aware of connectedness and similarity, not difference. He recognises 'how crowded and complex his own body was' (*CCC*, 90). Similarly, the spontaneous sensuousness marking his experience of the rainstorm in Virgilia's company arises from the sense that the wash of heavy rain sets the two young people temporarily 'outside the permitted and the ordinary' of civilised life (*CCC*, 91). Water's purgative power, one should note, will also organise much of the novel's narrative resolution.

Access to the experience of nature is not, however, the most important consideration in determining an individual's relationship with the work of civilisation. Neither Fergus nor Virgilia gives evidence of experiencing civilising education as a significant impediment to self-actualisation. Fergus learns to go against social convention, and eventually against the law, but never manifests doubt as to the rightness of his feelings and impulses. In Virgilia's case, civilising education contributes appreciably to her self-assurance and to her building of a coherent sense of self. Both Virgilia and Fergus, however, are securely placed, even privileged, with respect to social standing. Adair's self-scrutiny and self-doubt, his sense of his own dividedness and inadequacy, are consistently linked to the tenuousness of his social placement, as a loosely adopted orphan in a relatively distinguished household. The problem of class accounts for much of his uneasy relationship with life and with his intimates, and more particularly, his tendency to see his body and body-centred drives as adversarial rather than empowering. Malouf evidently sees that the civilising process, and the Enlightenment that does so much to organise it, are uneven in the distribution of their benefits – just as the law is in the extension of its protections.

In the course of his career, Malouf has faced some criticism with respect to his critical awareness of class. Wallace-Crabbe offers an early assertion of the author's 'deep-laid conservatism', both of vision and of form.[4] Sharrad, with a much fuller view of the overall career, still finds some limitation in what he sees as Malouf's middle-class perspective.[5] The 1996 novel, however, is alert about questions of class and goes so far as to denounce, implicitly, the violence that inheres in class-based social divisions. The case against classism has Adair as a focal point, but not as the main one. Carney, in this respect, is more revelatory.

Carney's masquerade-for-pay, performed for a blind girl on an estate near Limerick, is probably the most startling and insolubly cryptic episode in the novel. Carney is clearly called upon to impersonate someone previously known to the girl, probably a family member – also perhaps a potential suitor. But the family's motive in setting up the illusory encounter remains a mystery. Is the girl inconsolable about a recent death, a real loss that Carney's impersonation is intended to deny? Is there some question of a family legacy, teetering undecidedly, in which the girl has a fulcrum role? Most probably the mystery's insoluble character is part of its point. A personal history is likely to have its moments of deep shadow, and this is more particularly the case if one is, like Carney, a member of an underclass, a man accustomed to being moved, directed, instructed by others more powerful and possessed of means. Carney's underclass status is immediately emphasised. He situates his tale in his history as an agricultural day-labourer, revealingly observing, 'It was best, you know, to look – as if you wouldn't give trouble.' Once engaged, on rather strange terms, he concedes, 'I was there to be hired. I couldn' do nothing but follow' (*CCC*, 63). This felt lack of agency and authority leads on to the representation of Carney as, socially speaking, nothing but body, nothing but a hireable, manageable hunk of flesh and energy, rather like 'the bull with a ring through its nose' that he sees upon arriving at the estate. The clothing covering this workable body does nothing to dignify it – 'I was all rags' – and Carney therefore is summarily stripped, then scrubbed. (A dark irony will overtake this first instance of Carney's being startlingly clean; the second instance is on the morning of his death.) Carney then receives 'a gentleman's clothes', still bearing the trace of another wearer upon them (CCC, 64). His final instruction, just before the meeting with the girl, is a command 'to do and say nothing', a quite complete suppression of agency. This command to remain passive and silent, to say nothing during the meeting nor ever after anything about it, is the most telling aspect of the assignment; it completes Carney's social delineation as nothing but body. The silence and passivity of soulless flesh accords perfectly with his social status and entirely conforms with the unquestioning docility expected of him. Ironically, his reward is to be 'a sovereign' (CCC, 65); he will receive a sovereign for relinquishing his self-sovereignty.

Malouf, in his handling of Carney, presses close to what Giorgio Agamben (1998) conceives as 'nuda vita', bare or naked life, an ancient notion with very specific applications, which modern power generalises, to strip or disinvest human beings of human status and thus to place them outside the realm of social protection the human being inhabits by right. But for Malouf, the body is precisely where agency and the priority of personhood reside when these have been expunged from every other quarter of a human life. The gentleman's clothes fit Carney quite well, except for the shoes that pinch. These pinching shoes are the first sign of Carney's body's resistance to domination, the first sign that Carney's resistance is centred in his body. Once he is in the presence of the blind girl, this resistance – the body's refusal to be obscured in its specificity – becomes more acute. Carney's heart beats wildly, which he fears will give him away. Then he sweats profusely and feels convinced that his distinct personal odour will surely disclose the ruse. But still more significant is his body's fuller coming into being in response to the blind girl's searching touch: the imposter feels the contacted parts of him 'light up' and 'glow' (*CCC*, 68). Finally, Carney's 'stiff cock' confirms that the body retains its sovereignty, even if the man does not. And yet this truth of himself, which is his body's truth, remains out of reach. Indeed, it is quite clear that the social world, with its hierarchies, strategically alienates Carney from this truth. Carney never knows if he has been recognised, if the blind girl knew his body as his and as him.

Carney's name already links the character with fleshly, or carnal, knowledge and experience. Carney's role as focal point in a broadly drawn economy of bodies lends credence to Taylor's conviction that *Conversations* represents the body 'as the site and origin of a comprehensive identity – both personal and national'.[6] The body is the first realm of the proper, 'the primary metonymy of place',[7] the first place where one always must be if one is to be anywhere else at all. But 'convicts were no longer British subjects according to law but human property of the Crown'.[8] Most convicts transported to Australian penal colonies had offended against property: in other words, their offence against propriety is an offence against property, and thus a reminder of how closely these two ideas are linked. Civilisation is thoroughly, inescapably material in its most essential manifestations; it describes, and also prescribes, the proper articulation of a body's relation with other bodies, with pertaining objects and with place. Australia, however, is a nation whose original human building blocks typically were both displaced and dispossessed of themselves. To *be* property rather than owning it, to be stripped of the claim to be one's own (which must precede any claim to havings that are one's own), to be both forcefully appropriated and forsaken – such conditions of being are peculiar ingredients for the eventual concoction of a national identity. But one must note that Adair perceives in Carney a 'settled savagery' (*CCC*, 32). This teasingly oxymoronic phrase deftly sketches a possible form for colonial (and eventually postcolonial) Australian subjectivity. Carney resists, is obliged to resist, social control and civilised domestication, and yet he has, in a strange and seemingly inhospitable land, established a place for himself; he has made the place into his own place. His case is just one more in evidence that, in Australia, 'the earth had taken the unaccustomed seed' (CCC, 59).

Fergus is another who cannot situate himself within the social systems of property and propriety; however, he confronts these systems from the opposite end of the social hierarchy. Maes-Jelinik affirms that Fergus's development is orientated upon, and manifests, his 'ontological oneness with nature',[9] which goes some way to explaining a character increasingly at odds with social order and constraint. Folkloric conceptions of the natural world's mystery and power colour Fergus's life from start to finish. He begins as a wood-spirit or changeling, 'uncanny', tearless, with luminous skin and a gripping blue-eyed gaze – 'an angel maybe, maybe the opposite' (CCC, 54). He graduates to the status of young centaur, long-legged, wild-maned, impetuous and independent, his entire nature 'deeply attuned to the nature and being of horses' (CCC, 92). Finally, he fulfils his mythic destiny by becoming another of Australia's heroically styled bushrangers, a new version of Jack Donahoe or Ben Hall or Ned Kelly, and thus returning to the woods, or at least the 'bush', from which he first emerges. A main structuring device of Malouf's story is the step-by-step bringing together of Fergus, the man of breeding, name and property, with Dolan, the rough outlaw struck down in a sudden ambush and buried in an unmarked grave in an unnameable place. As with the case of Adair and Carney, however, it is not Fergus but Garrety, the underclass character, who best reveals the man-of-nature's opposition to the rule of law.

Garrety role as a liminal figure is first announced by Langhurst's sense of him as 'a clean, quick animal' (CCC, 12). He is an animal that, unlike Langhurst, is well adjusted to being an animal; an animal that, although 'clean', has an animal's strong, distinguishing smell. Quite promptly, the text records Garrety's 'dark, almost gypsy features' (CCC, 20), then affirms that he is 'as good a tracker as any black' – indeed, 'uncanny' in his skill (*CCC*, 26). Even Jonas is 'spooked', and one learns that 'Garrety's knowledge came from a source that [Jonas] did not care to recognise' (*CCC*, 27). The suggestion here is that Garrety has somehow struck upon mystical and sacred forms of Aboriginal knowledge and that Jonas does not wish to acknowledge such a possibility. Garrety, the preternaturally skilful interpreter of nature and landscape, is to be read as a crossover phenomenon in relation to culture, even as he will ultimately be a crossover case in his relation to the law. He knows the land better than any white man should and even testifies to an occasional initiation into the dream-time, as when he finds himself in a paddock, on an ordinary afternoon, suddenly wading in blood. He realises, 'I'd stepped into a place where something terrible had happened, or was goin' t' happen' (*CCC*, 125).

The Garrety who lies down, prematurely but prophetically, in a freshly dug grave is curiously Christlike. The details of his presentation – his long hyper-extended body, with 'every bone in his rib-cage visible above the concave belly' (*CCC*, 207), with salient cheekbones and hollow cheeks and an almost smile – recall the crucifixion figures of Flemish masters. The 'shine' of his face also conforms, as does the notion of his rising 'replenished', as if resurrected (*CCC*, 208). Certainly, the Garrety engraved in Langhurst's memory – 'hanging there on his elongated frame, then rising' (*CCC*, 210) – is unmistakably Christological. Such imagistic suggestion sustains a sense that Garrety's later crossover, and eventual death, will be a salutary sacrifice. Perhaps, in making sense of Australian colonial history, one must recognise that the saviour and the thief, immolated together, are in fact one, inseparable – or at least differently inflected versions of the same story. The figure of the sinner-saint or angelic animal also orders the conclusion of Carney's story, which images the condemned man bathing in a living stream, with 'sunlight on his shoulders and hair' (*CCC*, 216), his cleansed body ultimately 'dazzling' enough to renew the onlooker Langhurst's faith in 'the freshness and sanctity of things' (*CCC*, 218).

Garrety is also important as a hinge-figure bringing white colonial Australia into relationship with Aboriginal Australia.

Jonas's textual career follows Garrety's very closely. The very first mention of Jonas, bracketed between the earliest characterisations of Garrety, gives a basic statement of colonial Australian race thinking. The text blandly affirms that this black trooper and guide 'did not count' (*CCC*, 10) – in the plain sense of not being counted in the troop, not really being one of the group that numbered four (white) men before Snelling's death, and three after. Interestingly, however, almost all subsequent developments of the Aboriginal character arise as if in counterpoint to developments of Garrety. A brief account of Jonas's look-out duties immediately precedes the account of Garrety's uncanny scouting skill. And of course, Garrety's recounting of his dreamtime experience arouses a distressed, and very eerie, 'high-pitched wailing' from the previously silent, all but invisible Jonas (*CCC*, 125). Garrety and Jonas seem to be very intimately *in relationship*, although neither one is willing to acknowledge the fact. Malouf's conception of the two characters is ordered by the conviction, already amply deployed in preceding works, that one knows a place by inhabiting it, by deeply inhabiting it. The innovation of *Conversations* is in Malouf's according more *independent* capacity for inhabiting to a white Australian – more than ever previously, and as much capacity, seemingly, as an Aboriginal character can claim. Gemmy, in Malouf's preceding novel, reveals a marked capacity for inhabiting, but he acquires it through Aboriginal guidance and acculturation. Still earlier, in *Blood Relations* (1988), Malouf had strongly presented a race-inflected sense of subjectivity and difference. Part-Aboriginal Dinny declares to his white father, 'It's my skin, Willy. You're not in it' (*BR*, 66). In *Conversations*, by contrast, the shape and content of subjectivity are not so much a matter of race as of place, not of being in a certain skin but of a specific being in the world. Garrety's special capacities evidently arise out of the confluence of his special temperament with the land he inhabits – and without significant Aboriginal input in his formation. But Garrety's close alliance with the Australian land, although ostensibly autonomous, nonetheless sets him, like the Aborigine, at odds with the dominant forces in Australian social evolution. He will discover himself, and his violent death, as an outsider and outlaw.

Colonial Australian society in some instances conforms to and colludes with the governmental authorities and their 'lesser' and 'insufficient' law (*CCC*, 199, 219). The limited vision of the folk – again one can perceive Malouf's distrust of the human collective – is first manifested when rebel-cohort Luke Cassidy's body is put on display in a country pub. The local populace discovers a rare opportunity,

> to stare at a real bushranger, his jaw tied up with a strip of torn shirt, where it had been shot away taking with it most of his teeth: a sight fearsome enough to satisfy the imagination of the most pious shopkeeper or industrious freeholder as to the malignity of outlaws and the wisdom of the authorities in having them hunted down and exterminated. (*CCC*, 31)

One is immediately reminded of the child Ovid's confrontation with the hacked-off head of a wolf. Here, as in that earlier story, Malouf represents the other's horrifying aspect as a production of violence – not the other in its own autonomous being but the other violated, in imagination and in fact. The spectacle of the mutilated Luke Cassidy is not, however, an isolated instance of the violated other, of othering through violation. The same thematic is evident from the earliest presentation of Daniel Carney, whose abject body – the breath 'rackety, broken with phlegm', the eye 'puffed and closed', the flesh bruised, bloodied, sour and filthy (*CCC*, 4-5) – is a production of a violent beating and a virtually unattended confinement. The novel's presentation of the bushranger or runaway or rebel is closely linked with the figure of the convict, whose body, in Turcotte's view, 'is the abject component of the European self'.[10] But one must recall that the abject element is abjected, rendered abject; it is a production, not an accidental misfortune. If Adair draws, as he does, a personal, developmental profit from his encounter with Carney, it is precisely because he is able, finally, to identify with the abject other. Such identification, quite frequent in Malouf, goes against the typical function of abjection in identity formation, in which the self seeks to consolidate itself by isolating, alienating and expelling its abject components. By recognising and even admiring the unconquerable vitality of Carney's damaged and repellent flesh, Adair is able to work through, and hopefully past, a lifelong history of disciplined resistance to the body's urgent hungers. Adair's response, however, is individual and uncommon; he is another of those few who respond creatively to the other's appeal.

The collective consciousness of colonial Australian society seems for the most part to be dominated and directed by power, by constituted colonial authority, but the collective unconscious is not. The unconscious is strongly marked by the ambivalent play of illicit dreams and desires, and seems to resist or elude authoritative social control, at least in some of its movements. In this respect, it counters the obfuscating and misleading discourses of power, the 'lyin'' which Carney denounces as 'just a way of holdin' us down' (CCC, 58). Malouf's story ends upon the remaking of Adair by the folkloric imagination, and of course the work of the popular mind is already pertinent to the conception of the fearsome yet darkly alluring bushranger. Various elements of fear and wonder find their way into the rumour-forged story of the 'more romantic, more outrageous' Adair, who is now 'of the devil's party' (CCC, 223), a convict's redeemer rather than his executioner. The small stream at Curlow Creek becomes Australia's fabulous inland sea; a boatful of renegades disguised as natives appears; a 'shadow Sydney' rises up and prospers in what had been the barren wastes of the continent's interior. Such details do not pertain to power's story, and they affirm, moreover, that power's story is not the only one, nor even the best one. Popularly generated narrative stops well short of Carney's terse denunciation of the ruses of the powerful, but it manifests significant degrees of resistance and clearly is sustained by the recognition that authoritative discourse never provides a whole story. A notably utopian urge characterises the folk narrative. It is a forging 'of what was not but ought to have been true' (CCC, 224); it looks toward a world of richer potential than that which the grim facts of history would make. If Malouf's Australia here appears as 'a repository of human illusions',[11] it is nonetheless clear that this character has its beneficial as well as detrimental aspects.

Yet Malouf does not see this cultural work of story production as distinctively Australian. One first confronts a 'world of folk-tales and old pagan superstitions' in Ireland, at Ellersley, and thus the text's implication may be that the energy of the Australian folk-imagination is in large part another aspect of Australia's Irish legacy. Thus, the name Adair is converted to O'Dare and gives expression to an almost parodic extremity of Irish derring-do. The O'Dare story is 'like all good stories, an old one in a new form' (*CCC*, 223), an Australian 'embodiment of Irish effrontery' (like the Irish bushranger-rebel), and one that the folk mind seems to steal from out of Adair's own dream. This dream may be a dream of place, engendered and nourished by imaginative response to the power of place, and for this reason key elements of Adair's unconfessed dream – the teeming inland sea, the strange boatmen, the promised release of 'a more obscure, endangered self' (*CCC*, 191) – find their place in the spontaneously generated Australian folk tale. But even so, one must note a kind of cross-fertilisation: Australia means a certain something to an Irishman, and the Irishman contributes a certain something to the meaning of Australia for Australians. Hassall argues that, for Adair and by extension for the European migrant, Australia emerges by the end of Malouf's novel as 'a therapeutic dream underworld where imported conflicts can be resolved and scripts rewritten in positive terms'.[12] This is quite true, but an incomplete truth. Adair and other migrant visitors do imaginatively remake Australia in accord with imported projects and concerns, but the importations and the imaginings do participate in very real ways in the making of Australia.

Malouf's thought and imagination maintain, in *Conversations*, the relational and transactional aspects established in earlier works, which necessitates a careful evaluation of Andrew Taylor's startling suggestion that what is new in the 1996 novel is that 'wholeness is now the realisation and totalisation of identity, not its other'. One must question whether wholeness should be understood in this way, and indeed whether 'whole-ness' is the right word for the state of being at which Adair (or any other of the novel's characters) arrives. That which is new and different, in relation to Malouf's preceding works, is acceptance, of the self and of the social world, of the tensions, contradictions, misguidedness and bedevilling multifacetedness that inhere in both the personal and the social realms. Adair, to take him as the key example, is hardly whole at the novel's end, though he bears with him the hope of a more integrated future life. He is, as he has always been, divided between his personal sense of self and his socially assigned identity – between Adair and O'Dare, to use the novel's own final way of specifying this division. But, crucially, Adair makes his peace with this division, accepts it as his human lot. Malouf's typifying distrust of the human collective, of which Adair clearly has his share, is also met with greater acceptance, even with a certain good humour: the human world is a mixed bag, containing both good and bad; one learns to live with it, as one must. Working from this sense of acceptance, one can then see that the novel's resolution contains another new key point of emphasis, something very like whole-ness, but which would be better named as communion. In so naming the newly emphasised element, however, one reaffirms the decisive importance of others and of the other, rather than putting the other aside in favour of a newly valorised 'realisation and totalisation' of individual identity.

The 'warm, spoiled loaf', in the eating of which Adair finally finds 'a kind of blessing', is perhaps Malouf's most optimistic expression of the relationship of the individual to the collective. Communion and community, the desire for them and their real availability, are affirmatively evoked. Yet the old ambivalence is still evident: the loaf is spoiled, after all, and it is *a kind of* blessing rather than a blessing plain and simple. (One recalls the 'mixed blessing' of commonplace and communal experience in *The Great World*.) Even the taste of the loaf is both salty and sweet, a kind of divided or contradictory experience, and yet 'refreshing' (*CCC*, 232). Bread, however, is a basic metonym for flesh. Indeed, it is the flesh-symbolising food by which one achieves communion. Thus Adair, by eating of his spoiled loaf, emerges out of his alienation into commonality and communion – the whole deeply shared realm of human experience; he also, in the same moment, in the same act, returns peaceably and pleasurably to that body, his own, from which he has been on the run for the entire duration of his narrative life. Finding or recreating the body, as much as finding or recreating community, is certainly among the novel's core concerns. Although the body, as an ordering theme, is contingent with the theme of community, it is not subordinate. Mending the body disarticulated by social prohibitions and regulations seems in fact to be a necessary preparation for a meaningful communion with one's fellows. Principally, and most fundamentally, it is *as* bodies – as whole integrated bodies – that we commune.[13]

The short stories

'A Medium', the final story of the *Antipodes* collection, offers a statement about narrative that is generally useful in dealing with Malouf's short fiction: 'There is no story, no set of events that leads anywhere or proves anything – no middle, no end' (*A*, 160). Significantly, there *is* invariably a beginning for every story; only the progressive, teleological development, through the middle to the end, is dismissed as illusory. A story then is a matter of beginning; one may even say a story is all beginning. This critical, theoretical position becomes particularly interesting once one recognises that one of the author's most typical short-fiction themes is coming of age. And in Malouf's narratives of coming of age – this is especially true in the later collection *Dream Stuff* – the focal characters characteristically do not come of age, do not move cleanly, unambiguously into more clearly mapped, more stable and secure modes of being. They carry across the threshold at least a portion of their former confusions and ambivalences.

The imaginative territory of 'Southern Skies' is similar to that of '12 Edmondstone Street'. The central family is set apart, subculturalised, by the parents' adherence to old-world values, which the son of the family feels obliged to resist. The problem of adolescence has a quite conventional shape, but is handled with subtlety and sensitivity, and engagingly linked with questions of cultural migrancy from old to new worlds. (The relationship between old Europe and new Australia is an ordering concern of *Antipodes*, though it receives little attention in *Dream Stuff*.) The young narrator anxiously, eagerly, waits 'for life somehow to declare itself', but no such declaration, no great glorious event ever occurs. He fears that the field of the world's possibilities may be narrower than he hopes; therefore, he doesn't wish 'to discover the limits of the world'. At the same time he feels trapped within himself, within the closely circumscribed concerns – 'my vanity, my charm, my falseness, my preoccupation with sex' (A, 13) – that compose his sense of self. Presented, in an important moment, with photographs of the 'Old World' known to his parents and to the Professor, the young man is unable to make the passage into a realm of experience that is new and different, but which is also, ironically, the place of his birth and the very foundation of his personal heritage. The problem is recognisably adolescent: 'No matter how hard I tried to think my way out into other people's lives, into the world beyond me, the feelings I discovered were my own' (A, 18). Yet this problem is also of abiding import in Malouf, linking with much of the author's other work by emphasising the need for self-overcoming and transformation, for breaking away from the established forms of self and 'out into' other worlds, other lives.

In Malouf one tends quite frequently to move from one unstable, unmastered version of self into another. Thus, when the boy looks through the Professor's telescope and discovers a world that seems, gloriously, to be without limits, he nonetheless fails to solve his genealogical problem. The Professor, who represents the virtues and shortcomings of the 'Old World', offers himself, in the classical Greek manner, as both mentor and lover. Yet, due no doubt to the limitation of his own grasp of the situation, the Professor does not understand his action as the giving of knowledge and pleasure to another adult. The young man therefore is left feeling that he has made a crucial passage in his perception of his life and of himself, and yet that this passage brings him no closer to the Professor. His sense of alienation from the Professor remains unmended: he blissfully receives from the Professor his moment of 'bursting into the life of things'; however, he must bear away with him the burden of a 'misapprehension' he does not know how to set right, and rides off on his bicycle (the totem of his adolescence), 'bounc[ing] unsteadily' over uneven ground (*A*, 25). Both Indyk and Sharrad read the story too optimistically: Indyk sees 'two types of sexual initiation', but finds that the story finally favours 'homosexual initiation', which it represents in relation to a kind of 'cosmic rapture';[1] for Sharrad, more simply, 'Loss of childhood and an opening out into adult awareness are held together in a moment of grace'.[2] Yet even if the young protagonist has become, at story's end, more of an adult, he is no closer, it seems, to intimate understanding of the adults that share his world. He has seen himself 'from out there' (*A*, 24), from the perspective of the world's immensity, and this experience of himself as so very small and yet so inalienably a part of it all, of all that is, validates his being and liberates him from the constraining structures of the self, from the self as a constraining structure. But the space between himself and others, other people, remains a gap; in fact, the gap, if anything, widens.

Antipodes offers other stories that squarely confront the theme of coming of age. Gerry, the young man of 'Sorrows and Secrets', looks forward to a life-defining opportunity to show himself capable of 'noble action', but loses his way amid 'the variousness of the world and the number of paths open in each moment of it' (*A*, 50). His recognition finally is of 'the immensity of the darkness' that surrounds each of the world's 'individual fragments' (*A*, 53), of which he, unhappily, is one. Luke, in 'Out of the Stream', is occupied with 'the business of getting the body through and over into – ' (*A*, 83). The sentence's final dash is eloquent: the boy seeks a crossover into some new mode of life his adolescent confusion does not allow him to conceive clearly. Like Gerry, he resolves his story with a vision of darkness, a darkness that is just becoming somewhat familiar and thinkable, but that is nonetheless 'bigger than any ocean, bigger even than the sky with its scattered lights' (*A*, 85). Neither of these two young characters gives the impression of being doomed – and nor does the youth of 'Southern Skies' – but they do not manage to sort out and simplify the complexity of experience. In Malouf's view, this is not what maturation is, not how one matures. Life includes its moments of graduation, but one graduates, most typically, into new realms of difficulty and perplexity.

Other stories in *Antipodes* show aspects of the coming-of-age narrative, although their main thematic concerns are somewhat distinct from it. 'The Empty Lunch-Tin' examines a mother's abiding sense of absence and loss in relation to a son who died before coming of age. Both 'That Antic Jezebel' and 'Bad Blood' recount a failure to graduate effectively, to progress beyond the persona of one's youth. The stories of Australian experiences of Europe are notable in this respect. Cassie, in 'A Trip to the Grundelsee', discovers some obscure referent for her own inner gloom by glimpsing into some of Europe's darker aspects; her story ends with her adolescent daughters' ironically optimistic resolve: 'Europe was a place they would visit one day and see for themselves' (*A*, 35). In 'The Sun in Winter' a traveller from a young nation, Australia, encounters the representative of a European city that has witnessed, and in a measured sense outlived, its own agedness and death. The adult couple of 'A Change of Scene' worry insistently about what their child Jason has seen and understood of European violence, never really recognising that their own experience of this violence is itself a harrowing initiation, a rending of the unconsciously fostered membrane of their Australian innocence. But if coming of age is the archetypal instance of coming into new consciousness through trial, one can certainly make this more extended link with the whole *Antipodes* collection. 'The Only Speaker of his Tongue', for instance, counters the initiation of Australians in Europe, focusing on a northern European character whose ordeal is in the recognition of the scope of the violence exerted upon Aboriginal Australians, a violence that has decimated 'a whole alternative universe' (*A*, 69).

As suggested earlier, however, *Dream Stuff: Stories* shows a more consistent concern with coming of age – and with the failure to come of age. In this volume, coming of age is a mythology with which Malouf engages in order to disarticulate it. 'At Schindler's', the collection's first story, deals with coming of age most straightforwardly and optimistically, but even here the resolution is peculiar. Having acknowledged finally the loss

of his father, Jack recovers his place in the community of childhood, rather than turning immediately toward the adult world
(as one would expect him, conventionally, to do). On new terms,
he will rejoin the adults – his mother and Milt – awaiting him
at Schindler's, but his arrival will be 'not too late, not too early
either' (DS, 23). More immediately, he wishes to be with Arnold
and the other Garrett boys, as though his acceptance of difficult adult realities authorised an extension of the time of his
childhood. New knowledge gives him not the means to move
forward, but the inclination to hang back and to save what is
salvageable.

Jack enjoys and is enlivened by the 'broken continuities'
characterising the childhood and familial worlds of the seaside
community, and also by the 'temporary truth' that configures
their shifting alliances (DS, 9), but he resists the inscription of
these unstable patterns upon his own family and upon his deeper
understanding of himself. As in '12 Edmondstone Street' and The
Conversations at Curlow Creek, the body is the cryptic key to
experience, the main site of both clarity and confusion. Continuous only in its changefulness, it is the shape of oneself that one
is always growing into and growing out of at the same time. Jack
has a sense of 'his body as the immediate image of himself' and
therefore hopes to find in it the means of bridging discontinuity
and absence. He wishes to span with his own body the distance
between himself and his lost father, gone missing somewhere in
the south-east Asian tropics. The experience, he intuits, would
be self-fulfilling but also self-immolating: 'His limbs would be
stretched then across three thousand miles of real space till every
joint was racked, and he would experience at last the thing he most
hungered for' (DS, 9–10). Interestingly, Milt shares Jack's notion
of the body's centrality in matters of knowledge and experience.
An aspiring palaeontologist, he affirms that bodies have 'laws',
even 'a kind of – grammar – syntax' (DS, 11). (Unfortunately,
this ascription of terms such as 'grammar' and 'syntax' to the
simple, sensible Yank Milt somewhat strains verisimilitude of
characterisation.) Milt, however, also problematises Jack's sense
of a body-orientated order of things. Milt brings another body,

a distinctly different one, into the sphere of the family. For this reason, 'he unsettled the map Jack carried in his head' (*DS*, 13), becoming Jack's own and his mother's intimate, and thus taking the father's position in the layout of Jack's domestic world. Jack may share certain notions of the body with Milt, but he shares his actual body, his flesh and image, with his lost father – a fact that a lightning-illuminated mirror will reveal to him at the story's climax.

Milt's difference resides also in his being American, and thus for Jack the representative of a distant and dimly understood 'modernity' (*DS*, 15). In his whole mode of being, and most particularly in his being so entirely at home in his own flesh, Milt already inhabits a time and place in which Jack has yet to arrive – and in which he is not certain ever to arrive. This arrival, which would be a valid coming of age, is offered to Jack when he confronts Milt's most intimate claiming of the father's place. Watching the spectacle of the lovers' emphatically physical engagement with each other, Jack first recognises, and accepts, that the male partner is Milt and not his restored father, and then recalls his own experiences of 'a kind of freedom only his body had access to'. But if Jack finds something of himself and his life in the lovers' actions, he also sees, in a lightning-flash of recognition, his own isolation, his exteriority to the lovers' special carnal bond. As the mirror shows him, he stands apart, as his father does, from the intense connectedness he can only watch and witness. By taking up their shared bodily freedom, the lovers are distanced from Jack, not brought closer to him – they enter 'the far place to which their bodies had carried them'. Jack, for his part, becomes one with his father in a mirror image that is 'fantastically elongated' (*DS*, 21), thus recalling his earlier fantasy of stretching his body across space to reach his far-off father. Jack's coming into fuller consciousness about himself and his world has much the same character as that fantasy: it entails achieving what one deeply desires, but only by being stretched to breaking, tortured, 'racked' (*DS*, 9).

Jack's failure to come of age in a really self-fulfilling way is in keeping with the general thrust of *Dream Stuff*. Like Jack,

Amy of 'Closer' hopes to mend the uneasy circumstances of her childhood by restoring a lost (in this case banished) loved one, but she can only achieve her desire in a dream-vision, which she articulates at the very moment when her real loss is confirmed as definitive. The cadets of 'Night Training' unquestioningly accept that their innocence is 'appalling' (DS, 65), their youth 'ridiculous' (DS, 66) – so much so that both give in, with a quite entire passivity, to the violation of their youth and innocence. Sally, of 'Sally's Story', sees her young American clients as 'these boys, these men' (DS, 75), as though they are each of them suspended between boyhood and manhood. At times, they are 'little-mannish' and at times, unambiguously, they are 'these boys' and 'just boys' (DS, 76, 77). 'Jacko's Reach' recounts a community's attempt to disavow and obliterate a liminal space of youthful experience, which although it has been left behind, has remained unforgotten and unresolved. 'Lone Pine' focuses on two ageing characters who have failed somehow to take up their lives, to grow with and grow into their lives, and who die, murdered by hap, in the midst of their ineffectual attempt, finally, to live.[3] 'Great Day' tells of a family whose four adult and independent sons turn into 'boys again' when returning to their parental home (DS, 135). Angie, one of the sons' wives, also feels 'like a child' there (DS, 139). Her husband Ralph is introduced as 'a big fair fellow who had never grown out of the schoolboy stage of being all arms and legs' (DS, 140). Fran, formerly a wife of the Tyler clan, now divorced, is 'childlike, girlish or boyish, it was hard to say' (DS, 141). Her former husband, Clem, however, is the clearest example of the generalised eternal juvenility of the clan. Having confronted the figure of a child, playing chicken with him upon a benighted highway, he has crashed into confirmed childhood status. Well into his thirties he is impetuous and indulged, charmingly but worryingly unpredictable in his words and actions. The title story, 'Dream Stuff', however, presents the clearest instance of a protagonist's failure to come of age – indeed, of a whole life shaped by that failure – and its focal character is, ironically, an author, a maker of other lives but never of his own.

Novelist Colin Lattimer's story begins and ends with a desperate moment of childhood, in which Colin clings to a dying dog in that shadowy threshold space, the under-the-house, which is so tantalisingly and unsettlingly developed in '12 Edmondstone Street' and *Harland's Half Acre*. Intriguingly, the adult author's fictions share something of the under-the-house liminality; they present a 'mixture of openness and hidden, half-sought-for menace' (*DS*, 41). These fictions struggle ambivalently to remake in more manageable form the core memory of childhood, which is a tableau of grim suggestiveness and unresolved emotional strain:

> The occasion remained suspended at a point where he was still crammed into the close place under the floorboards, with the big dog warm in his arms and the whole weight of the house on his shoulders, while his father, dark-faced and wheezy with hay-fever, stretched a hand towards him, all the fingers tense to grasp or be grasped, and his brow greasy with sweat; as if he were the one who was trapped up there dying – the worm at his heart taking all his breath. (*DS*, 34–5)

This scene renders in condensed form all the key elements of Colin's refusal of his life – the too-close intimacies vying one against the other, the clinging to what one must lose and the reluctance to take up, and content oneself, with what remains. Mortality is ubiquitous: in the worm in the heart of the living dog, in the father's shortness of breath and sweaty brow (as if he is already in death throes), and in the boy's unwillingness to take the father's proffered hand, which he knows will close about his own and pull him into a world of finality and loss, of loss's finality. The basic themes of childhood's life-defining incident are recapitulated, in varied form, in Colin's young manhood. His guided tour of Athens, which should contribute to his sense of himself and his world, ends abruptly with the disappearance of his guide and thus offers a perfect short summary of a life without a coming of age: 'Things had been moving towards some event or revelation that at the last moment, for whatever reason, had been withheld' (*DS*, 41).

The unfulfilled, incomplete, under-defined character of Colin's life is thoroughly detailed. He is 'almost famous' (DS, 46). This 'almost' is crucial, it seems, because he repeatedly finds himself in situations where he is mistaken for someone else and his sense of himself is called into question. His self-elected Athens tour-guide 'seemed to have mistaken him for someone else' (DS, 39). The much later climactic incident of misrecognition in Brisbane begins with another Mediterranean man – 'Armenian, or Yugoslav' or 'Greek maybe, Lebanese' (DS, 53) – who presumes to offer himself as a guide, who presumes to know what Colin really wants, really is looking for. The half-mad stranger who subsequently waylays Colin brings a well-detailed private-life scenario providing Colin with a central role. The police who investigate the incident speak to Colin as if to 'a bemused and stubborn child' (DS, 53), as Colin's father had spoken to him when he refused to relinquish his mother's dying dog. These interrogators do not recognise Colin as an author – 'What sort of books, Colin?' – nor do they credit his claim to being 'local' – 'Didn't sound it' (DS, 54). Ironically, the police cannot believe that Colin is not wilfully involved, failing to recognise that a certain lack of wilful involvement typifies this man's character. Colin's account of himself, which the police find so dubious, is strangely consonant with the larger patterns of his life: he 'had stepped out of nowhere into a situation with which he had absolutely no connection' (DS, 54). Moreover, Colin comes to feel curiously at home in the false life that is foisted on him. In the distorting mirror of his jail cell, he reveals himself as 'a dead ringer of himself who for thirty years had lived a different and coarser life – maybe even that of the man he had been mistaken for' (DS, 56). Still more compellingly, when confronted finally with the woman with whom he has allegedly entertained a sexual affair, he feels 'a little shameful kick of desire' (DS, 59). Because Colin has never really laid claim to a life he might call his own, various lives seem to reach out to him, offering themselves, but he is never more than half able to take them up.

Throughout 'Dream Stuff' Colin, in relation to his own life, is shown to be one who is not quite there, halfway in and halfway out. Greenness, so powerfully evocative of life force, is represented ambivalently. The father's limited but psychologically troubling legacy has as its centrepiece 'a little green-bound pocket diary' (DS, 39). The green of Brisbane is first portrayed as 'Irresistible growth. Though it wasn't always an image of health or of fullness.' The 'green stuff' is also the 'dream stuff' (DS, 42), the marijuana associated with wonder, euphoria, but also with stupefaction, disorientation, loss of self. Whatever truth the green, dream-generating stuff reveals is linked with Brisbane's 'underground history'; it is 'an emanation in heavy light and in green, subaqueous air, of an aboriginal misery that no tower block or flyover could entirely obliterate' (DS, 43). The story's middle passages somewhat refresh its general mood, evoking 'the warm sunlight' of the young writer's 'Brisbane childhood'; indeed, the city of memory and imagination is 'brimming with sunlight'(DS, 44), a warm source of inspiration. And although Colin deplores the new Brisbane of steel, glass, and concrete, he senses that the light is unchanged and still offers 'the same promise of an ordinary grace' (DS, 36). This light, however, cannot entirely redeem the new Brisbane, whose less alluring details receive a quite insistent portrayal; the city of warm light is also the repository of 'the accumulated debris and filth of nearly a million souls' (DS, 58). Toward the end of the story, a even more unpleasantly suggestive version of Brisbane appears; in this final imaging Brisbane is once again 'out of sight, underground', and now 'Unkillably, uncontrollably green. Swarming with insects and rotting with a death that would soon once again be life, its salt light, by day, blinding to the eye and deadening of all thought, its river now, under fathoms of moonlight, bursting with bubbles, festering, fermenting' (DS, 61). The green of life is both rich and squalid and, for Colin at least, more squalid than rich.

When, in the story's final passages, Colin returns to the scene of childhood loss, one finally sees clearly the structure of Colin's failure – or is it a refusal? – to accept and take up the human life that is offered to him. The heart that gives 'a regular reassuring thump against his ribs' is, crucially, not his own; it is the dog's worm-gnawed but not yet failing heart (*DS*, 63). In Malouf's imagining, this is how it should be; this is the rightness of experience that Colin has lost and never recovered. The heart whose beating one feels most acutely should not be one's own; it should be the other's. The other's beating heart, the other's life, provides the key to one's own heart, the most illuminating connection to one's own life.

'Dream Stuff' is not an entirely successful story, but its shortcomings may be revelatory. Pierce affirms that Malouf is always alert to the social 'web of connections' that binds the human being, but adds that the world of dream, of organising importance in *Dream Stuff*, 'is essentially an antisocial or an asocial realm'. Extending from this primary observation, Pierce rightly notes in the collection's title story 'an uncertain control of working-class idiom': the ascription of words like 'feller' and 'gizzard' to Colin's late-twentieth-century urban Australian assailant is unconvincing, even 'discordant'. This stylistic problem manifests, in Pierce's view, Malouf's hedging of sympathy for 'fringe dwellers', and thus a disappointing 'shift of demeanor' and 'a sourer tone'.[4] This supposed waning of sympathy for Australian society's marginal elements may go some way to accounting for a curious randomness ascribed to acts of violence in Colin Lattimer's story, in 'Jacko's Reach', and in 'Lone Pine'. While being detained by police, Colin sees 'drunks, derelicts, young toughs' and 'young Aboriginals', all of whom the narrative voice characterises as 'the agents, or victims or both, of a violence that was random but everywhere on the loose' (*DS*, 56). The suggestion that violence, though 'random', arises among society's marginal elements and then spills out, as it were, beyond their ranks, must disturb some of the story's interpreters. One must wonder if this is meant to be a specific and subjectively limited rendering of Colin's view, which is compromised by his will to see his own encounter with violence as entirely senseless. But even so, the problem remains that other representations of violence as random occur in *Dream Stuff*. The narration of 'Lone Pine' looks toward the climactic random murder of two white suburbanites by remarking upon the migrant 'tribes' of Australia's highways, which include a boy in a passing car 'putting up two fingers in the shape of a gun and mouthing Bang, Bang, You're Dead' (*DS*, 103). 'Jacko's Reach' includes a character described as 'the sort of girl that acts of violence, which haunt the streets like ghosts on the lookout for a body they can fill, are deeply drawn to' (*DS*, 97). Again one must wonder if this natural association of violence with a certain version of femininity is to be ascribed only to the popular mind, the narrative 'we'.[5]

A faltering of style in Malouf's rendering of lower-class speech is quite clear, whether or not one accepts Pierce's interpretation of its meaning.[6] But the additional, potentially related problem of Malouf's representations of random violence is more difficult to judge. As suggested previously, the author may be representing a *misconceived* sense of randomness pertaining to the view of those members of society who are not marginal, who are relatively comfortable and who do not wish to see themselves, potentially, as intended victims. This more favourable evaluation receives some support from 'Blacksoil Country', *Dream Stuff*'s second last story, which presents violence as systemic rather than random, as the predictable expression of an unjust and divided society.

Indyk emphasises the problematic function of paternal legacies in Malouf's work. Certainly, Colin Lattimer's underdeveloped and unresolved relationship with his father is a key to his stunted character, but 'Blacksoil Country' presents a truly sinister version of paternity, the father who takes life from the son rather than giving it, which recalls but also intensifies the portrayal of Clem Harland in *Harland's Half Acre*. Jordan McGivern's father progresses fatally toward a murderous moment that is self-defining, self-consolidating, the moment of life in which he feels 'most sure of himself, most free' (*DS*, 125). Here is a violence that is anything but random; it is deeply motivated and delivers no less a reward than freedom. It is as if the father's fatal gunshot destroys not only the Aborigine it strikes down, but the 'nigger' the father perceives, yet disavows, in himself, the blackness of a humiliating servitude to which he had thought himself eternally condemned. The murder offers the father 'a new way of being inside his own skin' (DS, 126), a new way of inhabiting his world, and a new and astonishing social success. This social aspect of Pa's triumph confirms the systemic character of his violence; as Scheckter remarks, 'racist distinction' yields the strange fruit of 'solidarity and success in a harsh land',[7] though it should be added that the land's harshness is in large part created by the settler perception of it. The grace, however, that Pa takes up is taken from another, from the Aborigine he kills, and also from his own son, who has lived until this moment under the protection of a grace – Jordan calls it 'magic' – bestowed by the Aborigines. Jordon recognises that the murder has placed his family and himself 'outside the rules', and that the rules have always been 'their rules' (DS, 127) – Aboriginal rules, which stand beyond the white man's control both in their grace and in their punishments.

The crime against the Aborigine is also a crime against the land. 'Blacksoil Country' reproduces the wild, troubling land that *Remembering Babylon*'s Queensland settlers confront. It is uncannily occupied, 'crowded with ghosts'; it nags the settler with the sense of being 'watched or tracked' (DS, 116). As in the 1993 novel, the project of settlement has tenuous, undefined aspects: 'When we come it was to settle. To manage and work a run of a thousand acres, unfenced and not marked out save on a map that wouldn't have covered more than a square handkerchief of it and could show nothing of what it was' (DS, 116–17). In keeping with the settler community of *Remembering Babylon*, Pa assumes an aggressive, exclusionary stance: 'Ourselves and no other' (DS, 117). Yet, already in the metonymy of its naming, the land is Aboriginally black, and it is perhaps this inescapable association that disposes the father against the land, that leads him to hate his relationship with it. Obliged always to work land he does not own, the father feels he is being 'treated like a bloody nigger' (DS, 118). The father also shows some of Colin Lattimer's distaste for the land's greenness, for the stark force of life that is in it; he is pictured looking into the land, squinting into 'the glare of green' (DS, 121). For the mother too, the land poses

itself as a problem: she finds it is 'too far' from established settlement; she begins her part in the narrative refusing to consider
the land, 'as if it wasn't there' (*DS*, 121). Only Jordon responds
to the land's peculiar but powerful allure, finally uniting himself
with the land he loves, mixing in his 'white grains with its many
black ones'; his mother too learns from her loss, now 'raising
her eyes to the land and gazing off into the brimming heart
of it' (*DS*, 130). This sense of the world's fullness, a fullness it
reveals only to initiated eyes, comes at a strange moment and at
a strange cost. Jordon takes on the character of the glad martyr.
The brutal violence marking the story's progress, which culminates in the retributive decimation of local Aboriginal tribes, is
reconstrued as part of the process of the white settlers' inhabiting of the new land.

The story's resolution, which accepts violence as the paradoxical cost of settlement, and tacitly posits this acceptance on the
part of all *white* participants, tends to reproblematise Malouf's
more general representation of violence. Noteworthily, 'Blacksoil
Country' is the only story in *Dream Stuff* to reach further back
in time than the mid-twentieth century. *Antipodes* is also set in
the later twentieth century, with the sole exception of 'The Only
Speaker of his Tongue'. Both these exceptional cases consider and
condemn white Australia's violence against Aboriginal peoples,
but both also situate this violence in a relatively remote past. In
the stories of Australian contemporaneity, violence is typically
random – or at least is perceived in this way by the narrative
voices. One must therefore ask, is not contemporary violence
an extension of the legacy of past violence; and does Malouf,
in his stories, deliberately or inadvertently raise this question?
Certainly, Malouf's address to the question is deliberate and
searching in his 1993 novel, but it is not clear that he continues
to remember Babylon thoroughly throughout the course of his
career.

'Great Day', the final story of the *Dream Stuff* collection,
and by far the longest, works hardest to grasp and represent
Australia's modern character. Significantly, this story also gives
strongest expression to Malouf's continental consciousness, his

sense that the Australian nation is distinguished by its inhabiting of a continent. This notion is evident, in flashes, in other stories. The liminal space known as 'Jacko's Reach' reveals its symbolic and cultural importance partly by giving children (and thus also the adults who subsequently remember childhood experience) a primary sense of 'the three hundred million square miles' that compose Australia. In 'Lone Pine' Harry considers, in a trivial quizzical mood, the immense distances his paper run has carried him through – when cumulatively measured. But he later comes upon a more direct and disturbing sense of his country's daunting expansiveness, 'the distances, the darkness, the changes as you slipped across unmarked borders' (*DS*, 103). But in 'Great Day' a deranged but also an enlightened recognition of conti- nental consciousness marks Clem Tyler, who has this orientation of mind forced upon him by his near-fatal highway accident: 'the whole continent – the whole three million square miles of rock, tree-trunk, sand, fences, cities – came bursting through the windscreen into his skull' (*DS*, 142). As in the concluding passages of *Remembering Babylon*, in this story one senses that, for modern Australians, arriving at some kind of continental consciousness is a prerequisite for coming into fuller awareness of self, of one's world, of one's place in this world – a prerequisite for an effective coming of age. And as in the 1993 novel, one senses the strain of pursuing this particular path of self-actuali- sation: one's place of being, the continent, is both insular and yet almost inconceivably expansive.

Ned, a child of the Tyler clan, manifests a nascent version of continental consciousness early in the story. He is pleased to consider himself first as being 'like a native' and subsequently as 'a spirit of the place', while ranging around on his grandfather Audley's land: 'He was filled with a superior sense of belonging here, of knowing every rock and stump on this hillside as if they were parts of his own body.' He thinks of the day-trippers he encounters as 'tourists' and rather resents what he considers their trespass (*DS*, 148–9). However, he is nonetheless alert to the potential symbolic importance of the beach bonfire they build in the course of their national holiday: 'The idea of a bonfire on every beach and the whole map of Australia outlined with fire was powerfully exciting to him. The image of it blazed in his head' (*DS*, 153).

Ned's vision looks forward to Clem's final conception of a coherent Australian nation, which involves the coming to voice, out of a primordial silence, of 'all this – this land mass, this continent' (*DS*, 180). As in the case of the young narrator of 'Southern Skies', Clem's special vision requires him to adopt the perspective of 'Out there' (*DS*, 179), both above and distant, a view from the heavens, or more denotatively, from outer space. However, whereas the earlier adolescent viewer attains a sense of singularity and participation, Clem's main theme is multiplicity. Clem recalls the earlier Digger Keen in desiring a perfect accumulation of life signs. 'Nothing is lost,' he affirms; 'Nothing ever gets lost' (*DS*, 181). He calls upon his listeners to imagine themselves in the position of the perfect receiver, the receiver that catches everything, loses nothing: 'If we imagined ourselves out there and concentrated hard enough, really concentrated, we could hear it too, all of it, the whole sound coming towards us, all of it.' He concludes by affirming his belief that this universal receptivity, this all-encompassing attentiveness, is 'possible' (*DS*, 181) – not sure, not even probable perhaps, but possible. Malouf's will evidently is to share this measured confidence; his story ends by evoking the coming of daylight 'on other beaches, in coves all round the continent, round the vast outline of it' (*DS*, 185). The vision recalls the concluding passages of *Remembering Babylon*. One gets a similar sense of looking toward a luminous threshold, toward a new dawning of consciousness, 'a new day coming' (*DS*, 185). But the vision is less compelling than previously, because the writing now evokes a simultaneous dawn for a continental nation, and thus belies the plain fact of continental vastness. Dawnings, whether of daylight or of consciousness, do not occur simultaneously for all inhabitants of a continental nation. Malouf's vision, in this moment of its imagining, is too unguardedly optimistic; the author finally presses beyond Clem's measured hope, but does so somewhat ineffectively.

The story's problems are not, however, only in its final gesture. By imagining in relation to the time stretches that pertain to modern astrophysics, Clem strikes on something very similar to the dreamtime. The present is fully inhabited by the past, as by the future:

> the receiver doesn't even know as yet that we've arrived – us whites, I mean. Our heartbeats haven't even got there yet. But that doesn't matter ... because we *are* here, aren't we? Others were here, now they're gone. But their heartbeats are still travelling out ... It doesn't matter one way or another, which people, the living or the dead, it's all the same. (*DS*, 180)

Aspects of this passage are certainly problematic, and debatable. Some voices within the Australian community would affirm that it very much matters 'which people' and that the erasure of differences, and their histories, can never be other than the achievement of a great receiver beyond culture, beyond the press of the social world, in the cool quiet reaches of outer space. The emphatic, almost smug, confidence in the assertion that white Australians '*are* here' may also rankle, as it seems to use a voice at once naïve and knowing to sweep aside the difficult history that founds this indisputable being here. Moreover, the difficult history is resolved by adopting an understanding of time that belongs to Aboriginal Australians.

The beauty of Clem's idea – and it does have its share of beauty – resides in large part in its being aurally rather than visually ordered. Unlike Ned's early vision, unlike the story's final dawning, both of which evoke what can ultimately be rationalised and mapped, Clem's version of continental consciousness has to do with what one can hear, or rather with what can be heard if one finds the will and the means to listen. Clem imagines the reception of auditory signals, heartbeats from within living beings, rather than the projected outlining of an image. While the eye reads surfaces, the ear or receiver, at least ideally, can pick up the indices of inner realities, of the depths of being. Clem's heartbeats represent multiplicity, but also unity, unity in diversity, millions of beats merging in 'a single hum' of shared life (*DS*,

180); they represent coherence, things different that nonetheless associate and hold together. This imagining anticipates a beginning – Malouf's investment in beginnings is considerable – a new attentiveness and participation. An inaugural spirit drives Clem, who seeks to discover life's accumulations rather than its dispersals, what is retained rather than lost. His dream is of an ear of universal receptivity. And indeed, the hope for a brighter future for the Australian nation may well have more to do with what its people learn to hear than with what they learn to see.

Critical overview and conclusion

Scholarly criticism of Malouf's work began in the later 1970s following the publication of the award-winning poetry collection *Neighbours in a Thicket* in 1974 and of *Johnno* in 1975. The pace of critical publication increased appreciably by the mid-1980s, when notable articles by such as Martin Leer, Laurie Hergenhan, Maryanne Dever, and Patrick Buckridge began to appear. *An Imaginary Life* claimed the lion's share of attention until the mid-1990s when *Remembering Babylon* became, and subsequently has remained, the main topic-text for Malouf criticism.

Philip Neilsen's *Imagined Lives* of 1990 is the first substantial monograph on Malouf, a work of enduring importance that has amply assisted in the writing of this present book. Comprehensive in scope, Neilsen's criticism presents a broad range of references and perspectives, but is limited by its early appearance in the later stage of Malouf's mid-career. This limitation has been somewhat amended by the publication in 1996 of a new edition including an analysis of *Remembering Babylon*. The reading of the 1993 novel is not, however, Neilsen's most incisive and makes evident a notable gap in his assembly of critical approaches: explicitly postcolonial critique is virtually absent in Neilsen, and such critique is fairly much indispensable to the effective evaluation of *Remembering Babylon*. This novel, moreover, casts a retrospective light on Malouf's preceding works, revealing more clearly the pertinence of the postcolonial perspective in their interpretation. Neilsen successfully discerns some of Malouf's abiding concerns – notably, the articulation of Australianness, myth-making, the world-making power of language, the relationship between nature and culture – and his analyses are subtle and elucidating. Yet one is left wondering about the postcolonial component, which may be a key to understanding the interconnectedness and integrity of Malouf's vision. To his credit, however, Neilsen notes Malouf's bias toward masculine experience and critically evaluates its consequences. Malouf wishes to challenge prescribed gender roles, but also makes use of 'conventional' ascriptions and even 'stereotyping', especially in relation to femininity, and thus enjoys only a 'mixed success' with female characterisation.[1]

Karin Hansson's *Sheer Edge* appeared in 1991, but it does not profit from Neilsen's findings and does not therefore further a general understanding of Malouf's achievement as much as it might. Hansson skilfully locates a number of Malouf's most typifying figurative devices. She considers Malouf as a postcolonial writer and reads portions of his work with clarity, but her criticism's effectiveness is impeded by her sense of the author's project as a quest for identity. Identity, certainly, is an issue in Malouf, and his sense of what it might involve is complex, but it is also, most commonly, the aspect of a Malouf character's self-understanding that needs to be re-evaluated and transformed, not stabilised, consolidated, and defined.

Ivor Indyk published his important monograph *David Malouf* in 1993, *Remembering Babylon*'s publication year, and Indyk unfortunately does not include analysis of this key novel. Indyk's approach, one may add, is no more postcolonial than Neilsen's, but he is nonetheless one of the best critics of Malouf's style and of his stylistic development – most notably, the development of the emblematic technique, which Indyk is the first to recognise and delineate. Contributing significantly to a general understanding of Malouf, he takes it upon himself to account for Malouf's marked interest in masculine experience with an intensity of attention no other critic has shown, before or since. His analysis of certain specific topics, such as paternity and masculine succession, is unmatched, but more importantly, he examines the place of male homosexual desire in Malouf. In the fictions, this desire generally finds expression in suggestive, imagistic ways, and Indyk is fully able to locate and explicate all pertinent instances. One might conclude that Indyk is perspicaciously reading the unconscious of Malouf's texts, if it were not the case that Malouf's poetry occasionally portrays a sexuality that is quite clearly homosexual. Indyk, however, gives relatively little attention to the delineation of desire in the poetry. Although his case for conceiving homosexual desire as the author's predominant concern is not entirely convincing, Indyk clearly demonstrates that it is a matter of recurrent address. Indyk's sense that Malouf works 'in areas of experience that have been granted only a tentative legitimacy' rings true,[2] but rings as true in relation to other foregrounded concerns such as 'other history'. Indyk's analysis nonetheless reveals a significant aspect of Malouf's unsettling of conventional conceptions of masculine experience and sociability.

As Foucault has cogently argued, an increasingly intensified drive to specify and assign 'sexualities' characterises Western modernity.[3] Malouf's literature, however, is distinguished by its attempt to portray a more utopian breadth of perspective upon experience. Desire, which in Malouf is most commonly but not exclusively a male's desire, has many forms and facets; erotic feeling may arise in response to a man or a woman or, for that matter, in response to animals (Jim Saddler's birds and Janet's bees suggest themselves), or landscapes (the expansive grasslands of Ovid's final moments; Jock McIvor's transfigured Queensland). Renderings of explicit sexual desire and of explicitly sexual actions are, moreover, relatively infrequent in Malouf's fictions, which make up the main bulk of his literary production. This characteristic of his work does not reflect prudery – indeed, he generally seems quite comfortable about bodily and libidinal life – but rather his acute interest in the experiences of desire and erotic feeling that precede and eventually inform the concrete, real-world acts that constitute sexual practice. For Malouf, the experience of desire is richer and more multiform than its enactments. He sees that desire is for the other, for otherness, and does not prescribe or advocate the lineaments the other may manifest. Indyk's work is instrumental in directing critical attention toward the question of desire in Malouf, thus enabling a recognition of the notable multiplicity and multifacetedness in Malouf's tracings of desire, of the erotic.

No other substantial critical monographs on Malouf have appeared since Indyk's. In 1997, Claudia Egerer published *Fictions of (In)Betweenness*, an engaging work of postcolonial criticism, but one that affords Malouf quite circumscribed attention, considering him in conjunction with J. M. Coetzee and Louise Erdrich. Amanda Nettelbeck's *Reading David Malouf* of 1995 is a less significant critical contribution than the same author's articles on Malouf. In 1994, however, Nettelbeck edited and published an important collection, *Provisional Maps: Critical Essays on David Malouf*. The collection seems to promise a markedly postcolonial orientation: Nettelbeck's Introduction promptly puts forward a lengthy quotation from Gayatri Spivak, which affirms the world- and subject-structuring function of language. Although several of the essays are not, upon examination, notably inflected by postcolonial critique, Nettelbeck's own contributions, along with her other articles published elsewhere, also in the first years of the 1990s, do much to initiate a postcolonial view of Malouf. For Nettelbeck, Malouf intervenes creatively in a troubled transitional moment in Australian national history, when the drive to propound nation-defining myths is beginning to give way to a more critical attitude to projects of national myth-making. Very concerned with encouraging the enunciation of multiple voices and perspectives, Nettelbeck stresses that to assert one version of national history is to leave aside, to exclude, other competing narratives of the nation. In Malouf she finds, and favours, a notably plural presentation of history. She notes, as several other critics have done, Malouf's attraction to continuity, but sees that he does not produce visions of continuity through elisions or effacements of difference. He is a myth-maker, but one who encourages reinterpretation of myths arising out of national and colonial history. The prefix 're' figures very prominently in Nettelbeck's writing (an effect of her postcolonial commitment); she finally situates Malouf's envisioning of Australia in a compromise between reconception and recuperation.

Nettelbeck's collection includes work by two other notably productive Malouf critics, Andrew Taylor and Peter Pierce, both of whom subsequently contributed to the 2000 collection of essays on Malouf published in *World Literature Today*. In his 1994 writing, Pierce coordinates with Nettelbeck, giving much of his attention to Malouf's engagement with history. He importantly notes in *Remembering Babylon* an increased anxiety about lost or misrepresentative histories, a new sense of memory's fragility. In his essay of 2000, Pierce focuses on the then newly published *Dream Stuff*, situating Malouf in a transitional moment of his imaginative career but also voicing notable dissatisfaction with the new work, particularly with respect to its representation of class.[4] Taylor, in 1994, expresses thoughtful reservations about Malouf's attempt to reconceive history in *The Great World*. In 2000, he reinvigorates the understanding of Malouf as post-Romantic, emphasising the author's conception of language and (more innovatively) considering how his figuring of the body may be of Romantic derivation. Taylor's publication on Malouf is particularly substantial and varied, however, and includes a crucial article, published in 1999, reflecting upon a possible reconception of identity, both personal and national, in *The Conversations at Curlow Creek*.[5]

The Malouf-focused issue of *World Literature Today* coordinates with, and commemorates, Malouf's election as the sixteenth laureate of the University of Oklahoma's Neustadt International Prize for Literature. Commentary on the award-winner begins with an encomium (by Ihab Hassan), which suggests that the assembled essays may be more celebratory than searching. Upon examination, however, the collection does provide an appreciably broad and perceptive consideration of Malouf's publications, returning to and developing various key topics that have emerged in Malouf criticism: language and especially the function of naming, the portrayal of landscape, the boundary and its transgression, difference and reconciliation, the body, memory, history, and myth, among others. Somewhat surprisingly (given the celebratory status of the occasion), noteworthy reservations about Malouf's achievement find their place in the criticism: that of Pierce, as noted above, and also that of Paul Sharrad. In both these cases, the dissatisfaction arises most specifically in relation to *Dream Stuff: Stories*, which suggests that this work is not perhaps to be ranked among the author's best.

In 2002, Alice Brittan published an article on *Remembering Babylon* in *PMLA*, marking Malouf's real (and somewhat tardy) arrival in high-profile scholarly publications outside Australia. Brittan's writing examines her topic-text as an articulation of a complex settler-colony economy, thus confirming Malouf as a productive site for postcolonial critique. Brittan aligns with a postcolonial critical thrust gaining momentum through the 1990s in publications by Nettelbeck, Bill Ashcroft, Gareth Griffiths, Les Spinks, and others. The tendency both in and outside Australia is increasingly, it would seem, to seize on Malouf in relation to a broad-based, internationally orientated postcolonial studies.

This present study, now at its conclusion, strives to give due attention to Malouf's place, already well established, within the international field of postcolonial writing, but without losing sight of Malouf's specificity and the specificity of his Australian context. With respect to time spans, Malouf's writing career quite closely coincides with the emergence and rise to prominence of contemporary postcolonial theory and critique. The relationship between postcolonial scholarship and Malouf's literary production deserves some close and specific attention.

In relation to the dominant lines of development in postcolonial theory, Malouf corresponds but does not entirely conform. For Claudia Egerer, Malouf's fictions 'reside' in postcolonial theory's 'center/margin debate', but 'somewhat uneasily', as she acknowledges at the outset. Egerer guides herself through an enlightening engagement with Malouf, using Edward Said and Homi Bhabha – especially Bhabha, and especially his Freud-inflected notion of 'unhomeliness' – but concludes finally by observing that Malouf's works 'exceed the framework of postcoloniality in their destabilization of notions of political and human agency'.[6]

Bill Ashcroft has made good use of Pierre Bourdieu's appreciably postcolonial sociology to analyse the inhabiting of colonial space in *Remembering Babylon*. Following Bourdieu's notion of *habitus*, Ashcroft argues that place is 'a *constantly negotiated* network of relationships' (30). Emphasis, for Ashcroft, must therefore fall on the boundary, which figures like Gemmy reveal as tenuous and provisional, subject to 'slippage'. Pursuing his use of Bourdieu, Ashcroft asserts, 'To inhabit place is to inhabit power', and therefore the act of transforming place must contest power's established claims. Human subjects disarticulate and transform the forms of power, redirect and put them to new use. Habitation, inhabiting, is a 'practice' that recreates place; power works '*through* people as well as *upon* them'.[7] Postcolonial theory and analysis thus enable Ashcroft's argument, making it a very productive critical intervention, but without yet subordinating Malouf's overall handling of space to pre-existing theory.

This present study opens by asserting Malouf's characterising concern with otherness, a concept that certainly resonates with the inaugural articulations of postcolonial theory. Discussion of *An Imaginary Life*, in Chapter 3, introduces the notion of the othered other, the other deformed and made threatening by fear and disavowal, by refused recognition, and this key conception of the social construction of otherness remains pertinent in subsequent discussion of abjection. Said's *Orientalism*, and most particularly in the chapter 'Orientalizing the Oriental', argues that imperial discourse works in large part by deformation of the cultural other, and that this deformation has a consolidating function with respect to imperial subjectivity. (Interestingly, *Orientalism* and *An Imaginary Life* were first published in the same year, 1978.) In a seminal essay, Spivak extends this line of thinking, arguing very cogently that the representation of the colonial subject in imperial discourse always and necessarily entails an othering; this othering has a disavowed self-constitutive function, representing the plurality of the colonial world as a singular 'Other of Europe as Self'.[8] Said and Spivak provide starting points for the critical reading of Malouf, but where they see and specify the problematic configuration that imperialism and its legacies make of the category of the other, Malouf finds what he evidently considers a key to late-modern, postimperial salvation. The other, as encountered in Malouf, eludes self-constitutive construction by the self. Rather than focusing on falsifications or mythologised deformations of the other (which he does nonetheless register), Malouf stages otherness as the challenge of becoming and the promise of new (or renewed) life. His work emphasises, as postcolonial high theory does not, that the other is a real force arising to confront any given configuration of self; it is not a counter-construct or paranoid projection, although these are both possible responses to the challenge the other unremittingly presents. Postcolonial theory's diagnosis of the imperial West's violent shaping of the understanding of otherness provides an interpretative context for the reading of Malouf, but his work certainly is not a literary reiteration of postcolonial theory's findings. Malouf's version of the other, moreover, shows a closer affiliation with continental philosophy as represented by Heidegger and (still more pertinently) Levinas.

By stressing the importance of language as the principal framework and vehicle for the making of worlds, by affirming the materiality of language and its active intervention in the field of social relations, Malouf's work affiliates with post-Foucauldian postcolonial scholarship. One may again mention Said here – and Robert Young, whose history-focused analysis of European constructions of hybridity is more useful, for the study of Malouf, than Homi Bhabha's better known psychoanalytic treatment of the same topic. More significantly, however, Malouf's understanding of the dynamics of the social collective resonates in important ways with postcolonial analyses of imperial social formations and particularly with postcolonial theory of the nation. Corrosively critical of the legacy of colonial government – one may immediately recall *Remembering Babylon* and *The Conversations at Curlow Creek* – Malouf sees that the nation, if it is not to function merely as a principal myth-figure legitimising domination, needs to discover itself as a cultural composite of diverse constituencies. However, he acknowledges, with Said, that culture, 'a system of discriminations and evaluations', is also invariably 'a system of exclusions'.[9] Like Bhabha, Malouf conceives of the nation as tenuously defined by 'transgressive boundaries' – boundaries that are made and unmade, defined and effaced, by acts or events of transgression. For Malouf, as for Bhabha, 'the margins of the nation displace the centre'.[10] The nation's most characteristic difference is not its difference from other nations but from itself; it is *internally* marked by cultural difference and … heterogeneous histories'.[11]

Postcolonial high theory, as initiated by such as Said, Bhabha, and Spivak, does not specifically address the contexts of the settler society. Theory and criticism focused on the settler society has arisen, notably in Australian scholarly communities, to address specific topics relating to it: the subjectivity of the settler, the representation and self-representation of the indigene, the conception and construction of the New World place, and the special centre/margin relationship that develops between Europe and the societies of settlement. In the work of the more prominent scholars – Helen Tiffin, Bill Ashcroft, Stephen Slemon, Alan Lawson, among others – discussion has tended to hinge on issues of representation and discourse. Malouf has found some place in this body of work, although not so ample a place as one might expect. Part of the reason for this lack of prominence may be in the recognition that Malouf stands apart, in an important way, from a dominant impetus of much postcolonial critique.

Much of Malouf's writing affirms – at times tacitly, at times explicitly – his belief in the abiding importance of Europe as a resource and a measure. The European legacy provides him with his principal standards of style, giving rise to what has been called his 'international style'. More crucially, he understands Australian culture and society as derived, in large part, from Europe and particularly from Great Britain. He goes further than ever previously – and perhaps too far – in making this case in his 2002 essay 'Made in England: Australia's British Inheritance', but

Anglo-Celtic Australia, its history and actuality, is prominently present in the texts that precede the late-arriving essay. One must nonetheless recognise that Malouf's Ango-Celtic Australia insistently differs from itself even as it deploys its multiple group-defining contingencies and recognitions: Digger differs radically from Vic, and also from Mac; Adair differs radically from Carney, and also from Fergus. And as Malouf's career develops through the 1980s and 1990s, the Anglo-Celtic component of Malouf's narratives increasingly confronts instances of diversity that challenge its dominance and any presumptive, self-ascribed integrity to which it may pretend. Malouf's Australia does not finally cohere around an Anglo-Celtic model. Beginning most notably in the publications of the 1980s – *Harland's Half Acre* stands out in this respect, as does *Blood Relations* – Malouf's fiction shows an increased representation of non-Anglo-Celtic Europeans and also Aborigines, who disrupt the settled perspectives of Anglo-Celtic characters and thus their group-identification. If the postcolonial aspect of Malouf's writing does not reside in the rejection or radical contestation of Europe, it is at least potentially present in a mobilisation of the European legacy in the plural – European lega*cies* – a mobilisation, moreover, that is contingent upon and inflected by non-European cultural presences.

But to stop short of representing Malouf as more politically invested than he is, one should note a certain bold literariness – bold because it does not meet with favour in all critical circles – that marks much of his work. *Child's Play*, in particular, stands out as a literary experiment, in the postmodern rather than postcolonial vein, and it merits attention largely as an impressive literary performance. The work's political investments are not notable, nor readily decipherable. It is certainly preoccupied with representing an experience of modernity, but a large part of the work's modern spirit inheres in its attempt to stage pure literature, to show what a late-twentieth-century imagination can do with the medium of words. An intensely literary ambition is also unmistakably present in *An Imaginary Life*, the author's first great success in fiction, and again in *Remembering*

Babylon – although this last clearly has sociopolitical concerns that override the urge to mere fine writing. This present study has not given focused attention to Malouf's literary or artistic achievement, but it has pursued its course believing in the pertinence of that achievement, with a sense that's Malouf's literary merit is part of what makes his works challenging and worthwhile sites of critical endeavour.

Malouf's staging of ethical imagination, however, has been the close and continuous concern of this criticism. For some of his critics, and for Malouf one must assume, it is not always clear what relation Malouf's ethical vision has with his politics – or with present-day political configurations more generally. Somewhat paradoxically, Malouf gives intense attention to individual subjectivity, yet also considers individual subjectivity as an ultimately untenable categorisation of human being. The category of the subject must be posited, as a useful fiction, in any given moment of experience, but the subject only sustains its relationship with living being through encounter, connection, and exchange with instances of the other, the not-I, and through the transformations thereby provoked. If I am to live, I must change; if I am to change, it must be through you, repeatedly through you, always through you – this briefly summarises Malouf's ethics of subjectivity. With politics, however, comes the question of power: Malouf, in the sociocultural worlds where he speaks and acts, and his personae and his characters, in those imagined worlds where they speak and act, must confront differences of power pertaining to individuals and groups. For Malouf, the most important instance of power is the power to represent, oneself and, still more crucially, others. Power of access, of imaginative access to the experience and knowledge of others, is a power Malouf cannot do without. The question, then, for his proper evaluation, does not reside in his claim to such power – which in any case he has asserted, tacitly but repeatedly, throughout his career – but in the effectiveness with which he exercises it. The measure of this effectiveness must return one, curiously and somewhat awkwardly, to the realm of the aesthetic. If Malouf's imaginative ventures are convincing and compelling, his success must be, at least in part, an achievement of his artistry, but must also be an achievement of attentive, nuanced reading. In the imaginative scope and diversity of his work, and most particularly in his sophisticated deployment of language powers, Malouf makes his appeal for such reading.

Notes

Chapter 1

1   Carolyn Masel, 'Late Landings: Reflections on Belatedness in Australian and Canadian Literatures', *Recasting the World: Writing after Colonialism*, ed. Jonathan White, Baltimore and London: The Johns Hopkins University Press, 1993, 180–2.

2   Philip Neilsen, *Imagined Lives: A Study of David Malouf*, St Lucia: University of Queensland Press, 1990, 4.

3   See Chapter 2, pages 22–5, for the detailed analysis of Auden's influence.

4   Carolyn Bliss, 'Reimagining the Remembered: David Malouf and the Moral Implications of Myth', *World Literature Today* 74.4, 2000, 725.

5   Amanda Nettelbeck, Introduction, *Provisional Maps: Critical Essays on David Malouf*, ed. Amanda Nettelbeck, Nedlands: Centre for Studies in Australian Literature, University of Western Australia, iii.

6   Amanda Nettelbeck, 'Imagining the Imaginary in *An Imaginary Life*', *Southern Review: Literary and Interdisciplinary Essays* 26.1, 1993, 28.

7   Ray Willbanks, Interview, 'David Malouf', *Australian Voices: Writers and Their Work*, Austin: University of Texas Press, 1991, 151.

8   Bliss, 'Reimagining', 725.

9   Samar Attar, 'A Lost Dimension: The Immigrant's Experience in the Work of David Malouf', *Australian Literary Studies* 13.3, 1988, 314.

10 Bob Hodge and Vijay Mishra, *Dark Side of the Dream: Austra-*

lian Literature and the Postcolonial Mind, North Sydney: Allen & Unwin, 1991, 196–7.

11   Russell West, 'Exile as Origin: Definitions of Australian Identities in Malouf's *12 Edmondstone Street*', *Anglia: Zeitschrift für Englische Philologie* 119.1, 2001, 80.

12   Neilsen, *Imagined*, 1, 182.

13   John Scheckter, 'Dreaming Wholeness: David Malouf's New Stories', *World Literature Today* 74.4, 2000, 741.

Chapter 2

1   Neilsen, *Imagined*, 5.

2   Ken Gelder and Paul Salzman note that Malouf espouses the idea that literary 'excitement' in Australia shifts from poetry to fiction (*The New Diversity: Australian Fiction 1970–88*, Melbourne: McPhee Gribble, 1989, 3).

3   Ivor Indyk *et al.*, Introduction, *David Malouf: A Celebration*, ed. Ivor Indyk, Canberra: National Library of Australia, 2001, 1–4.

4   Martin Leer, 'At the Edge: Geography and the Imagination in the Work of David Malouf', *Australian Literary Studies* 12.1, 1985, 11.

5   Barnard Turner, 'On Frontiers: The "Nationalism" of David Malouf's Poetry and Its Implications for a Definition of "Commonwealth Literature"', *Nationalism vs. Internationalism: (Inter)National Dimensions of Literatures in English*, eds Wolfgang Zach and Ken Goodwin, Tübingen: Stauffenburg, 1996, 497.

6   Chris Wallace-Crabbe, 'Imitations of Secular Grace', *Meanjin* 40.4, 1981, 500–2.

7   Turner, 'Frontiers', 502.

8   Leigh Dale and Helen Gilbert, 'Edges of the Self: Topographies of the Body in the Writing of David Malouf', *Provisional Maps*, ed. Nettelbeck, 80, 90. Dale and Gilbert's analysis has a very political anti-imperial thrust, which should be noted. Their argument, more fully stated, is that Malouf's body-in-metaphor eschews 'imperial reduction' and portrays 'an otherness which exceeds textual containment' ('Edges', 88).

9   Wallace-Crabbe, 'Imitations', 501

10   Paul Sharrad, 'A Delicate Business: David Malouf's Shorter Prose', *World Literature Today* 74.4, 2000, 759–68; Paul Kavanaugh, 'With

Breath Just Condensing on It: An Interview with David Malouf', *Southerly: A Review of Australian Literature* 3, September 1986, 253.

11   W. H. Auden, *Collected Poems*, ed. Edward Mendelson, London: Faber and Faber, 1994, 247.

12   Auden, *Collected*, 541.

13   Auden, *Collected*, 247.

14   Auden, *Collected*, 248.

15   Auden, *Collected*, 157.

16   Ivor Indyk, *David Malouf*, Melbourne: Oxford University Press, 1993, 78.

17   Critics, however, have suggested limitations to Malouf's imaginative outreach. Leer finds in the poetry a frequent failure to 'grasp the "other"' but also 'miraculous moments of touching' ('Edge', 12). Turner finds that Malouf's poetry 'brackets experiences of plurality' in the Australian ethnic landscape ('Frontiers', 501).

Chapter 3

1   Maryanne Dever begins to suggest this critical orientation, stating that the novel is partly about 'Dante's desire to be a writer' ('Secret Companions: The Continuity of David Malouf's Fiction', *World Literature Written in English* 26.1, 1986, 69).

2   Ivor Indyk, *David Malouf*, 7.

3   Stephen Kirby, 'Homosocial Desire and Homosexual Panic in the Fiction of David Malouf and Frank Moorhouse', *Meanjin* 46.3, 1987, 392; Neilsen, *Imagined*, 15, 32.

4   Andrew Taylor, '*The Bread of Time to Come*: Body and Landscape in David Malouf's Fiction', *World Literature Today* 74.4, 2000, 715–23.

5   Eve Kosofsky Sedgwick, *Between Men: English Literature and Male Homosocial Desire*, New York: Columbia University Press, 1985; *The Epistemology of the Closet*, Berkeley: University of California Press, 1990.

6   Ivor Indyk, *David Malouf*, 8.

7   Particularly in the self-doubt Johnno engenders in Dante one can see the importance of the double or *Doppelgänger* motif, which is emphasised by Neilsen and by Hodge and Mishra.

8   Indyk, *David Malouf*, 41.

9   Kirby, 'Homosocial'.

10   *The Practice of Everyday Life*, trans. Stephen Rendell, Berkeley: University of California Press, 1984.

11   Avis G. McDonald, one of several critics to assert the centrality of language in Malouf's Ovid tale, affirms that synecdoche provides the governing logic of the work's overall composition ('Beyond Language: David Malouf's *An Imaginary Life*', *ARIEL* 19.1, 1988, 53).

12   Patrick Buckridge, 'Colonial Strategies in the Writing of David Malouf', *Kunapipi* 8.3, 1986, 57.

13   Suzie O'Brien, 'Raising Silent Voices: The Role of the Silent Child in *An Imaginary Life* and *The Bone People*', *SPAN* 30, 1990, 91.

14   Gareth Griffiths, '*Being There*; Being There: Kosinski and Malouf', *Past the Last Post: Theorizing Post-Colonialism and Post-Modernism*, eds Ian Adam and Helen Tiffin, Calgary: University of Calgary Press, 1990, 154.

15   Ovid's final 'I am there' has been variously interpreted, most engagingly, however, in relation to Heideggerian philosophy. Carmen Concilio suggests that 'I am there' alludes to Heidegger's 'da-sein' ('The Magic of Language in the Novels of Patrick White and David Malouf', *Coterminous Worlds: Magical Realism and Contemporary Post-Colonial Literature in English*, eds Elsa Linguanti, Francesco Casotti, and Carmen Concilio, Amsterdam: Rodopi, 1999, 42). Neilsen also works from Heidegger, placing Ovid's final enunciation 'beyond time and place' and interpreting it as an affirmation of 'the completeness of life in death' (*Imagined*, 64).

16   Malouf, it should be noted, remains committed to his notion of a 'speech of silence'. In interview,in 1994 (by which date sixteen years and several Malouf books had followed upon *An Imaginary Life*), the author reaffirms his belief in the special value of a 'language of gesture' or 'of silence' that arrives at understanding without the mediation of words (Nikos Papastergiadis, 'David Malouf and Languages for Landscape: An Interview', *ARIEL* 25.3, 1994, 91).

17   A more fully detailed account of identification, the imaginary, and the relation of the imaginary to the later-arising symbolic order of language can be found in Jacques Lacan's *Ecrits: A Selection*, trans. Alan Sheridan, New York: W. W. Norton, 1977.

18   Amanda Nettelbeck's Lacanian reading discerns 'a Romantic affirmation of the pre-symbolic', but also an exploration of subject

construction in and by the symbolic ('Imagining', 37–8). Andrew
Taylor argues that Ovid in exile suffers a symbolic castration (a
loss of 'tongue'), and then saves himself by learning 'the language
of the pre-Oedipal imaginary' ('Postmodern Romantic: The Imaginary in David Malouf's *An Imaginary Life*', *Imagining Romanticism: Essays on English and Australian Romanticisms*, eds Deirdre
Coleman and Peter Otto, West Cornwall, CT: Locust Hill, 1992,
288). However, this notion of pre-Oedipal language is conceptually
as paradoxical as Malouf's own 'speech of silence'.

19   Emmanuel Levinas provides the most thoughtfully elaborate
understanding of the other's appeal/*appel*, which is to be understood as a calling out to, a calling toward, a call for approach – ultimately a calling into being for the human subject. Closely related
to the appeal is Lévinas's sense of the importance of face-to-face
encounter, which Malouf seems also to share. In face-to-face
encounter, one enacts a full recognition of the other as other and an
openness to the other's appeal. Face-to-face is the originary ethical
stance, the self-constituting acceptance of responsibility for the
other (*Otherwise than Being or Beyond Essence*, trans. Alphonso
Lingus, Dordrecht, Boston, London: Kluwer Academic, 1991).

20   In *Fly Away Peter*, Jim Saddler and Imogen Harcourt are both
loners, both set apart by a personal passion (birds for him, photog-
raphy for her), and both are exceptionally receptive to instances of
newness and difference they chance to encounter. Jock McIvor, in
Remembering Babylon, learns to see north Queensland's strange
beauty and to feel sympathy for the stranger Gemmy Fairley, but
only through the sacrifice of his comfortable (and yet constraining)
bonds with the settler society he inhabits.

21   Stephen Woods, 'David Malouf's *Child's Play* and "The Death of
the Author"', *Australian Literary Studies* 13.3, 1988, 322, 327.

22   Griffiths, '*Being*', 156.

23   Dever, 'Secret, 67.

24   Julie Copeland, 'Interview with David Malouf', *Australian Literary
Studies* 10.4, 1982, 429.

25   Laurie Hergenhan, 'Discoveries and Transformations: Aspects of
David Malouf's Work', *Australian Literary Studies* 11.3, 1984,
337.

26   Tony Thwaites, 'The Site of the Beholder: David Malouf's *Child's
Play*', *Southern Review: Literary and Interdisciplinary Essays*
20.1, 1987, 30.

27   Marina van Zuylen argues that the victims of 'monomania' use

'obsessive strategies ... to keep the arbitrary out of their lives' (*Monomania: The Flight from Everyday Life in Literature and Art*, Ithaca and London: Cornell University Press, 2005, 1). Malouf's terrorist conforms, to a notable degree, to this characterisation of the obsessive personality.

28   Neilsen, *Imagined*, 67.

29   Neilsen, *Imagined*, 67.

30   Thwaites, 'Site', 34.

31   Indyk, *David Malouf*, 63, 87.

32   Edward Hills, '*La Maison Onirique*: David Malouf's First House', *Meridian* 16.1, 1997, 3.

33   Hills, 'Maison', 3.

34   Indyk, *David Malouf*, 81.

35   Attar, 'Lost', 313, 320.

36   Graham Huggan, '(Un)Co-Ordinated Movements: The Geography of Autobiography in David Malouf's *12 Edmondstone Street* and Clark Blaise's *Resident Alien*', *Australian and New Zealand Studies in Canada* 3, 1990, 61.

37   Huggan, '(Un)Co-Ordinated', 64.

Chapter 4

1   Gelder and Salzman, *New*, 144.

2   Karin Hansson, *Sheer Edge: Aspects of Identity in David Malouf's Writing*, Lund: Lund University Press, 1991, 139.

3   Amanda Nettelbeck, 'Rewriting an Explorer Mythology: The Narration of Space in David Malouf's Work', *Provisional Maps*, ed. Nettelbeck, 102, 104, 111.

4   Andrew Taylor, '*The Great World*, History, and Two or One Other Things', *Provisional Maps*, ed. Nettelbeck, 36, 37.

5   Michel Foucault establishes the concept of counter-memory to designate the various dissonant elements which individual or cultural memory does not assimilate and incorporate, and which may therefore unsettle accepted versions of the past (*Language, Counter-Memory, Practice: Selected Essays and Interviews*, Ithaca: Cornell University Press, 1977).

6   Neilsen, *Imagined*, 106.

7   Neilsen, *Imagined*, 96.

8   Neilsen, *Imagined*, 122.

9   Taylor, '*Bread*', 720.

10 Neilsen, *Imagined*, 123, 139.

11 Neilsen, *Imagined*, 141.

12 Indyk, *David Malouf*, 96.

13 Robert Ross, '*Harland's Half Acre*: A Portrait of the Artist as a Young Australian', *World Literature Today* 74.4, 2000, 735, 737.

14 Leer, 'Edge', 20.

15 Neilsen, *Imagined*, 127–8

16 Peter Knox-Shaw, 'An Art of Intersection: David Malouf's *Kunstlerroman, Harland's Half Acre*', *Antipodes* 5.1, 1991, 38.

17 Gelder and Saluzman, *New*, 144–5. Neilsen specifically rebuts the Gelder and Salzman position (*Imagined*, 157), as does Ross, though not quite so directly ('*Harland's*', 734).

18 Julia Kristeva, *Powers of Horror: An Essay on Abjection*, trans. Leon S. Roudiez, New York: Columbia University Press, 1982, 4.

19 Kristeva, *Powers*, 9.

20 David Kerr, 'Uniting the Hemispheres: David Malouf's Fictions', *Australian Literature Today*, New Delhi: Indian Society for Commonwealth Studies, 1993, 66.

21 Dever, 'Secret', 122.

22 Neilsen, *Imagined*, 133.

Chapter 5

1   Lacan in his *Ecrits* portrays the imaginary order of experience as preceding the symbolic order, but also, paradoxically, as a retrospection provoked by accession to the symbolic.

2   Peter Knox-Shaw observes that Malouf aims for a dismantling of prevailing established patterns of literature and culture, an initiative that is already evident in *Fly Away Peter* but more fully apparent in *The Great World* ('Malouf's Epic and the Unravelling of a National Stereotype', *Journal of Commonwealth Literature* 26.1, 1991, 79–100).

3   Indyk remarks that Vic recalls Willy, the central character of

Malouf's 1988 play *Blood Relations*, in his renunciation of the past and resulting feeling of discontinuity, which spur the need for action.

4   Knox-Shaw describes *The Great World* as 'an analysis of the social instrumentation of will' ('Malouf's', 98). It might be more strictly accurate to say that Vic's characterisation entails such analysis.

5   Amanda Nettelbeck, 'Myths of a Nation: History as Narrative Invention in David Malouf's *The Great World*', *Myths, Heroes and Anti-Heroes: Essays on the Literature and Culture of the Asia-Pacific Region*, eds Bruce Bennett and Dennis Haskell, Nedlands: Centre for Studies in Australian Literature, University of Western Australia, 1992, 141.

6   Neilsen, *Imagined*, 152.

7   Buckridge, 'Colonial', 181.

8   Shelagh Rodgers, 'The Other History that Never Gets Recorded', *Australian and New Zealand Studies in Canada* 5, 1991, 95.

9   Knox-Shaw, 'Malouf's', 81.

10 Taylor, *'Great'*, 48.

11 Taylor, *'Bread'*, 718.

12 Indyk, *David Malouf*, 103.

13 Neilsen, *Imagined*, 177.

14 In learning something of what it means to think black, Digger recalls the part-Aboriginal Dinny of Malouf's 1988 play *Blood Relations*. Dinny claims he 'had to start thinkin' black at twenty', following years of 'white' education (*BR*, 66).

15 Knox-Shaw, first recalling that 'digger' is a self-ascribed nickname of the Australian trooper in World War I, argues that the digger-image tended to encourage 'conformism' and to elide 'cultural difference', and that the digger is definitionally 'white' and 'male' (83). Malouf's character, Knox-Shaw suggests, may be intended as 'a redeemed version of the digger stereotype' ('Malouf's', 86).

16 Neilsen, *Imagined*, 157. Neilsen offers quite extensive discussion of the links between Malouf and Carter. Carter's most pertinent works concerning the theory and analysis of space are *The Road to Botany Bay* (1987), *Living in a New Country* (1992). and *The Lie of the Land* (1996).

17 Xavier Pons, 'Broken Lines, Broken Lives: Discontinuities in David Malouf's *The Great World*', *Commonwealth Essays and Studies* 16.2, 1993, 87.

18   Amanda Nettelbeck, 'Narrative Invention as "Spatial History" in *The Great World*', *Australian and New Zealand Studies in Canada* 7, 1992, 52.

19   Pons, 'Broken', 80.

Chapter 6

1   Germaine Greer, 'Malouf's Objectionable Whitewash', *Age*, 3 November 1993.

2   Peter Craven, 'An Ad for Philistinism', *Australian*, 10 November 1993.

3   Peter Otto, Review, 'Forgetting Colonialism (David Malouf, *Remembering Babylon*)', *Meanjin* 52.3, 1993, 546, 553.

4   Veronica Brady, 'Redefining Frontiers: "Race", Colonizers and the Colonized', *Antipodes* 8.2, 1994, 94.

5   Suvendrini Perera, 'Unspeakable Bodies: Representing the Aboriginal in Australian Critical Discourse', *Meridian* 13.1, 1994, 17, 18, 22.

6   Gia Metherell, 'Babylon Not Always Remembered Fondly', *Canberra Times*, 24 May 1996.

7   Sheila Whittick, 'Excavating Historical Guilt and Moral Failure in *Remembering Babylon*: An Exploration of the Faultlines in White Australian Identity', *Commonwealth Essays and Studies* 19.2, 1997, 99.

8   Marc Delrez and Paulette Michel-Michot, 'The Politics of Metamorphosis: Cultural Transformation in David Malouf's *Remembering Babylon*', *The Contact and the Culmination*, eds Marc Delrez and Benedicte Ledent-Benedicte, Liege, Belgium: L3–Liege Language and Literature, 1997, 155, 157.

9   Michael Mitchell, 'Armed Angels: Visible Darkness in Malouf and Golding', *World Literature Today* 74.4, 2000, 771.

10   Bliss, 'Reimagining', 731–2.

11   It should be noted that some critical voices, from the beginning, have asserted that Malouf makes effective interventions in cultural and racial politics. Taylor affirms Malouf's interest, especially in *Remembering Babylon*, 'in challenges to political and linguistic demarcations' ('*Great*', 35). For Claudia Egerer, Malouf consistently wrestles with 'the problematics of marginality' (*Fictions of*

(In)Betweenness, Goteborg, Sweden: Acta Universitatis Gothoburgensis, 1997, 139). Alice Brittan characterises the 1993 novel as 'an exploration of the cultural contours and lines of force that … continue to shape and fissure Australian society in the present day' ('B-b-british Objects: Possession, Naming, and Translation in David Malouf's *Remembering Babylon*', PMLA 117, 2002, 1169).

12   Brittan, 'B-b-british', 1159–61.

13   This problem of finding appropriate designations for Gemmy signals his centrality within the novel's overall examination of the perturbed relationship, in migrant colonial contexts, between words and things. For detailed discussion of this issue, see Xavier Pons, 'Reconciling Words and Things: Language Allegories in David Malouf's *Remembering Babylon*', *Commonwealth Essays and Studies* 27.1, 2004, 99–110.

14   Indyk, *David Malouf*, 47.

15   Paul Carter, *Living in a New Country*, London: Faber & Faber, 1992, 160.

16   Brady, 'Redefining', 96.

17   Whittick's, 'Excavating', 93–4.

18   Les Spinks makes in this respect a quite crucial point: 'difference is always already inscribed at the heart of identity' ('Allegory, Space, Colonialism: *Remembering Babylon* and the Production of Colonial History', *Australian Literary Studies* 17.2, 1995, 171).

19   Malouf's one important preceding use of the hammer image has, however, a distinct meaning. *Blood Relations* opens with the central character, Willy, hammering crates shut, an action suggesting Willy's aggressive, repressive (and ultimately absurd) will to define and contain his property.

20   Perera, 'Unspeakable', 18.

21   Neilsen, *Imagined*, 212–13.

22   Pierce pertinently remarks that *Remembering Babylon* emphasises 'the fragility of the prop to self-hood that memory can afford', thus distinguishing this work from the preceding fictions, and notably the immediate predecessor *The Great World* ('Problematic History, Problems of Form, David Malouf's *Remembering Babylon*',' *Provisional Maps*, ed. Nettelbeck, 195).

23   Peter Pierce has presented a similar view, finding in Frazer's utopianism 'a well-intentioned if deluded desire' ('Problematic', 193).

24   Michael Mitchell coincides with this view of Gemmy, arguing that the character is 'a victim of the metropolis' and thus 'not a

representative of Aboriginal culture'; his hybridity is at best 'a hybridity of victimhood' ('Armed', 771).

25 Perera, 'Unspeakable', 18.

26 Brady claims that Janet's swarming experience suggests 'a new discovery of Australia' ('Redefining', 100), or at least a renewed discovery. This view accounts for the incident more satisfactorily than the hybridisation argument.

27 'The world is all edges', and often woundingly edgy, in 12 *Edmondstone Street* (*ES*, 54).

28 Bill Ashcroft states the problem of borders or boundaries more complexly: the boundary signifies 'limitation and contradiction', but also 'control'; however, 'the boundary is always subject to slippage and provisionality' ('Habitation', *New Literatures Review* 34, 1997, 34, 36).

29 Spinks, 'Allegory', 173.

30 Margery Fee, 'Who Can Write as Other?', *The Post-Colonial Studies Reader*, eds Bill Ashcroft, Gareth Griffiths, and Helen Tiffin, London and New York: Routledge, 1995, 244.

31 Chris Tiffin and Alan Lawson, *De-Scribing Empire: Post-Colonialism and Textuality*, London and New York: Routledge, 1994, 235.

Chapter 7

1 Malouf reveals here, as elsewhere, that one earns the right to a washing or cleansing by living a fully human life. Willy of *Blood Relations* affirms, 'Anything worth doing gets you mucky', but adds that it is always good to 'wash it off' (*BR*, 81, 82).

2 Stella Borg Barthet, 'Resistance and Reconciliation in David Malouf's *The Conversations at Curlow Creek*', *Resistance and Reconciliation: Writing in the Commonwealth*, eds Bruce Bennett, Susan Cowan, Jacqueline Lo, Satendra Nandan, and Jen Webb, Canberra: Association for Commonwealth Literature and Language Studies, 2003, 266.

3 Indyk makes a similar but rather darker observation when he discovers quite frequent evocations of 'malign feminine power' in Malouf (*David Malouf*, 95). Malouf's short story 'Eustace', however, presents an intense evocation of the power of femaleness and female sexuality without any suggestions of malignity. The main female characters are all children, but through their influence

the boy Eustace, very much concerned with maintaining control of self and world, repeatedly finds himself losing control of both.

4 Wallace-Crabbe, 'Imitations', 505.

5 Sharrad, Delicate', 759-68.

6 Andrew Taylor, 'Origin, Identity and the Body in David Malouf's Fiction', *Australian Literary Studies* 19.1, 1999, 13.

7 Bill Ashcroft, 'The Return of the Native: *An Imaginary Life* and *Remembering Babylon*', *Commonwealth Essays and Studies* 16.2, 1993, 53.

8 Brittan, 'B-b-british', 1159.

9 Hena Maes-Jelinek, 'David Malouf's "Voyaging Imagination": *The Conversations at Curlow Creek*', *Commonwealth* 23.1, 2000, 94.

10 Gerry Turcotte, 'Response: Venturing into Undiscoverable Countries: Reading Ondaatje, Malouf, Atwood and Jia in an Asia-Pacific Context', *Australian Canadian Studies* 16.2, 1997-98, 71.

11 Xavier Pons, 'Wrong Side of the Mirror: Exile in David Malouf's *The Conversations at Curlow Creek*', *Flight from Certainty: The Dilemma of Identity and Exile*, eds Anne Luyat and Francine Tolron, Amsterdam: Rodopi, 2001, 149.

12 Anthony J. Hassall, 'The Wild Colonial Boy: The Making of Colonial Legends in David Malouf's *The Conversations at Curlow Creek*', *Antipodes* 14.2, 2000, 148.

13 Delrez and Michel-Michot find in Malouf an 'ascensional materialism', a 'form of spirituality starting … from the reality of matter' ('Politics', 167). The portrayal of the body in *Conversations* conforms quite well to this critical description.

Chapter 8

1 Indyk, *David Malouf*, 64–5.

2 Sharrad, Delicate', 762.

3 John Scheckter stresses the importance, for the story's interpretation, of the elderly couple's poverty of life experience ('Dreaming Wholeness: David Malouf's New Stories', *World Literature Today* 74.4, 2000, 741–8).

4 Peter Pierce, 'What Dreams May Come: David Malouf's *Dream Stuff*', *World Literature Today* 74.4, 2000, 756–7.

5 The earlier use of the 'we' as a narrative voice, in 'The Prowler' of 1982, definitely favours the view that Malouf does not identify with the narrative voice of 'Jacko's Reach'. In 'The Prowler' the use of the narrative 'we' is very much in the Faulknerian mode (as in 'A Rose for Emily') and serves to reveal the often skewed, submerged dynamic of unconscious community life.

6 It should be noted that Pierce finds similar problems with 'proletarian speech' in 'Lone Pine' and even in certain texts of *Antipodes* ('Dreams', 757).

7 Scheckter, 'Dreaming', 747.

Chapter 9

1 Neilsen, *Imagined*, 145.

2 Indyk, *David Malouf*, 107.

3 Michel Foucault, *The History of Sexuality. Volume I: An Introduction*, trans. Robert Hurley, New York: Vintage, 1990.

4 For fuller discussion of Pierce's criticism of class representation, see Chapter 8, 174–5.

5 For fuller discussion, see Chapter 7, 155, 161–2.

6 Egerer, *Fictions*, 140, 178.

7 Ashcroft, 'Habitation', 36, 39–40.

8 Gayatri Chakravorty Spivak, 'Can the Subaltern Speak?', *Marxism and the Interpretation of Culture*, eds Cary Nelson and Lawrence Grossberg, Urbana: University of Illinois Press, 1988, 281.

9 Edward W. Said, *The World, the Text, and the Critic*, London: Faber, 1984, 11.

10 Homi K. Bhabha, 'Introduction: Narrating the Nation', *Nation and Narration*, ed. Homi Bhabha, London and New York: Routledge, 1990, 5-6.

11 Homi K. Bhabha, 'DissemiNation: Time, Narrative, and the Margins of the Modern Nation', *Nation and Narration*, 299.

Select bibliography

The primary bibliography is very selective with respect to Malouf's ample body of short essays, journalistic articles and reviews, and published lectures. The secondary bibliography lists the scholarly works and interviews that have served directly in the writing of this book. For comprehensive lists of primary and secondary materials, on Malouf and other Australian authors, the best resource is the AusLit database.

Works by David Malouf

POETRY COLLECTIONS

'Interiors', *Four Poets*, Melbourne: Cheshires, 1962.

Bicycle and Other Poems, St Lucia: University of Queensland Press, 1970.

Neighbours in a Thicket, St Lucia: University of Queensland Press, 1974

Poems 1975–76, Sidney: Prism, 1976.

Wild Lemons: Poems, Angus & Robertson, 1980.

First Things Last, London: Chatto & Windus, 1980.

Poems 1959–89, St Lucia: University of Queensland Press, 1992.

Selected Poems 1959–89, London: Chatto & Windus, 1994.

FICTION

Johnno (1975), New York: George Braziller, 1998.

An Imaginary Life (1978), New York: Vintage International, 1996.

Child's Play (1981), New York: Vintage International, 1999.

Child's Play with Eustace and The Prowler, London: Chatto & Windus, 1982.

Fly Away Peter (1982), New York: Vintage International, 1998.

Harland's Half Acre (1984), New York: Vintage International, 1997.

Antipodes (1985), Harmondsworth, Middlesex: Penguin, 1986.

The Great World (1990), New York: Vintage International, 1993.

Remembering Babylon (1993), Toronto: Vintage Canada, 1994.

The Conversations at Curlow Creek (1996), Toronto: Vintage Canada, 1998.

Untold Tales, Sydney: Paper Bark Press, 1999.

Dream Stuff: Stories (2000), Toronto: Vintage Canada, 2001.

AUTOBIOGRAPHY

12 Edmondstone Street (1985), Harmondsworth, Middlesex: Penguin, 1986.

PLAY

Blood Relations, Sydney: Currency Press, 1988.

LIBRETTI

Voss, first production at the Australian Opera, 1986.

Mer de Glace, first production at the Australian Opera, 1990.

Baa Baa Black Sheep: A Jungle Tale, London: Chatto & Windus, 1993.

Jane Eyre, London: Vintage, 2000.

ESSAYS AND MISCELLANEOUS

'A First Place: The Mapping of the World', *Southerly* 45.1, 1985, 3–10.

A Spirit of Play: The Making of Australian Consciousness, Sydney: ABC Books, 1998.

Introduction, Charlotte Brontë, *Jane Eyre*, World's Classics, Oxford: Oxford University Press, 1999.

'A Writing Life' (The 2000 Neustadt Lecture), *World Literature Today* 74.4, 701–5.

'Made in England: Australia's British Inheritance', *Quarterly Essay* 12, 2003, 1–66.

CRITICAL WORKS AND INTERVIEWS

Agamben, Giorgio, *Homo Sacer: Sovereign Power and Bare Life*, trans. Daniel Heller-Roazen, Stanford: Stanford University Press, 1998.

Ashcroft, Bill, 'The Return of the Native: *An Imaginary Life* and *Remembering Babylon*', *Commonwealth Essays and Studies* 16.2, 1993, 51–60.

Ashcroft, Bill, 'Habitation', *New Literatures Review* 34, 1997, 27–42.

Attar, Samar, 'A Lost Dimension: The Immigrant's Experience in the Work of David Malouf', *Australian Literary Studies* 13.3, 1988, 308–21.

Auden, W. H., *Collected Poems*, ed. Edward Mendelson, London: Faber and Faber, 1994 [1976].

Bhabha, Homi K., 'DissemiNation: Time, Narrative, and the Margins of the Modern Nation', *Nation and Narration*, ed. Homi Bhabha, London and New York: Routledge, 1990, 291–322.

Bhabha, Homi K., 'Introduction: Narrating the Nation', *Nation and Narration*, ed. Homi Bhabha, London and New York: Routledge, 1990, 1–7.

Bliss, Carolyn, 'Reimagining the Remembered: David Malouf and the Moral Implications of Myth', *World Literature Today* 74.4, 2000, 724–32.

Borg Barthet, Stella, 'Resistance and Reconciliation in David Malouf's *The Conversations at Curlow Creek*', *Resistance and Reconciliation: Writing in the Commonwealth*, eds Bruce Bennett, Susan Cowan, Jacqueline Lo, Satendra Nandan, and Jen Webb, Canberra: Association for Commonwealth Literature and Language Studies, 2003, 265–77.

Brady, Veronica, 'Redefining Frontiers: "Race", Colonizers and the Colonized', *Antipodes* 8.2, 1994, 93–100.

Brittan, Alice, 'B-b-british Objects: Possession, Naming, and Translation in David Malouf's *Remembering Babylon*', *PMLA* 117, 2002, 1158–71.

Buckridge, Patrick, 'Colonial Strategies in the Writing of David Malouf', *Kunapipi* 8.3, 1986, 48–58.

Carter, Paul, *Living in a New Country*, London: Faber & Faber, 1992.

Concilio, Carmen, 'The Magic of Language in the Novels of Patrick White and David Malouf', *Coterminous Worlds: Magical Realism and Contemporary Post-Colonial Literature in English*, eds Elsa Linguanti, Francesco Casotti, and Carmen Concilio, Amsterdam: Rodopi, 1999, 29–45.

Copeland, Julie, 'Interview with David Malouf', *Australian Literary Studies* 10.4, 1982, 429–36.

Craven, Peter, 'An Ad for Philistinism', *Australian*, 10 November 1993.

Dale, Leigh and Helen Gilbert, 'Edges of the Self: Topographies of the Body in the Writing of David Malouf', *Provisional Maps: Critical Essays on David Malouf*, ed. Amanda Nettelbeck, Nedlands, Australia: Centre for Studies in Australian Literature, 1994, 85–100.

de Certeau, Michel, *The Practice of Everyday Life*, trans. Stephen Rendell, Berkeley: University of California Press, 1984.

Delrez, Marc and Paulette Michel-Michot, 'The Politics of Metamorphosis: Cultural Transformation in David Malouf's *Remembering Babylon*', *The Contact and the Culmination*, eds Marc Delrez and Benedicte Ledent, Liège, Belgium: L3–Liège Language and Literature, 1997, 155–70.

Dever, Maryanne, 'Secret Companions: The Continuity of David Malouf's Fiction', *World Literature Written in English* 26.1, 1986, 62–74.

Egerer, Claudia, *Fictions of (In)Betweenness*, Goteborg, Sweden: Acta Universitatis Gothoburgensis, 1997.

Fee, Margery, 'Who Can Write as Other?', *The Post-Colonial Studies Reader*, eds Bill Ashcroft, Gareth Griffiths, and Helen Tiffin, London and New York: Routledge, 1995.

Foucault, Michel, *Language, Counter-Memory, Practice : Selected Essays and Interviews*, Ithaca: Cornell University Press, 1977.

Foucault, Michel, *The History of Sexuality. Volume I: An Introduction*, trans. Robert Hurley, New York: Vintage, 1990.

Gelder, Ken and Paul Salzman, *The New Diversity: Australian Fiction 1970–88*, Melbourne: McPhee Gribble, 1989.

Griffiths, Gareth, '*Being There*; Being There: Kosinski and Malouf', *Past the Last Post: Theorizing Post-Colonialism and Post-Modernism*, eds Ian Adam and Helen Tiffin, Calgary: University of Calgary Press, 1990, 153–66.

Greer, Germaine, 'Malouf's Objectionable Whitewash', *Age*, 3 November 1993.

Hansson, Karin, *Sheer Edge: Aspects of Identity in David Malouf's Writing*, Lund: Lund University Press, 1991.

Hassall, Anthony J., 'The Wild Colonial Boy: The Making of Colonial

Legends in David Malouf's *The Conversations at Curlow Creek*', *Antipodes* 14.2, 2000, 145–51.

Hassan, Ihab, 'Encomium: David Malouf', *World Literature Today* 74.4, 2000, 710–12.

Hergenhan, Laurie, 'Discoveries and Transformations: Aspects of David Malouf's Work', *Australian Literary Studies* 11.3, 1984, 328–41.

Hills, Edward, '*La Maison Onirique*: David Malouf's First House', *Meridian* 16.1, 1997, 3–14.

Hodge, Bob, and Vijay Mishra, *Dark Side of the Dream: Australian Literature and the Postcolonial Mind*, North Sydney: Allen & Unwin, 1991.

Huggan, Graham, '(Un)Co-Ordinated Movements: The Geography of Autobiography in David Malouf's *12 Edmondstone Street* and Clark Blaise's *Resident Alien*, *Australian and New Zealand Studies in Canada* 3, 1990, 56–65.

Indyk, Ivor, *David Malouf*, Melbourne: Oxford University Press, 1993.

Indyk, Ivor, Introduction, *David Malouf: A Celebration*, ed. Ivor Indyk, Canberra: National Library of Australia, 2001, 1–4.

Kavanagh, Paul, 'With Breath Just Condensing on It: An Interview with David Malouf', *Southerly: A Review of Australian Literature* 3, September 1986, 247–59.

Kerr, David, 'Uniting the Hemispheres: David Malouf's Fictions', *Australian Literature Today*, ed. R. K. Dhawan, New Delhi: Indian Society for Commonwealth Studies, 1993, 61–73.

Kirby, Stephen, 'Homosocial Desire and Homosexual Panic in the Fiction of David Malouf and Frank Moorhouse', *Meanjin* 46.3, 1987, 385–93.

Knox-Shaw, Peter, 'An Art of Intersection: David Malouf's *Kunstlerroman, Harland's Half Acre*', *Antipodes* 5.1, 1991, 31–9.

Knox-Shaw, Peter, 'Malouf's Epic and the Unravelling of a National Stereotype', *Journal of Commonwealth Literature* 26.1, 1991, 79–100.

Kristeva, Julia, *Powers of Horror: An Essay on Abjection*, trans. Leon S. Roudiez, New York: Columbia University Press, 1982.

Lacan, Jacques, *Ecrits: A Selection*, trans. Alan Sheridan, New York: W. W. Norton, 1977.

Leer, Martin, 'At the Edge: Geography and the Imagination in the Work of David Malouf', *Australian Literary Studies* 12.1, 1985, 3–21.

Levinas, Emmanuel, *Otherwise than Being or Beyond Essence*, trans. Alphonso Lingus, Dordrecht, Boston, London: Kluwer Academic, 1991.

Lévi-Strauss, Claude, *Tristes Tropiques*, trans. John and Doreen Weightman, New York: Penguin, 1992.

McDonald, Avis G., 'Beyond Language: David Malouf's *An Imaginary Life*', *ARIEL* 19.1, 1988, 45–54.

Maes-Jelinek, Hena, 'David Malouf's "Voyaging Imagination"': *The Conversations at Curlow Creek*', *Commonwealth* 23.1, 2000, 89–98.

Masel, Carolyn, 'Late Landings: Reflections on Belatedness in Australian and Canadian Literatures', *Recasting the World: Writing after Colonialism*, ed. Jonathan White, Baltimore and London: The Johns Hopkins University Press, 1993, 161–89.

Metherell, Gia, 'Babylon Not Always Remembered Fondly', *Canberra Times*, 24 May 1996.

Mitchell, Michael, 'Armed Angels: Visible Darkness in Malouf and Golding, *World Literature Today* 74.4, 2000, 770–7.

Neilsen, Philip, *Imagined Lives: A Study of David Malouf*, St Lucia, University of Queensland Press, 1990.

Neilsen, Philip, *Imagined Lives: A Study of David Malouf* (2nd edition), St Lucia, University of Queensland Press, 1996.

Nettelbeck, Amanda, 'Myths of a Nation: History as Narrative Invention in David Malouf's *The Great World*', *Myths, Heroes and Anti-Heroes: Essays on the Literature and Culture of the Asia-Pacific Region*, eds Bruce Bennett and Dennis Haskell, Nedlands: Centre for Studies in Australian Literature, University of Western Australia, 1992, 132–41.

Nettelbeck, Amanda, 'Narrative Invention as "Spatial History" in *The Great World*', *Australian and New Zealand Studies in Canada*, 7, 1992, 41–52

Nettelbeck, Amanda, 'Imagining the Imaginary in *An Imaginary Life*', *Southern Review: Literary and Interdisciplinary Essays* 26.1, 1993, 28–38.

Nettelbeck, Amanda, Introduction, *Provisional Maps: Critical Essays on David Malouf*, ed. Amanda Nettelbeck, Nedlands: Centre for Studies in Australian Literature, University of Western Australia, 1994, i–ix.

Nettelbeck, Amanda, 'Rewriting an Explorer Mythology: The Narration of Space in David Malouf's Work', *Provisional Maps: Critical Essays on David Malouf*, ed. Amanda Nettelbeck, Nedlands:

Centre for Studies in Australian Literature, University of Western Australia, 1994, 101–15.

Nettelbeck, Amanda, *Reading David Malouf*, Sydney: Sydney University Press/Oxford University Press, 1995.

O'Brien, Suzie, 'Raising Silent Voices: The Role of the Silent Child in *An Imaginary Life* and *The Bone People*', *SPAN* 30, 1990, 79–91.

Otto, Peter, Review, 'Forgetting Colonialism (David Malouf, *Remembering Babylon*)', *Meanjin* 52.3, 1993, 545–58.

Papastergiadis, Nikos, 'David Malouf and Languages for Landscape: An Interview', *ARIEL* 25.3, 1994, 83–94.

Perera, Suvendrini, 'Unspeakable Bodies: Representing the Aboriginal in Australian Critical Discourse', *Meridian* 13.1, 1994, 15–26.

Pierce, Peter, 'Problematic History, Problems of Form: David Malouf's *Remembering Babylon*', *Provisional Maps: Critical Essays on David Malouf*, ed. Amanda Nettelbeck, Nedlands: Centre for Studies in Australian Literature, The University of Western Australia, 1994, 183–96.

Pierce, Peter, 'What Dreams May Come: David Malouf's *Dream Stuff*', *World Literature Today* 74.4, 2000, 751–7.

Pons, Xavier, 'Broken Lines, Broken Lives: Discontinuities in David Malouf's *The Great World*', *Commonwealth Essays and Studies* 16.2, 1993, 79–87.

Pons, Xavier, 'Wrong Side of the Mirror: Exile in David Malouf's *The Conversations at Curlow Creek*', *Flight from Certainty: The Dilemma of Identity and Exile*, eds Anne Luyat and Francine Tolron, Amsterdam: Rodopi, 2001, 140–52.

Pons, Xavier, 'Reconciling Words and Things: Language Allegories in David Malouf's *Remembering Babylon*', *Commonwealth Essays and Studies* 27.1, 2004, 99–110.

Rodgers, Shelagh, 'The Other History that Never Gets Recorded', *Australian and New Zealand Studies in Canada* 5, 1991, 94–6.

Ross, Robert, '*Harland's Half Acre*: A Portrait of the Artist as a Young Australian', *World Literature Today* 74.4, 2000, 733–8.

Said, Edward W., *Orientalism*, New York: Vintage, 1979.

Said, Edward W., *The World, the Text, and the Critic*, London: Faber, 1984.

Scheckter, John, 'Dreaming Wholeness: David Malouf's New Stories', *World Literature Today* 74.4, 2000, 741–8.

Sedgwick, Eve Kosofsky, *Between Men: English Literature and Male*

Homosocial Desire, New York: Columbia University Press, 1985.

Sedgwick, Eve Kosofsky, *The Epistemology of the Closet*, Berkeley: University of California Press, 1990.

Sharrad, Paul, 'A Delicate Business: David Malouf's Shorter Prose', *World Literature Today* 74.4, 2000, 759–68.

Slemon, Stephen, 'Unsettling the Empire: Resistance Theory for the Second World', *World Literature Written in English* 30.2, 1990, 30–41.

Spinks, Les, 'Allegory, Space, Colonialism: *Remembering Babylon* and the Production of Colonial History', *Australian Literary Studies* 17.2, 1995, 166–74.

Spivak, Gayatri Chakravorty, 'Can the Subaltern Speak?', *Marxism and the Interpretation of Culture*, eds Cary Nelson and Lawrence Grossberg, Urbana: University of Illinois Press, 1988, 271–313.

Taylor, Andrew, 'Postmodern Romantic: The Imaginary in David Malouf's *An Imaginary Life*', *Imagining Romanticism: Essays on English and Australian Romanticisms*, eds Deirdre Coleman and Peter Otto, West Cornwall, CT: Locust Hill, 1992, 275–90.

Taylor, Andrew, '*The Great World*, History, and Two or One Other Things', *Provisional Maps: Critical Essays on David Malouf*, Nedlands: Centre for Studies in Australian Literature, University of Western Australia, 1994, 35–50.

Taylor, Andrew, 'Origin, Identity and the Body in David Malouf's Fiction', *Australian Literary Studies* 19.1, 1999, 3–14.

Taylor, Andrew, '*The Bread of Time to Come*: Body and Landscape in David Malouf's Fiction', *World Literature Today* 74.4, 2000, 715–23.

Thwaites, Tony, 'The Site of the Beholder: David Malouf's *Child's Play*', *Southern Review: Literary and Interdisciplinary Essays* 20.1, 1987, 17–35.

Tiffin, Chris, and Alan Lawson, *De-Scribing Empire: Post-Colonialism and Textuality*, London and New York: Routledge, 1994.

Turner, Barnard, 'On Frontiers: The "Nationalism" of David Malouf's Poetry and Its Implications for a Definition of "Commonwealth Literature"', *Nationalism vs. Internationalism: (Inter)National Dimensions of Literatures in English*, eds Wolfgang Zach and Ken Goodwin, Tübingen: Stauffenburg, 1996, 495–502.

Turcotte, Gerry, 'Response: Venturing into Undiscoverable Countries: Reading Ondaatje, Malouf, Atwood and Jia in an Asia-Pacific Context', *Australian Canadian Studies* 16.2, 1997–98, 65–72.

van Zuylen, Marina, *Monomania: The Flight from Everyday Life in Literature and Art*, Ithaca and London: Cornell University Press, 2005.

Wallace-Crabbe, Chris, 'Imitations of Secular Grace', *Meanjin* 40.4, 1981, 500–6.

West, Russell, 'Exile as Origin: Definitions of Australian Identities in Malouf's *12 Edmondstone Street*', *Anglia: Zeitschrift für Englische Philologie* 119.1, 2001, 77–92.

Whittick, Sheila, 'Excavating Historical Guilt and Moral Failure in *Remembering Babylon*: An Exploration of the Faultlines in White Australian Identity', *Commonwealth Essays and Studies* 19.2, 1997, 77–99.

Willbanks, Ray, Interview, 'David Malouf', *Australian Voices: Writers and Their Work*, Austin: University of Texas Press, 1991, 143–57.

Woods, Stephen, 'David Malouf's *Child's Play* and "The Death of the Author"', *Australian Literary Studies* 13.3, 1988, 322–33.

Young, Robert J. C., *Colonial Desire: Hybridity in Theory, Culture and Race*, London and New York: Routledge, 1995.

Index

Note: 'n.' after a page number indicates the number of a note on that page.